Architects of Civilization

In this brilliant, incisive survey of Greek philosophy, Rex Warner presents selections from the outstanding classical thinkers whose ideas have shaped and stimulated the whole course of Western culture down through the ages.

Thales, Zeno, Pythagoras, Heraclitus, Anaxagoras, Plato, Aristotle, Epicurus, Lucretius, Marcus Aurelius, Plotinus—Rex Warner interprets their major philosophical ideas, summarizes their lives, and places their writings in proper historical context.

Here is a stimulating body of philosophical thought on such subjects as metaphysics, astronomy, cosmology, ethics, politics, and the great philosophies of conduct, a remarkable record of man's never ending effort to explain the world about him through the use of reason.

A specialist in classical literature, Rex Warner has taught in England, Egypt and Greece. Some of his most valuable works have been translations from Greek literature—Aeschylus's Prometheus Bound, Euripides' Hippolytus and Helen, Xenophon's Anabasis, and Ovid's Metamorphoses. He has also written novels and a biography of Julius Caesar, The Young Caesar, which was hailed as "brilliant" by the critics.

Other MENTOR Books on Ancient Greece

THE GREEK PHILOSOPHERS

REX WARNER

A MENTOR BOOK

Published by THE NEW AMERICAN LIBRARY

FIRST PRINTING, AUGUST, 1958

ACKNOWLEDGMENTS

The author wishes to thank the following publishers and authorized representatives for their kind permission to reprint from the books indicated below:

ADAM AND CHARLES BLACK LTD. (LONDON)
John Burnet, *Early Greek Philosophy.*

THE CLARENDON PRESS (OXFORD)
Epicurus, *Principal Doctrines,* translated by Cyril Bailey in *Epicurus, the Extant Remains;* Lucian, *Hermotimus,* translated by H. W. and F. G. Fowler in *The Works of Lucian of Samosata;* Plato, *Gorgias,* translated by Benjamin Jowett.

J. M. DENT & SONS LTD. (LONDON)
Aristotle, *Metaphysics,* translated by John Warrington. (Everyman's Library.)

E. P. DUTTON & CO., INC.
Aristotle, *Metaphysics,* translated by John Warrington. (Everyman's Library.)

HARVARD UNIVERSITY PRESS (The Loeb Classical Library)
Aristotle, *Nicomachean Ethics,* translated by H. Rackham; Aristotle, *Physics,* translated by P. H. Wicksteed and F. M. Cornford; Epictetus, *Discourses,* translated by W. A. Oldfather; Sextus Empiricus, *Against the Ethicists,* translated by R. G. Bury in *Sextus Empiricus.*

LONGMANS, GREEN & CO., LIMITED (LONDON)
Plotinus, *Enneads,* translated by W. R. Inge in *The Philosophy of Plotinus.*

THE MACMILLAN COMPANY (NEW YORK)
John Burnet, *Early Greek Philosophy.*

OXFORD UNIVERSITY PRESS (LONDON)
Marcus Aurelius, *Thoughts,* translated by John Jackson.

JOHN CLIVE GRAVES ROUSE
Plato, *The Republic* and *Meno* from *Great Dialogues of Plato,* translated by W. H. D. Rouse, edited by Eric H. Warmington and Philip G. Rouse, published by The New American Library of World Literature, Inc. © 1956 by John Clive Graves Rouse.

LIBRARY OF CONGRESS CATALOG CARD NO. 58-12836

MENTOR BOOKS are published by
The New American Library of World Literature, Inc.
501 Madison Avenue, New York 22, New York

PRINTED IN THE UNITED STATES OF AMERICA

Author's Note

I have attempted here to present a serviceable sketch of Greek philosophy from its beginnings in Ionia to its decline under the Roman empire, allowing the philosophers so far as possible to speak for themselves. The subject is vast, and the reader should not forget that what is provided here is no more than a sketch.

I have given a good deal of space to Plato and Aristotle, but their work is so pre-eminent both in scale and in value that I should like to explain why I have not given them more. The reason is that they are the subjects of separate volumes in this series, in which the treatment of their thought can properly be expanded beyond the limits of the present work.

In the writing of this book I have been aided more than I can say by the advice, guidance and practical help of my friend Mr. Geoffrey Warnock, of Magdalen College, Oxford. If there are any merits in the work, then he is entitled to his full share of credit. As for the defects, they, poor things, are my own.

REX WARNER

Contents

CHAPTER I

The Pre-Socratic Philosophers

1. The Great Innovation

The Greeks invented, among other things, science and philosophy. The first scientists and philosophers lived during the sixth century B.C. on the Greek coast of Asia Minor and in the Greek cities of southern Italy. Later, during the fifth and fourth centuries, the important center of thought was Athens. But by this time science and philosophy were studied everywhere in the Greek world. These studies shaped the civilization of Rome and, in many respects, the theology and ethics of the Christian churches. They were revived in something more like their original form at the time of the Renaissance. They have transformed the whole of mankind.

It would be an exaggeration to say that before the time of Thales of Miletus men were incapable of rational thought, but there would be some truth in the statement, since before his time it does not appear that anyone asked those precise questions out of which science and philosophy were to develop. The questions were "What is everything made of?", "How do things come into being, change and pass away?", "What permanent substance or substances exist behind appearances?" And these questions, of course, led on to others connected with the existence of the gods, the laws of nature and the duties or purpose of man upon the earth.

The originality was both in the asking of the questions themselves and in the assumption made with regard to how they could be answered. It was assumed, for the first time in history, that the investigator was dealing with a universe that was a "cosmos"—that is to say an orderly system governed by laws which could be discovered by logical thought and by observation.

Of course this assumption, in a limited way, had been made previously. No form of civilization at all would be possible if it were not generally believed, for example, that spring would invariably follow winter. And the civilizations of Mesopotamia and of Egypt, with both of which the Greeks were acquainted, had already made remarkable discoveries on the basis of the observed regular movements in nature. The Babylonians were able to predict eclipses, though, being ignorant of their true causes, they did not know whether a particular eclipse would in fact be visible from Babylonia. They watched for the eclipses at the right times and regarded it as a good omen if the eclipse did not appear. There was, as it were, on the one side a certain number of observed recurrent phenomena, and on the other side a great realm of experience which was regarded as unpredictable and irrational, though in some ways open to influence by means of magic or religious observances.

It was a state of affairs at which the Roman poet Lucretius, a contemporary of Julius Caesar, writing some five hundred years after the original revolution of thought, looked back. He wrote:

There was a time when the life of men was something evidently quite foul. Mankind was groveling on the ground, pressed down beneath the heavy weight of superstitious awe. This superstitious awe (Religion, one may call it) proudly showed her head in every quarter of the sky and with an aspect of terror stood over and looked down on mortal man. It was a man from Greece who first dared to raise defiantly his mortal eyes and then to take his stand against her. He could not be suppressed by stories about the gods or by thunderbolts or by a sky full of the menace of thunder. On the contrary, these things were an incentive to the cutting genius of his mind. They made him all the more ready to be the first man on earth to want to break through the bolts fitted across the doors of reality. And so this vital vigor of his spirit won a total victory. His campaign carried him far beyond the flaming barriers of the sky. By sheer force of intellect he was able to wander over the whole of infinity. From this journey he brings back to us the fruits of victory—the knowledge of what can and what cannot come into existence, what are the fixed limitations to the powers of each individual thing and the sharply drawn line of definition. So now it is the turn of Religion to be cast down and trampled under foot. As for us, the victory has raised us up to the skies.

Lucretius, of course, was writing of Epicurus, and Epicurus was not "the first man who dared to raise his eyes." Then, too, Lucretius writes with the rather exaggerated fervor of a convert. It is by no means true that Greek philosophy is necessarily anti-religious. Yet still the general picture given by Lucretius is not far from the truth. Something really unique and revolutionary had happened when Thales, for whatever reasons, came to the conclusion that there was a fundamental substance and that this substance was water. As for superstition, it had certainly not died out at the time of Lucretius and it has not died out yet. Nevertheless it is impossible to deny that the "victory" was a real one.

As for the precise doctrines of many of these early philosophers, there is often considerable difficulty in discovering them and in understanding them. Partly the difficulties proceed from lack of material. Partly the difficulty is in the nature of things, since this new invention of rational thought only gradually invented its own vocabulary. The early thinkers did not call themselves "philosophers" and took some time before they became logicians. Such notions as "substance," "matter," "mind," "element," "atom," "force"—even "thing" and "event"—were not ready to hand; the words for them did not exist. Words had to follow thought, so that it is impossible that the *original* thought should have been clearly and neatly expressed.

Nor, of course, was there at first any close distinction between philosophy and science. There was not even (in spite of what Lucretius says) a distinction between these and religion. The investigation was into *Phusis,* the nature of things—what things are, how they come into being. And here Lucretius writes well about "the fruits of victory."

2. Thales of Miletus

The great innovation began in the Greek city of Miletus at the beginning of the sixth century B.C. Miletus was a great seafaring power. Her colonies surrounded the shores of the Black Sea and she founded the first Greek settlements in Egypt. There is evidence that the temperament of the Milesians, as of all the Ionian Greeks, was in every way adventurous, exploratory and individualistic.

The very limited information of value which we possess about Thales of Miletus comes to us from a few references in Herodotus and Aristotle. Herodotus tells us that Thales proposed a plan for a federation of the Ionian states with its capital at Teos. A sensible idea like this seems more characteristic of these early thinkers, many of whom were actively engaged in politics, than does the later anecdote of Thales falling into a well because he was so occupied with looking at the stars. Philosophers were not regarded as being odd and unpractical eccentrics until the time of Aristophanes. Herodotus also tells us that Thales successfully predicted an eclipse which was visible in Asia Minor in May, 585 B.C. However, as his successor as leader of thought in Miletus, Anaximander, was certainly ignorant of the true cause of eclipses, we may assume that Thales was also ignorant and was merely applying the rule-of-thumb methods which had long been practiced in Babylonia. So too, though he is said to have been the "father" of geometry, there is in fact no evidence that he was, in the true sense, a mathematician at all. He may well have visited Egypt and have brought back from Egypt to Greece valuable and practical methods of mensuration. That is all.

His importance, then, lies in his teaching, and of this no less an authority than Professor John Burnet writes, "speaking strictly we do not know anything about the teaching of Thales at all." Aristotle indeed attributes to him the sayings that "all things are full of gods" and that "the magnet is alive since it has the power to move iron." But these sayings may easily be later attributions and, even

12

if one accepts them as genuine, they certainly do not provide sufficient evidence to justify us in describing Thales as a pantheist or in forming any theory as regards the particular sort of "life" which was held to animate the magnet.

We are left with the other statement attributed to Thales by Aristotle. This is that the fundamental substance from which all things proceed is water. How he arrived at this doctrine we do not know. A part may well have been played by all sorts of other considerations apart from the obvious ones—the observation of water appearing both as a liquid, as a solid and as a vapor, the phenomena of rain and of dew, the effect of water on the growth of vegetation, even the old myth that the ocean was the father of all things. What is really important is that the doctrine should have been expressed at all, that a man should have assumed the existence of a coherent universe and should have looked for one underlying reality as a substratum or cause for everything. There is a sense (as was suggested by Lucretius) in which it would be true to say that the distance between Thales and a modern atomic physicist is less great than the distance between Thales and the whole history of civilization before him.

3. Anaximander

Anaximander (born about 610 B.C.) was the first of the Greeks to write a book in prose. This book, though now lost, was available for a time to later philosophers. It is quite frequently referred to and its actual language is sometimes quoted. Those references (quoted by John Burnet,*) which have most relevance to Anaximander's general and original view of the problem which had been raised by Thales are as follows:

1. Anaximander of Miletos, son of Praxiades, a fellow-citizen and associate of Thales, said that the material cause

* *Early Greek Philosophy,* 4th edition. London: Adam & Charles Black; New York: The Macmillan Company, 1930, pp. 52-53.

and first element of things was the Infinite, he being the first
to introduce this name of the material cause. He says it is
neither water nor any other of the so-called elements, but a
substance different from them which is infinite, from which
arise all the heavens and the worlds within them.

2. He says that this is "eternal and ageless" and that it
"encompasses all the worlds."

3. And into that from which things take their rise they
pass away once more, "as is meet; for they make reparation
and satisfaction to one another for their injustice according to
the ordering of time" as he says in these somewhat poetical
terms.

4. And besides this there was an eternal motion, in which
was brought about the origin of the worlds.

5. He did not ascribe the origin of things to any alteration
in matter, but said that the oppositions in the sub-stratum,
which was a boundless body, were separated out.

Now with regard to these references it should again be
remembered that many of the terms ("material cause,"
"first element," for example) could not have been used
by Anaximander himself. We may assume his actual
language to have been "somewhat poetical" and can be sure
only that he did use the words "infinite," "boundless" and
that curious phrase about "injustice." Nevertheless it is
still possible to imagine how he thought, if not precisely
how he expressed himself.

It would seem that, having accepted the view of Thales
that there must be one primary substance, it occurred to
him to wonder why Thales had picked on water. Water is
just one of the kinds of things there are; so it, like everything else, must be merely one of the forms of some even
more fundamental "stuff." And, so far as visible substances are concerned, nothing else satisfies the required
conditions even as well as water.

By describing his primary substance as "the Infinite" or
"the non-limited," Anaximander meant something which
was not only "unlimited" in extent, but was also "unlimited" in the sense that it had no precise characteristics
or attributes. It was neither wet or dry, hot or cold, liquid
or solid. These and other opposites with which we are

familiar by means of our senses become "separated out" from the boundless substratum which, in itself, can never be observed or, except in its derivatives, experienced.

Now this doctrine of Anaximander is, in its own way, as revolutionary as was the original assumption by Thales that there actually was a substratum. It is certain that at this time there was no recognized distinction between philosophy and science; yet Anaximander, for the first time in history, is putting forward an argument which can be called purely philosophical rather than scientific. For the force of his doctrine rests only on logical argument and cannot be either proved or disproved by experiment. One can imagine experiments which could be designed to corroborate or to overthrow the theory of Thales. Water is visible and tangible. "The Infinite" or "the non-limited" is not.

It is interesting and important to notice that science itself could not have developed if scientists had not accepted this wholly "unscientific" argument of Anaximander. It is only very recently (not earlier than the seventeeth century) that scientists have found any good empirical evidence for the view that all the different things in the world are in some way "forms" of some unvarying substance which cannot be identified with any "thing" or "element." Yet, in spite of the lack of evidence, they continued to believe that this view must be the correct one. May it be that the distinction which we make, and which the ancient Greeks did not make, is a somewhat artificial one? Roughly, our distinction is this: science depends on observation and experiment and it produces "results"; philosophy depends on logical argument and need not produce "results" in any comparable sense. This is certainly not a distinction which Anaximander, or any other early Greek thinker, would have recognized. It is possible that their attitude may be more "modern" than ours.

Anaximander himself did not confine himself to "theory" —another word which had still to be either invented or invested with meaning. He was the first to attempt to draw a map and to construct a model which was intended to illustrate the movements and dimensions of the heavenly bodies. He decided, from his observation of or information about the breeding habits of sharks, that man, originally, was like another animal, namely a fish.

His mind was indeed far-ranging. He, rather than Epicurus, was the first to go "beyond the flaming barriers of the sky." Since "the Infinite" was, by definition, boundless, there were "innumerable worlds." They had come from and would disappear into "the unlimited." Some of them could be observed. Others could be imagined and many of their properties could be demonstrated. Certainly with regard to these worlds and to the other heavenly bodies he had definite ideas. He believed, for instance, that "The sun was a wheel 28 times the size of the earth, like a chariot-wheel with the felloe hollow, full of fire, showing the fire at a certain point through an orifice, as through the nozzle of a pair of bellows." He believed that the earth is suspended in space and, for some reason, that it is shaped like a cylinder. He had explanations for the phenomena of thunder, lightning and the winds. Altogether he is a fine example of that particular daring of thought, both in its penetration and in its wide horizons, which Lucretius so much admired.

4. Anaximenes

The third of the philosophers of the school of Miletus is Anaximenes. We have no precise dates for his life and know only that he was a younger "associate" of Anaximander. Like Anaximander he wrote a book and seems to have employed a style that was less poetical than that of the elder philosopher. The important references to him from later sources are quoted by Burnet (*op. cit.*, p. 73) and are as follows:

1. Anaximenes of Miletus, son of Eurystratus, who had been an associate of Anaximander, said, like him, that the underlying substance was one and infinite. He did not, however, say it was indeterminate, like Anaximander, but determinate; for he said it was Air.

2. From it, he said, the things that are, and have been, and shall be, the gods and things divine, took their rise, while other things came from its offspring.

3. "Just as," he said, "our soul, being air, holds us together, so do breath and air encompass the whole world."

4. And the form of the air is as follows. Where it is most even, it is invisible to our sight; but cold and heat, moisture and motion, make it visible. It is always in motion; for, if it were not, it would not change so much as it does.

5. It differs in different substances in virtue of its rarefaction and condensation.

6. When it is dilated so as to be rarer, it becomes fire; while winds, on the other hand, are condensed Air. Cloud is formed from Air by felting;* and this, still further condensed, becomes water. Water, condensed still more, turns to earth; and when condensed as much as it can be, to stones.

In comparing Anaximenes with Anaximander perhaps our modern distinction between the philosopher and the scientist may be of use. It appears that Anaximenes was more of a scientist and less of a philosopher than his predecessor. He was interested in how things worked rather than in what they were. Thus he was not trying to answer quite the same question as that which had occurred to the mind of Anaximander. When Anaximander thought of the primary substance or substratum, he was asking himself "What is it that every particular thing is a form of?" This question, it would seem, can only be answered (if it can be answered at all) by saying "Some stuff which is not itself of any particular kind." This stuff, indeed, must be "unlimited" in the sense of being "indeterminate," and, as an answer to the question, "air" is no improvement on "water."

But the question which Anaximenes asked himself seems to have been of a more "practical" or "scientific" kind. He was interested not in what is more fundamental than any kind of thing, but simply in what particular kind of thing is most fundamental. It is, of course, very likely that he was himself quite unaware that these are different questions.

* "Felting" is the regular term for this process with all the early cosmologists.

So far as his own particular question is concerned, air seems to be as good a speculative answer as any. The theory of rarefaction and condensation as being the factors which account for difference cannot be original. (Thales must have held the same view about water.) Much more significant is the view, which we have expressed in Anaximenes' own words, that "just as our soul, being air, holds us together, so do breath and air encompass the whole world." Here life is directly connected with the primary substance. Later theories of a more mystical nature—theories, for instance, of a "world-soul"—could look back for support to this doctrine of Anaximenes.

Curiously, Anaximenes with his "scientific" approach and his comparatively clear style was less fruitful as a scientist than was the more philosophical and "poetical" Anaximander. Anaximander had held that the cylindrical earth remains suspended in space because there is no reason why it should move in any one particular direction rather than in another. Anaximenes reverted to the flat-earth theory. For him the earth and the heavenly bodies are flying saucers, or rather saucers floating on air. Neither of the two theories would be regarded today as correct; but the theory of Anaximander held more promise.

5. Pythagoras

What is known as "the school of Miletus" ends with Anaximenes. That these particular Ionian Greeks proceeded for the time being no further with their speculations and discoveries may be associated with the fact that before the death of Anaximenes the Persians had occupied the Greek Asiatic coast.

The next "schools" of philosophy appear in the Greek cities of southern Italy and the next philosophers are also Ionians. Of them one of the most important, and elusive, is Pythagoras, who came from the island of Samos, probably about 531 B.C., settled in southern Italy and there founded what amounted to a religious order. His society appears to have had political as well as religious and philosophical aims. It was certainly suppressed at some date between

460 and 400 B.C., though survivors of the society carried on their teaching in mainland Greece. With some of these Socrates was acquainted and their doctrines undoubtedly influenced Plato. It is impossible to say what precisely Pythagoras believed himself and very difficult to be sure of what his followers believed. One certain fact seems to be that he, for the first time, made philosophy into something which we would call a religion or a way of life. Thus his attitude was a completely different one from that of the thinkers of Miletus who were great exemplars rather of curiosity than of any feeling that they needed in any way to be "saved." They spoke, certainly, about "gods" and, as we have seen, Thales is said to have pronounced that "all things are full of gods." But, however this statement may be understood, it cannot be presumed to mean anything mystical. We translate the Greek word *theos* as "god," and there are some Greeks (Aeschylus and Plato for example) who sometimes use the word in a sense not unlike that which we attach to it. As a rule, however, *theos* means either some "force" or the personification in mythology of some force. It would be quite natural for an early cosmologist, looking objectively at the sun or at the moon or at the stars, and having come to some speculative conclusions about their substance, to pronounce that they were "divine." This would not mean that he acknowledged any personal feeling other than scientific curiosity for these heavenly bodies. As for the particular gods (Zeus, Hera, Aphrodite and so on) the early Ionian philosophers do not seem to have speculated upon their existence or their functions. One may suppose that they presumed them to exist, though it is difficult to see what part they could have played in a universe composed entirely of water, air or the unlimited. Later, as we shall see, it was regarded as reasonable to suppose that "the gods" exist, but have nothing whatever to do with mankind.

However in the seventh and sixth centuries B.C. there seems to have taken place, particularly in Attica and in the Greek cities of Italy and Sicily, something that can be described as a religious revival. We find that "the gods" themselves (and in particular Apollo and Dionysus) are taken much more seriously than they were by the adventurous scientists of Ionia. We find also a different outlook on man. A real distinction is now made between the soul and the body. "Ecstasy"—"the stepping out of oneself"—is acknowledged as a fact and investigated as a hint of some "divine" origin of the soul. There is speculation about life after death, and rules are laid down for pure living which may ensure benefits both here and hereafter.

We are not concerned here with the origin of this religious revival or with what exactly is meant by "Orphism" or with what "the mysteries" were. It is sufficient to point out that this religious movement had its effect on Pythagoras and, through him, on the subsequent history of philosophy. With him philosophy enters, as it were, another sphere. Instead of being simply "curiosity" or "science" it becomes "a way of life," a religion itself or a substitute for one. Yet it remains concerned with the problem first raised by Thales. The underlying substance or principle is still sought for.

In discussing Pythagoras it will be convenient to distinguish between what we know of him as a religious teacher and what we know of him as a philosopher; but again we must remember that he and his followers did not make this distinction. They simply regarded philosophy and mathematics as "good for the soul," as, in fact, the best and highest form of purification. It seems to have been Pythagoras who first defined "the three lives" by comparing all men to those who attend the Olympic Games. The lowest class are those who come there simply to buy and sell; next are the actual competitors; and the highest class is that of those who are simply there to watch (*theōrein*, from which our "theory" and "theoretical" are derived). This idea of the dignity, even the sanctity, of the contemplative or philosophical life is a new idea and was to be further developed. It is a moral idea and implies the consideration of man's duty with regard to his soul and the souls of others. This was not a consideration that had occurred to the inquirers of Miletus, but it was to play a most important part in the discussions of Socrates and in the later semi-religious systems of Stoicism and Epicureanism.

Of the actual religious doctrine of Pythagoras we do not know very much. It seems certain that he believed in the transmigration of souls or in "being born again." It is likely that he taught his followers to abstain from animal flesh on the grounds that there was a kinship between men and animals, though it is impossible to say whether this belief derived from primitive notions of tabu or from the rational reflection that the soul of one of one's deceased friends might be inhabiting the body of some animal killed for the table. We hear too of a number of rather curious prohibitions and injunctions, such as:

Do not eat beans.
Do not touch a white cock.
Do not stir the fire with iron.
When you get out of bed, roll up the bedclothes and smooth out the impress of the body.

These are curiosities. The higher discipline of the school was connected with music and mathematics. Either Pythagoras himself or one of his followers certainly discovered the proof of the theorem which bears his name (the discovery is said to have been celebrated by the sacrifice of an ox) and laid the foundations both of arithmetic and geometry. It is impossible to discuss here the strictly mathematical side of the doctrine. (An excellent account will be found in Samuel Sambursky's *The Physical World of the Greeks.**) Here we are chiefly interested in how the Pythagoreans attempted to answer the question propounded first by Thales; and it seems certain, from the following account given of them by Aristotle, that they really did hold the view that "things are made of numbers." It was a view which influenced Plato and which, in its more mystical form, has had a long history. It is possible also to maintain that the Pythagoreans laid the foundations of modern mathematical physics. Yet to say that "things are made of numbers" is, of course, to go much further than to say that there are numerical relations between things or even that the laws of the universe can

* New York: The Macmillan Company; London: Routledge & Kegan Paul, Ltd., 1956.

be expressed in mathematical terms. To the Pythagoreans, excited, as was natural enough, by their discoveries, there was something sacred in numbers themselves. Numbers and their arrangements expressed quality as well as quantity. This will become clear from the words of Aristotle (*Metaphysics I*). It should be noted that Aristotle in writing about "the so-called Pythagoreans who led the field in mathematics and whose studies convinced them that the principles of that science were of universal application," is writing of an already developed school. Pythagoras himself has become a legendary figure.

So far we have been discussing material and efficient causes as understood by the early philosophers. Contemporary with and even prior to them were the so-called Pythagoreans, who led the field in mathematics and whose studies convinced them that the principles of that science were of universal application.

Numbers, of course, are of their very nature the first of those principles; and the Pythagoreans thought they saw in numbers, rather than in fire or earth or water, many resemblances to things which exist and which come into being. They also realized that the properties and ratios of musical scales depend on numbers. In a word, they saw that other things, in respect of the whole of their natures, resemble numbers, and that numbers are the primary elements of the whole of nature. Hence they considered the principles of numbers as the principles of all things, and the whole universe as a harmony or number. Moreover, they collected and systematized all the instances they could find of correspondence between (1) numbers or harmonies and (2) the properties and relations of the heavens and the whole universal order. If anything was lacking to complete their theories, they quickly supplied it. They held, for instance, that ten is a perfect number and embraces all the powers of number. On this view they asserted that there must be ten heavenly bodies; and as only nine were visible they invented the "counter-earth" to make a tenth.

I have discussed these theories in greater detail elsewhere. My purpose in referring to them now is only to discover what causes were recognized by the Pythagoreans and how they compare with my own list. Well, the Pythagoreans evidently treated numbers both as the material principle and as that which makes things what they are temporarily or permanently.

They also held (1) that the principles of number are the Even (or Unlimited or Indefinite) and the Odd (or Limited or Definite); (2) that Unity (because it is both even and odd) is produced out of these two and number out of Unity; and (3) that number, as I have said, constitutes the whole sensible world.*

6. Xenophanes

Xenophanes, also from Ionia, probably left his native city of Colophon at the time of the Persian conquest in 545 B.C. He may then have been about twenty-five. The rest of his long life (he lived to be over ninety) was spent in the Greek cities of the West, mainly, it seems, in Sicily. He wrote in poetry and a considerable number of his verses have survived.

He seems to have been rather a critic of ideas than an original philosopher; but his criticism is important. It was concerned with both social and theological ideas and is much more typical of the active, practical spirit of Ionia than are the more mystical (though much more fruitful) views of Pythagoras.

We know from Pindar, a contemporary of Xenophanes, how strongly and beautifully developed was the cult of athletes in the Greek cities of Sicily and Italy. Victory in the Olympic Games was something which brought to the victor almost divine honors—the gods themselves, in the fine poetry written to commemorate these victories, are often given the qualities of athletes. Xenophanes applies both to the social and to the religious theory the keen edge of Ionian rationalism. "Our art," he says (by which he means scientific inquiry, economic and political efficiency) "is a great deal more useful than the strength of men and horses." It is the same view as that which we meet later in Aeschylus, who makes Prometheus declare that the future dispensation, the way of progress, is to be by means of intelligence rather than of brute force.

Most remarkable are Xenophanes' criticisms of the

* Aristotle, *Metaphysics*, translated by John Warrington. London: J. M. Dent and Sons; New York: E. P. Dutton & Co., Inc., 1956, pp. 64-65. (Everyman's Library.)

established mythological ideas of the gods. These attacks of his on anthropomorphism need no explanation. The fragments are from his *Satires* or *Silloi* and are quoted by Burnet (*op. cit.*, p. 119).

1. Homer and Hesiod have ascribed to the gods all things that are a shame and disgrace among mortals, stealings and adulteries and deceivings of one another.

2. But mortals deem that the gods are begotten as they are, and have clothes like theirs, and voice and form.

3. Yes, and if oxen and horses or lions had hands, and could paint with their hands, and produce works of art as men do, horses would paint the forms of the gods like horses, and oxen like oxen, and make their bodies in the image of their several kinds.

4. The Ethiopians make their gods black and snub-nosed; the Thracians say theirs have blue eyes and red hair.

Xenophanes' own views about the gods seem to have taken the form of a kind of pantheism. The relevant fragments are as follows:

5. One god, the greatest among gods and men, neither in form like unto mortals nor in thought. . . .

6. He sees all over, thinks all over, and hears all over.

7. But without toil he swayeth all things by the thought of his mind.

8. And he abideth ever in the selfsame place, moving not at all; nor doth it befit him to go about now hither now thither.

These fragments (5-8) seem to show merely a development of the thought expressed in the previous fragments (1-4). The full statement is something like this: "The stories of the gods told by Horace and Hesiod are both immoral and scientifically absurd. All that we know is the material universe and this, in its totality, is the only thing that can be called divine."

Later thinkers, and in particular Parmenides, made a philosophical system out of the idea of "the One." Xenophanes must be considered as an interesting and influential critic of established ideas rather than as the founder of any "school."

7. *Heraclitus*

Of the life of Heraclitus of Ephesus we know very little. He seems to have written his work about 500 B.C. and is said, instead of publishing it, to have deposited it in the temple of Artemis in his native city. He writes disparagingly of other philosophers and is clearly convinced that he has discovered something which had eluded everyone up to his time. His style is prophetic and even in antiquity he was known as "the Dark." How wide, various and deep was his outlook may be indicated by the fact that when we read today the fragments which have survived we are reminded sometimes of a Hebrew prophet, sometimes of an oracle, sometimes of William Blake, sometimes of T. S. Eliot and sometimes of such modern thinkers as Hegel, Marx or Bertrand Russell. Indeed it seems in this case a mistake to attempt to explain the thought before the reader has had an opportunity of feeling the impact of the remarkably original style in which it is expressed. The following quotations are again from Burnet (*op. cit.,* pp. 132-41) and I have kept his numbering:

1. It is wise to hearken, not to me, but to my Word, and to confess that all things are one.
4. Eyes and ears are bad witnesses to men if they have souls that understand not their language.
7. If you do not expect the unexpected, you will not find it; for it is hard to be sought out and difficult.
10. Nature loves to hide.
16. The learning of many things teacheth not understanding, else would it have taught Hesiod and Pythagoras, and again Xenophanes and Hekataios.
19. Wisdom is one thing. It is to know the thought by which all things are steered through all things.
20. This world, which is the same for all, no one of gods or men has made; but it was ever, is now, and ever shall be an ever-living Fire, with measures of it kindling, and measures going out.
21. The transformations of Fire are, first of all, sea; and half of the sea is earth, half whirlwind. . . .

22. All things are an exchange of Fire, and Fire for all things, even as wares for gold and gold for wares.

24. Fire is want and surfeit.

25. Fire lives the death of air, and air lives the death of fire; water lives the death of earth, earth that of water.

26. Fire in its advance will judge and convict all things.

29. The sun will not overstep his measures; if he does, the Erinyes, the hand-maids of Justice, will find him out.

41, 42. You cannot step twice into the same rivers; for fresh waters are ever flowing in upon you.

43. Homer was wrong in saying: "Would that strife might perish from among gods and men!" He did not see that he was praying for the destruction of the universe; for, if his prayer were heard, all things would pass away. . .

46. It is the opposite which is good for us.

47. The hidden attunement is better than the open.

61. To God all things are fair and good and right, but men hold some things wrong and some right.

62. We must know that war is common to all and strife is justice, and that all things come into being and pass away [?] through strife.

69. The way up and the way down is one and the same.

70. In the circumference of a circle the beginning and end are common.

71. You will not find the boundaries of soul by travelling in any direction, so deep is the measure of it.

80. I have sought for myself.

81. We step and do not step into the same rivers; we are and are not.

91a. Thought is common to all.

91b. Those who speak with understanding must hold fast to what is common to all as a city holds fast to its law, and even more strongly. For all human laws are fed by the one divine law. It prevails as much as it will, and suffices for all things with something to spare.

95. The waking have one common world, but the sleeping turn aside each into a world of his own.

98, 99. The wisest man is an ape compared to God, just as the most beautiful ape is ugly compared to man.

100. The people must fight for its law as for its walls.

104. It is not good for men to get all they wish to get. It is sickness that makes health pleasant; evil, good; hunger, plenty; weariness, rest.

125. The mysteries practised among men are unholy mysteries.

126. And they pray to these images, as if one were to talk with a man's house, knowing not what gods or heroes are.

127. For if it were not to Dionysus that they made a procession and sang the shameful phallic hymn, they would be acting most shamelessly. But Hades is the same as Dionysus in whose honour they go mad and rave.

It is clear from these few extracts that we are in the presence of a confident and original thinker. Heraclitus has been called, not without reason, "the first mental philosopher." His "Word" is something different from "inquiry." Mere knowledge is not enough for him. He claims to be able to see into the nature of things and to have discovered a universal law, something that is "common," so long as one is "awake." This law is, for the first time, connected with man's own nature ("I sought for myself") and also with something which Heraclitus calls "God." (Fragments 98, 99 are a neat answer to Xenophanes.) Here he seems to reject both the easy pantheism of Xenophanes and the mysticism of "the religious revival" as exemplified by Pythagoras. His "Word" is neither purely theoretical nor a form of expiation or otherworldliness. It is very definitely "engaged." It is not "the Word" of St. John, but it is nearer to this than are the mathematical or magic symbols of the Pythagoreans.

There is without doubt a peculiar grandeur about his vision of the world and, though it is expressed enigmatically enough, it has influenced and stimulated thinkers and poets from his day to our own. For this reason Heraclitus is perhaps all the more difficult to understand. It is likely, for instance, to confuse rather than to enlighten us if we try to explain the dictum "Hades and Dionysus are the same" by imagining that Heraclitus was interested in the same considerations as those of Blake when he wrote "The Marriage of Heaven and Hell." We shall be on safer ground if we proceed rather more historically and assume that Heraclitus must certainly have *begun* to think about the problems which had been raised by earlier thinkers, in particular the thinkers of Miletus. He too must have begun by asking himself what is the fundamental "stuff" of which everything is made. He too was looking for the unity behind variety and change.

His originality is in coming to the conclusion that the unity *is* variety, that what is fundamental is not a "stuff" but a process. The images he gives of this process are those of a river or of a flame. Of these things it is possible to say both that they do and they do not persist. One cannot step into the same river twice, yet it remains a river. Nothing exists statically. There is no "stuff." Yet the process, or movement, of existence continues forever and identifiable shapes are visible in the stream or flame.

This is a different way of looking at things altogether from that of the Milesians. Anaximander certainly speaks of an "eternal motion" and explains change by the "reparation" which things make to each other for their "injustice." But he and the others are always thinking of some underlying "stuff" (even if it is called "the unlimited") which is in motion. If there were no motion, the "stuff" would still be there, though in an undifferentiated state. Heraclitus, on the other hand, as is made quite clear by fragment 43, believes that without motion, or "strife," nothing would exist at all. So far from accepting Anaximander's view of "reparation" and "justice," he proclaims (fragment 62) that "strife is justice."

His fire, therefore, cannot be understood in at all the same way as the water or air of the others. True that he uses some phrases which recall the "scientific" preoccupations of the Milesians. His fire has its intake and its outgiving; it has to change into earth and water and then change back again into itself. But these detailed explanations are insignificant compared with his grand idea of the universe as subsisting not on any kind of "stuff" or material, but on motion or on "an attunement of opposite tensions." As we have seen, he believes that man too is part of the general law of the universe. The state of man depends on tension and the right mixture of opposites.

One may find, of course, some kind of analogy in modern science, which regards matter as involving incessant motion and energy for its very existence. (Even "the one" of the atom is "many.") And there are other analogies with some modern philosophical theories, e.g., the theory of Russell that a "thing" is really "a class of events"—an idea explicitly intended by Russell to eliminate the notion of *substance*. But it is impossible to say to what extent Heraclitus thought and argued at all in the same way as a modern scientist or philosopher. Again it should be said that the distinctions between science, philosophy and religion could scarcely have been present to his mind. "Dark" indeed he is. No doubt he would have considered it natural that his "darkness" has been the source of so much illumination. He had not discovered "the Law of Contradiction" (that was the achievement of Parmenides); he declared however that such a law cannot aptly be applied to a consideration of the universe or of the soul.

8. Parmenides

Heraclitus, though influenced by the Milesians, cannot be said to belong to any "school." Another "school" however, known as the Eleatic, now arose in the Greek West. The founder of this school was Parmenides, a native of the Greek city of Elea in southern Italy. He is said to have made laws, which were greatly respected, for his native city, and to have come to Athens in his sixty-fifth year and conversed with the young Socrates. This must have been in about 450 B.C. He is said too to have been converted to the philosophical way of life by a Pythagorean to whom he afterwards built a shrine as a hero. He wrote in verse and, though from a literary point of view his verse is less "poetical" than the prose of Heraclitus, it is verse of considerable fervor. Quite obviously the philosophical way of life means much to him, though it does not mean what it meant to Pythagoras or what, later, it was to mean to Lucretius. Parmenides seems unique in having been inspired with rapture by pure logic. He was the first logician and may be described as the first philosopher in the modern sense of the word. His system depends entirely on logical deduction and has little or nothing in common with the speculative "science" of the Milesians or with what (for want of a better word) we may call the intuitive method of Heraclitus. It is to be noted that Plato, with his own respect for method, takes Parmenides more seriously than any of his predecessors.

Parmenides' poem begins with an allegorical description of his journey by chariot from the abode of Night to that of Day. Here he is met by a goddess (he is "a youth" at the time) who defines for him the methods of thought and introduces him to the Way of Truth. The second part of the poem, "The Way of Opinion," merely describes the views of others. As Parmenides did not believe in them himself, we shall only be concerned with the first part.

Here he (or the goddess) distinguishes between three ways of thought. They are (1) that It is, (2) that It is not, (3) that It both is and is not. (3) must obviously refer to the method of Heraclitus. Parmenides vigorously asserts that the only possible way of thought is (1). It is impossible, he says, to think or to believe in "nothing" as something which exists. There cannot "be" such a thing as emptiness. There can be no spaces between objects, no temporal beginnings or endings of things. The universe is one single, continuous object. Motion and change are inconceivable, and, if our senses suggest that things do move and do change, then our senses are deceiving us.

We may perhaps explain the doctrine of "that It is" more clearly by using rather more modern terms. The basic idea is this: (1) Any intelligible name must be the name *of* something which exists. (This idea, incidentally, is common in philosophy well into the twentieth century.) (2) Therefore a sentence of the form "— does not exist" must always be meaningless or self-contradictory. It is meaningless if the blank is filled by what is not a name of something existing; it is contradictory if it is filled by a real name. (3) Therefore all views must be rejected which either say or imply that something (anything) does not exist; for that "cannot be thought."

It follows that what exists must be temporally infinite; to say otherwise would entail referring to "what is not" as preceding and following it, and that makes no sense. Spatially it is concluded that "what exists" is finite and spherical, though it is rather difficult to see why Parmenides believed this. Presumably it was because "bounded by nothing" was to him a meaningless idea; yet it seems that this could also be taken as a reason for denying that "what exists" is spatially bounded at all.

Now there is something quite new in this rigid, and enthusiastic, application of a supposed principle of logic, leading, as it does, to such startling conclusions as that change and motion are illusions of the senses. The conclusions are shown in their most striking form by Parmenides' follower Zeno in his famous paradoxes. The logical method, however—a method which depends entirely on thought and not at all on experiment or observation—is the creation of Parmenides. I am quoting from Burnet (*op. cit.,* pp. 174-75) the passages from the poem which define the doctrine of "that It is."

One path only is left for us to speak of, namely, that *It is*. In this path are very many tokens that what is is uncreated and indestructible; for it is complete, immovable, and without end. Nor was it ever, nor will it be; for now *it is*, all at once, a continuous one. For what kind of origin for it wilt thou look for? In what way and from what source could it have drawn its increase? . . . I shall not let thee say nor think that it came from what is not; for it can neither be thought nor uttered that anything is not. And, if it came from nothing, what need could have made it arise later rather than sooner? Therefore must it either be altogether or be not at all. Nor will the force of truth suffer aught to arise besides itself from that which is not. Wherefore, Justice doth not loose her fetters and let anything come into being or pass away, but holds it fast. Our judgment thereon depends on this: *"Is it or is it not?"* Surely it is adjudged, as it needs must be, that we are to set aside the one way as unthinkable and nameless (for it is no true way), and that the other path is real and true. How, then, can what *is* be going to be in the future? Or how could it come into being? If it came into being, it is not; nor is it if it is going to be in the future. Thus is becoming extinguished and passing away not to be heard of.

Nor is it divisible, since it is all alike, and there is no more of it in one place than in another, to hinder it from holding together, nor less of it, but everything is full of what is. Wherefore it is wholly continuous; for what is, is in contact with what is.

Moreover, it is immovable in the bonds of mighty chains, without beginning and without end; since coming into being and passing away have been driven afar, and true belief has cast them away. It is the same, and it rests in the self-same place, abiding in itself. And thus it remaineth constant in its place; for hard necessity keeps it in the bonds of the limit that holds it fast on every side. Wherefore it is not permitted to what is to be infinite; for it is in need of nothing; while, if it were infinite, it would stand in need of everything.

The thing that can be thought and that for the sake of which the thought exists is the same; for you cannot find thought without something that is, as to which it is uttered. And there is not, and never shall be, anything besides what is, since fate has chained it so as to be whole and immovable. Wherefore all these thing are but names which mortals have given, believing them to be true—coming into being and passing away, being and not being, change of place and alteration of bright colour.

Since, then, it has a furthest limit, it is complete on every side, like the mass of a rounded sphere, equally poised from the centre in every direction; for it cannot be greater or smaller in one place than in another. For there is nothing that could keep it from reaching out equally, nor can aught that is to be be more here and less there than what is, since it is all inviolable. For the point from which it is equal in every direction tends equally to the limits.

9. Empedocles

Empedocles, a native of the Greek city of Akragas in Sicily, was born probably about 493 B.C. and may have lived until about 433. His activities and his character alike seem to have been extraordinarily various. He was an aristocrat and also a champion of the democracy. He was offered and declined the kingship of Akragas. He was exiled and recited at Olympia his poem "The Purifications," in which he claimed to be a god. He was a keen observer—much more of a "scientist" than Parmenides—and he was also a kind of magician. He was a considerable poet and one of the founders of the new art of rhetorical and balanced prose. He had an important influence on medicine. He was an evolutionist and may be credited with the invention of the theory of "the survival of the fittest." He seems to have followed, at least to some extent, the Pythagorean way of life. "Wretches," he exclaims, "utter wretches, keep your hands from beans!" (Burnet, *op. cit.*, fragment 141, p. 226.) Some idea of his own notion of himself may be gained from another passage from the "Purifications" (Burnet, *op. cit.*, p. 221-22).

112. Friends, that inhabit the great town looking down on the yellow rock of Akragas, up by the citadel, busy in goodly works, harbours of honour for the stranger, men unskilled in meanness, all hail. I go about among you an immortal god, no mortal now, honoured among all as is meet, crowned with fillets and flowery garlands. Straightway, whenever I enter with these in my train, both men and women, into the flourishing towns, is reverence done me; they go after me in countless throngs, asking of me what is the way to gain; some desiring oracles, while some, who for many a weary day have been pierced by the grievous pangs of all manner of sickness, beg to hear from me the word of healing.

We may notice here, apart from the claim to divinity, a great confidence in the power of wisdom to bring about results. And in fact Empedocles' theory of the four (or six) elements has proved very much more capable of useful development than have the various theories of "the One."

His philosophy is expressed in the poem "On Nature," of which 350 verses survive. His problem, it seems, was, while repairing the theory of Parmenides about "what is," to reconcile it with the apparent facts of change and of motion. And (though Burnet does not accept this view) his method appears to be based on a kind of compromise between Parmenides and Heraclitus. He accepts the idea of the permanency of "what is," but insists also on the permanency of a "process." In doing so he abandons the original Milesian hypothesis of a single substratum and

comes forward with the view that the world is composed
not of one "stuff" but of four "roots" or elements—fire, air,
water and earth. These, as seems natural to a person of his
temperament, are given divine names, though they are
examined both experimentally and logically. Three of these
"roots" had already been put forward as the ultimate reality
by Empedocles' predecessors. In adding earth to the list and
in asserting the existence of four elements rather than one
"stuff," he may have been actuated simply by a kind of
common sense; and those who, whether from a logical or
an aesthetic impulse, wish to see all things explained by one
hypothesis must deplore the pluralism. Yet it was a pluralism which led to results and which, unlike the splendid
monism of Parmenides, did, if not make, at least account
for, sense. In a way, too, it was the first step towards the
atomic theory. But more remarkable than the theory of
the four "roots" is the theory which is intended to account
for change and motion, for the process of development and
dissolution. Here Empedocles proclaims the existence of
two "things" which he calls Strife and Love. We should,
without question, call these "things" "forces." As Sambursky says, "Empedocles was the first to distinguish matter from force." And this is probably true, though it may
be possible to find some such distinction in Heraclitus.
However, though the distinction is a real one, the fragments show that Empedocles himself was scarcely aware
of it. His "forces" are to him material. They have weight,
length and breadth. How he thought of them we do not
know. But do we know how we think of our own "forces"?

Strife and Love, or, as we should say, attraction and
repulsion, account for change and motion. The elements
are compounded under their influence and their influence
can be imagined in more dimensions than the "upward
and downward path" of Heraclitus. The cyclical process
of the "Sphere" in which we live can be imagined or
demonstrated as follows. Love is the unifier and Strife the
divider. Four distinct historical periods must follow each
other.

1. The period in which Love is supreme and Strife is
outside the sphere. In this period all the elements are

mixed together. Nothing is distinguishable from anything else.

2. The period when Strife begins, as it were, to invade. In this period the elements are separated and, with Love still active, come together in various combinations, including some very odd ones (e.g., heads without necks, men with the heads of oxen, etc.).

3. The period when Strife is supreme. The four elements are now distinct and separate. Nothing can exist except fire, air, water and earth. Love is outside the sphere.

4. The period when Love, in its turn, begins to invade and the elements are again brought to mingle with each other in various associations. Obviously the kind of world which we know can only exist in periods 2 and 4. There are good reasons for believing that Empedocles thought that our world is in period 2.

This theory was evidently worked out in great detail. Perhaps its most interesting applications are in the realm of biology. Empedocles' theory of sensation and of vision was to have a long future and was taken up both by Plato and Aristotle and by the atomists. The theory is that "effluences" come to us from things and by "fitting into the forces" of the various organs of sense communicate to us vision, taste, smell, etc.

In the following extracts (taken from Burnet, *op. cit.*, pp. 205 ff.) it has seemed advisable, however, to give more space to the general theory of this remarkable man than to his detailed applications of it.

6. Hear first the four roots of all things: shining Zeus, life-bringing Hera, Aidoneus and Nestis whose tear-drops are a well-spring to mortals.

8. And I shall tell thee another thing. There is no substance of any of all the things that perish, nor any cessation for them of baneful death. They are only a mingling and interchange of what has been mingled. Substance is but a name given to these things by men.

16. For even as they (Strife and Love) were aforetime, so too they shall be; nor ever, methinks, will boundless time be emptied of that pair.

17. I shall tell thee a twofold tale. At one time it grew to be one only out of many; at another, it divided up to be many instead of one. There is a double becoming of perishable things and a double passing away. The coming together of all things brings one generation into being and destroys it; the other grows up and is scattered as things become divided. And these things never cease continually changing places, at one time all uniting in one through Love, at another each borne in different directions by the repulsion of Strife. Thus, as far as it is their nature to grow into one out of many, and to become many once more when the one is parted asunder, so far they come into being and their life abides not. But, inasmuch as they never cease changing their places continually, so far they are ever immovable as they go round the circle of existence. . . .

But come, hearken to my words, for it is learning that increaseth wisdom. As I said before, when I declared the heads of my discourse, I shall tell thee a twofold tale. At one time it grew together to be one only out of many, at another it parted asunder so as to be many instead of one;—Fire and Water and Earth and the mighty height of Air, dread Strife, too, apart from these, of equal weight to each, and Love in their midst, equal in length and breadth. Her do thou contemplate with thy mind, nor sit with dazed eyes. It is she that is known as being implanted in the frame of mortals. It is she that makes them have thoughts of love and work the works of peace. They call her by the names of Joy and Aphrodite. Her has no mortal yet marked moving round among them, but do thou attend to the undeceitful ordering of my discourse.

For all these are equal and alike in age, yet each has a different prerogative and its own peculiar nature, but they gain the upper hand in turn when the time comes round. And nothing comes into being besides these, nor do they pass away; for, if they had been passing away continually, they would not be now, and what could increase this All and whence could it come? How, too, could it perish, since no place is empty of these things? There are these alone; but, running through one another, they become now this, now that, and like things evermore.

35, 36. But now I shall retrace my steps over the paths of song that I have travelled before, drawing from my saying a new saying. When Strife was fallen to the lowest depth of the vortex, and Love had reached to the centre of the whirl, in it do all things come together so as to be one only; not all at once, but coming together at their will each from different quarters; and, as they mingled, Strife began to pass out to the furthest limit. Yet many things remained unmixed, alternating with the things that were being mixed, namely, all that Strife not fallen yet retained; for it had not yet altogether retired perfectly from them to the outermost boundaries of the circle. Some of it still remained within, and some had passed out from the limbs of the All. But in proportion as it kept rushing out, a soft, immortal stream of blameless Love kept running in, and straightway those things became mortal which had been immortal before, those things were mixed that had before been unmixed, each changing its path. And, as they mingled, countless tribes of mortal creatures were scattered abroad endowed with all manner of forms, a wonder to behold.

57. On it (the earth) many heads sprung up without necks and arms wandered bare and bereft of shoulders. Eyes strayed up and down in want of foreheads.

60. Shambling creatures with countless hands.

61. Many creatures with faces and breasts looking in different directions were born; some, offspring of oxen with faces of men, while others, again, arose as offspring of men with the heads of oxen, and creatures in whom the nature of women and men was mingled, furnished with sterile parts.

10. Anaxagoras

Anaxagoras, an Ionian from Clazomenae, came to Athens in 480 B.C., quite possibly as a member of Xerxes' invading army or navy. At this time he was probably about twenty years old. He was the first philosopher to settle in Athens and he lived there for thirty years. He was a friend and a teacher of Pericles and, probably in 450 B.C., was accused before the Athenian courts by Pericles' political opponents. The charges were that he was a pro-Persian and that his attitude to the gods was irreligious. He had taught that the sun was a red-hot stone and that the moon was made of earth. However he had not the scruples of Socrates about evading prison and, probably with the help of

Pericles, he was able to leave Athens and to return to Ionia. He settled at Lampsacus and lived there for about twenty-five years. As a mark of respect to his memory, the anniversary of his death was long kept as a holiday in Lampsacus for schoolchildren.

His work was read first with enthusiasm and finally with disappoint... ent by the young Socrates. The only fragments which survive seem to have come from the first book of this work, in which he deals with his general principles. There is still controversy among scholars about precisely how these principles are to be understood.

His approach to the problem of substance and change seems to have been like that of Empedocles (though without his mystical, Pythagorean attitude). He too accepts the view of Parmenides that nothing can be added to or taken away from what is. He too is concerned to explain motion and change. It is quite likely (see fragment 17) that he had read the poem of Empedocles. Certainly his idea of "mingling" and "separation" reminds one of the Sicilian philosopher (though this idea may also be derived from Anaximenes).

He did not believe in either one or four "roots" or elements. Nor is he an atomist. He held the view that matter is a continuum, infinitely divisible and that, however much it may be divided, each part will contain elements of everything else. Thus the difference between, say, fire and earth, or a piece of gold or a grain of wheat, is accounted for simply by the fact that in fire there is *more* fire than there is in earth, and in gold *more* gold than there is in wheat; yet there is *some* fire in earth, *some* earth in fire, *some* wheat in gold and *some* gold in wheat. It seems probable, too, that the opposites—the hot and the cold, the moist and the dry, etc.—were also regarded as "things" and hence part of the constitution of the "seeds."

As for the problem of how these seeds ever came together into the forms we know—the problem of motion, growth and change—Anaxagoras assumes the existence of an external cause which he calls *Nous* or "Mind." In doing so he earned the applause of Aristotle who, simply because he made this assumption, says that he, compared with all the other philosophers whom we have been discussing, was like a sober man among a crowd of drunkards. Socrates too, according to Plato, was delighted when he first read that Anaxagoras had made Mind the cause of all things. However he was quickly disillusioned by discovering that though Anaxagoras did indeed use Mind as a kind of *deus ex machina* to account for the original rotatory movement which gave rise to the formation of the world, his real interests were much more what we would call "scientific." He only used Mind as a hypothesis when he could think of nothing else. We should note too that Anaxagoras' *Nous,* like the Love and Strife of Empedocles, is imagined as a substance (fragment 12). It is therefore impossible to maintain that Anaxagoras introduced, except verbally, anything which can be called a "spiritual" element into philosophy. The following fragments are quoted from Burnet, *op. cit.,* pp. 258 ff.

4. . . . . But before they were separated off, when all things were together, not even was any colour distinguishable; for the mixture of all things prevented it—of the moist and the dry, and the warm and the cold, and the light and the dark, and of much earth that was in it, and of a multitude of innumerable seeds in no way like each other. For none of the other things either is like any other. And these things being so, we must hold that all things are in the whole.

6. And since the portions of the great and of the small are equal in amount, for this reason, too, all things will be in everything; nor is it possible for them to be apart, but all things have a portion of everything. Since it is impossible for there to be a least thing, they cannot be separated, nor come to be by themselves; but they must be now, just as they were in the beginning, all together. And in all things many things are contained, and an equal number both in the greater and in the smaller of the things that are separated off.

8. The things that are in one world are not divided nor cut off from one another with a hatchet, neither the warm from the cold nor the cold from the warm.

11. In everything there is a portion of everything except Nous, and there are some things in which there is Nous also.

12. All other things partake in a portion of everything, while Nous is infinite and self-ruled, and is mixed with nothing, but is alone, itself by itself. For if it were not by itself, but were mixed with anything else, it would partake in all things if it were mixed with any; for in everything there is a portion of everything, as has been said by me in what goes before, and the things mixed with it would hinder it, so that it would have power over nothing in the same way that it has now being alone by itself. For it is the thinnest of all things and the purest, and it has all knowledge about everything and the greatest strength; and Nous has power over all things, both greater and smaller, that have life. And Nous had power over the whole revolution, so that it began to revolve in the beginning. And it began to revolve first from a small beginning; but the revolution now extends over a larger space, and will extend over a larger still. And all the things that are mingled together and separated off and distinguished are all known by Nous. And Nous set in order all things that were to be, and all things that were and are not now and that are, and this revolution in which now revolve the stars and the sun and the moon, and the air and the aether that are separated off. And this revolution caused the separating off, and the rare is separated off from the dense, the warm from the cold, the light from the dark, and the dry from the moist. And there are many portions in many things. But no thing is altogether separated off nor distinguished from anything else except Nous. And all Nous is alike, both the greater and the smaller; while nothing else is like anything else, but each single thing is and was most manifestly those things of which it has most in it.

13. And when Nous began to move things, separating off took place from all that was moved, and so much as Nous set in motion was all separated. And as things were set in motion and separated, the revolution caused them to be separated much more.

17. The Hellenes follow a wrong usage in speaking of coming into being and passing away; for nothing comes into being or passes away, but there is mingling and separation of things that are. So they would be right to call coming into being mixture, and passing away separation.

21. From the weakness of our senses we are not able to judge the truth.

21a. What appears is a vision of the unseen.

11. Zeno and Melissos

We have seen how Empedocles and Anaxagoras attempted to restore the world of appearances which had been so nearly destroyed by the logic of Parmenides. At the same time the disciples of Pythagoras were continuing to pursue their method of analyzing reality into a system of numbers—numbers expressing points, lines or geometrical shapes and proportions. No one, in fact, had really faced the full force of Parmenides' assertion "As it was in the beginning is now and ever shall be." One cannot help feeling that in the systems of his successors the idea of motion, whether under the guise of condensation and rarefaction, "mingling" or *Nous,* has somehow slipped in through the back door.

Now, in the middle of the fifth century and in the youth of Socrates, the doctrine of Parmenides is once more vigorously asserted by Zeno, a pupil and fellow-townsman of Parmenides himself, and by Mclissos, a native of Samos.

Zeno, according to Plato, was born about 490 B.C. and visited Athens, in company with Parmenides, when he was about forty years old. Aristotle describes him as the inventor of dialectics and it is certainly true that, though the principles of dialectics are evident in Parmenides' own writing, Zeno was the first to give to what may be called either "logic-chopping" or "rational thought" a dramatic and a particularly incisive expression. His method was to take up the hypothesis of his philosophical opponent and from it to deduce contradictory conclusions. The effect of the method is to suggest that those who disagree with the doctrine of the Parmenidean "One" and try to "save appearances" will find themselves involved in difficulties much greater than those which they have been attempting to avoid.

His three best-known paradoxes may be summarized as follows:

1. You cannot get to the other side of a racecourse. To do so, you must first get halfway across, and to do this, you

must first get halfway to the halfway point, and so on *ad infinitum*. Therefore you can never start at all.

2. Achilles can never catch up with the tortoise. To do so he must first reach the point from which the tortoise started, and by that time the tortoise will have got a little further on. By the time he makes up this further distance, the tortoise will have moved a little more, and so on *ad infinitum*.

3. The arrow in flight is at rest. At any given moment it must occupy a space equal to itself. Therefore it cannot move.

Of these paradoxes the first two are directed against the hypothesis that matter or being is infinitely divisible, or, to be more precise, that a line is made up of an infinite number of points. The third paradox (and a fourth which, for reasons of space, I have omitted) is directed at the hypothesis that matter or being is made up of a finite number of indivisibles. We are left to conclude that if being is neither infinitely divisible nor composed of a finite number of divisibles, it must be, as Parmenides had concluded, a continuum. It may be thought that there is something obviously absurd about Zeno's arguments, and in a sense this is true. However, anyone who cares to investigate the enormous and still growing literature devoted to their discussion will soon realize that his logical knots are very skillfully tied.

The system of Parmenides is explained with at least as great clarity as that of Parmenides himself by Melissos of Samos, who also, in one important respect, makes an addition to the theory. Of Melissos himself we know nothing except that he commanded the Samian fleet against Athens in 442-440 B.C., defeated Pericles and, probably, was later defeated by him. He differs from Parmenides in concluding that "what exists" is infinite in space as well as in time. I must admit that I cannot understand why Parmenides did not come to this conclusion himself, since if his sphere had anything outside it, that "anything" must be "nothing," and there is no "nothing." We should note too an interesting line of thought in fragment 8. Here Melissos asserts that if one is going to believe in "a many" (and of course he thinks one should not) then each one of the many must have all the characteristics of the Parmenidean "One." It seems something of an exaggeration to say, as Burnet does of this statement, "In other words, the only consistent pluralism is the atomic theory"; but there is no doubt that the atomic theorists were influenced by this line of thought.

It may be interesting to read the following fragments in conjunction with those of Parmenides. The fragments are from Burnet, *op. cit.,* pp. 321 ff.

1a. If nothing is, what can be said of it as of something real?

1. What was was ever, and ever shall be. For, if it had come into being, it needs must have been nothing before it came into being. Now, if it were nothing, in no wise could anything have arisen out of nothing.

2. Since, then, it has not come into being, and since it is, was ever, and ever shall be, it has no beginning or end, but is without limit. For, if it had come into being, it would have had a beginning (for it would have begun to come into being at some time or other) and an end (for it would have ceased to come into being at some time or other); but, if it neither began nor ended, and ever was and ever shall be, it has no beginning or end; for it is not possible for anything to be ever without all being.

3. Further, just as it ever is, so it must ever be infinite in magnitude.

4. But nothing which has a beginning or end is either eternal or infinite.

5. If it were not one, it would be bounded by something else.

6. For if it is (infinite), it must be one; for if it were two, it could not be infinite; for then they would be bounded by one another.

7. So then it is eternal and infinite and one and all alike. And it cannot perish nor become greater, nor does it suffer pain or grief. For, if any of these things happened to it, it would no longer be one. For if it is altered, then the real must needs not be all alike, but what was before must pass away, and what was not must come into being. Now, if it changed

by so much as a single hair in ten thousand years, it would all perish in the whole of time.

Further, it is not possible either that its order should be changed; for the order which it had before does not perish, nor does that which was not come into being. But since nothing is either added to it or passes away or is altered, how can any real thing have had its order changed? For if anything became different, that would amount to a change in its order.

Nor does it suffer pain; for a thing in pain could not all be. For a thing in pain could not be ever, nor has it the same power as what is whole. Nor would it be alike, if it were in pain; for it is only from the addition or subtraction of something that it could feel pain, and then it would no longer be alike. Nor could what is whole feel pain; for then what was whole and what was real would pass away, and what was not would come into being. And the same argument applies to grief as to pain.

Nor is anything empty. For what is empty is nothing. What is nothing cannot be.

Nor does it move; for it has nowhere to betake itself to, but is full. For if there were aught empty, it would betake itself to the empty. But, since there is naught empty, it has nowhere to betake itself to.

And it cannot be dense and rare; for it is not possible for what is rare to be as full as what is dense, but what is rare is at once emptier than what is dense.

This is the way in which we must distinguish between what is full and what is not full. If a thing has room for anything else, and takes it in, it is not full; but if it has no room for anything and does not take it in, it is full.

Now, it must needs be full if there is naught empty, and if it is full, it does not move.

8. This argument, then, is the greatest proof that it is one alone; but the following are proofs of it also. If there were a many, these would have to be of the same kind as I say that the one is. For if there is earth and water, and air and iron, and gold and fire, and if one thing is living and another dead, and if things are black and white and all that men say they really are,—if that is so, and if we see and hear aright, each one of these must be such as we first decided, and they cannot be changed or altered, but each must be just as it is. But, as it is, we say that we see and hear and understand aright, and yet we believe that what is warm becomes cold, and what is cold

warm; that what is hard turns soft, and what is soft hard; that what is living dies, and that things are born from what lives not; and that all those things are changed, and that what they were and what they are now are in no way alike. We think that iron, which is hard, is rubbed away by contact with the finger; and so with gold and stone and everything which we fancy to be strong, and that earth and stone are made out of water; so that it turns out that we neither see nor know realities. Now these things do not agree with one another. We said that there were many things that were eternal and had forms and strength of their own, and yet we fancy that they all suffer alteration, and that they change from what we see each time. It is clear, then, that we did not see aright after all, nor are we right in believing that all these things are many. They would not change if they were real, but each thing would be just what we believed it to be; for nothing is stronger than true reality. But if it has changed, what was has passed away, and what was not is come into being. So then, if there were many things, they would have to be just of the same nature as the one.

9. Now, if it were to exist, it must needs be one; but if it is one, it cannot have body; for, if it had body it would have parts, and would no longer be one.

10. If what is real is divided, it moves; but if it moves, it cannot be.

12. *Leucippus*

Leucippus of Miletus was a contemporary of Melissos. He is said to have "heard" Zeno and may well have visited Elea, the headquarters of the "school" of Parmenides. By inventing the atomic theory he gave what seems much the most satisfactory answer to the question first posed by his fellow-countryman Thales, at least if that question is taken to be a "scientific" one; and, in his own peculiar way, he succeeded in reconciling the views both of the Ionians and of the Eleatics. His theory was developed by Democritus (born about 460 B.C.) and was later expanded into a system that was both philosophical and ethical by Epicurus. At this point I shall make no comment on the later developments. It is, in fact, impossible to distinguish clearly what parts of the development of the theory should be attributed to Leucippus and what to Democritus. Leucippus, however, must be credited with having taken the first and decisive step. He was bold enough to assert that "Nothing" "exists," and was thus able to offer an explanation of motion. He accepted Zeno's arguments against infinite divisibility and asserted the existence of ultimate particles, or "atoms" (a word which simply means "indivisibles"), each one of which had, as Melissos had suggested, the characteristics of the Parmenidean "One." Everything, he declared, was made up of atoms and the void (the void being "nothing") in different arrangements. The atoms themselves are invisible, though they are not all of the same size. Yet, though they have magnitude, they cannot be divided. The reason for this is that they, like the One of Parmenides, contain no empty space. The practical applications of this theory will be discussed later, when we come to consider Epicurus. Here it will be sufficient merely to notice Leucippus' revolutionary new use of the verb "to be." His essential principle that there can be a void—that there can *be* what is, in a sense, nothing— would have seemed an intolerable paradox to earlier thinkers, who were inclined to identify existence with *corporeal* existence. This bold unorthodoxy was an essential factor in his resistance to the logic of Parmenides and Zeno.

Only one fragment of Leucippus survives. It is "Nothing happens at random, but all things for a reason and of necessity." This is certainly evidence for a belief in determinism; but how far Leucippus himself went with his determinism we do not know. "Necessity" may still have been to him a "force" like the Love and Strife of Empedocles. Possibly the full determinism by which everything takes place simply because of the properties inherent from eternity in the atoms and in the void was the later development of Democritus. Leucippus' importance as a logician is well shown, however, by a passage from Theophrastus and a passage from Aristotle. These I quote from Burnet (*op. cit.,* pp. 333-35).

1. Leucippos of Elea or Miletos (for both accounts are given of him) had associated with Parmenides in philosophy. He did not, however, follow the same path in his explanation of things as Parmenides and Xenophanes did, but, to all appearance, the very opposite. They made the All one, immovable, uncreated, and finite, and did not even permit us to search for *what is not*; he assumed innumerable and ever-moving elements, namely, the atoms. And he made their forms infinite in number, since there was no reason why they should be of one kind rather than another, and because he saw that there was unceasing becoming and change in things. He held, further, that *what is* is no more real than *what is not*, and that both are alike causes of the things that come into being; for he laid down that the substance of the atoms was compact and full, and he called them *what is*, while they moved in the void which he called *what is not,* but affirmed to be just as real as *what is*.

2. Leucippos and Democritus have decided about all things practically by the same method and on the same theory, taking as their starting-point what naturally comes first. Some of the ancients had held that the real must necessarily be one and immovable; for, said they, empty space is not real, and motion would be impossible without empty space separated from matter; nor, further, could reality be a many, if there were nothing to separate things. And it makes no difference if any one holds that the All is not continuous, but discrete, with its parts in contact (the Pythagorean view), instead of holding that reality is many, not one, and that there is empty space. For, if it is divisible at every point there is no one, and therefore no many, and the Whole is empty (Zeno); while, if we say it is divisible in one place and not in another, this looks like an arbitrary fiction; for up to what point and for what reason will part of the Whole be in this state and be full, while the rest is discrete? And, on the same grounds, they further say that there can be no motion. In consequence of these reasonings, then, going beyond perception and overlooking it in the belief that we ought to follow the argument, they say that the All is one and immovable (Parmenides), and some of them that it is infinite (Melissos), for any limit would be bounded by empty space. This, then, is the opinion they expressed about the truth, and these are the reasons which led them to do so. Now, so far as arguments go, this conclusion does seem to follow; but, if we appeal to facts, to hold such a view looks like madness. No one who is made is so far out of his senses that fire

and ice appear to him to be one; it is only things that are right, and things that appear right from habit, in which madness makes some people see no difference.

Leucippos, however, thought he had a theory which was in harmony with sense, and did not do away with coming into being and passing away, nor motion, nor the multiplicity of things. He conceded this to experience, while he conceded, on the other hand, to those who invented the One that motion was impossible without the void, that the void was not real, and that nothing of what was real was not real. "For," said he, "that which is strictly speaking real is an absolute *plenum*; but the *plenum* is not one. On the contrary, there is an infinite number of them, and they are invisible owing to the smallness of their bulk. They move in the void (for there is a void); and by their coming together they effect coming into being; by their separation, passing away."

CHAPTER II

Socrates

We have seen that in the period from Thales until the middle of the fifth century the original "inquiry" of the Ionians became gradually differentiated into various branches of inquiry and various methods. True that a "philosopher"—a word only just beginning to come into use —was expected to be an astronomer and a mathematician as well as a logician; yet still the distinction between philosophy and science, dialectic and experiment is becoming clearer. Empedocles and Anaxagoras had conducted experiments with inflated skins in order to prove that air is corporeal. Medicine was beginning to make progress along lines which we should call "scientific." Xenophanes insists that his art is "useful." And on the other side we find, among the Pythagoreans, in Parmenides and others, an almost religious view of the contemplative life, a respect for "pure" thought as the highest activity of which man is capable. We find also that both what we may call the "scientific" and the "philosophical" attitudes are tending to come into conflict with conventional mythologic religion.

The question is often asked why it was that the Greeks, who had invented so rapidly so many of the basic principles of science, never went further with their application. Important discoveries, certainly, were made in astronomy, mechanics and medicine; but, on the whole, the tendency is towards theory and speculation and away from experiment and observation. In the end the magnificently constructed system of Aristotle, invested with the authority of St. Thomas Aquinas, becomes a positive impediment not only to science but even to the "inquiry" with which the whole process began.

The usual answer to this question is that the Greeks had "an aristocratic culture"; they would not soil their hands in a laboratory; they thought experiment an occupation only fitted for slaves. I do not believe that this answer is correct. Among many arguments against it one may adduce the activities of the extremely "aristocratic" Empedocles. A͏ ͏ophanes, certainly, makes fun of the whole idea of scientific experiment. He was pleasing an audience who liked to hear jokes about what we too, before our scientists became so powerful, liked to think of as "the absent-minded professor." It is the same attitude as that which we find in Swift's "Voyage to Laputa," and it derives from the belief not that science is "slavish," but that it is unimportant when compared with other activities.

In particular it seemed to the citizens of the new democracies of the fifth century much less important than politics. An Athenian, with his energy and intellectual curiosity, was eager indeed to explain the world and also to change it. But explanation was the work of philosophy, change of politics. And so the abstract principles, when they were "applied" at all, were applied not to the development of science but to the technique of living successfully in a political society.

The teaching of this technique was, in the middle and end of the fifth century, the work of traveling scholars, theorists and educators who are known as "sophists." They can scarcely be called philosophers and so will only concern us here in so far as they exercised an effect on the climate of opinion in which philosophy was to grow. An excellent account of their admirable educative work will be found in Werner Jaeger's *Paideia*.* They were the first grammarians, the first teachers of the art of persuasive prose, the first systematizers, one may say the first humanists. Though not, strictly speaking, philosophers themselves, they were connected with the philosophy both of

* Translated by Gilbert Highet. Oxford: Basil Blackwell & Mott Ltd., 1939, I, pp. 283 ff.

the past and of the future. Gorgias of Leontini, for instance—a special favorite in Athens—had been a pupil of Empedocles. He had written a treatise in which he maintained (1) that nothing exists, (2) that if anything does exist, it cannot be known, (3) that if it can be known, the knowledge cannot be communicated by language. He then, as an expert in balanced prose, devoted himself to the practical task of showing how prose can be, if not informative, at least influential. And this new art of rhetoric is far more than merely a question of style. It is necessary to find the right argument for the right person at the right occasion. Psychology is involved. One has to know what, in one's audience, can be attributed to "nature" and what to environment. The character of the individual takes on a new importance and so does the whole study of morality whether "natural" or imposed. Great systematic learning, a form of technique and the application of this technique to the practical problem of living are the characteristics of the sophists. One of the greatest of these, Protagoras, is credited with the statement "Man is the measure of all things." It is characteristic of the philosophical and religious skepticism of the movement that with regard to God he said that he was unable to state definitely either that He existed or that He did not exist.

Now, though it is quite true that the sophists were remarkable educators and that many of them had not only high cultural ideals but respectable ideas about morals, there was obviously, as Socrates perceived, a strange contradiction between their claim to be able to teach men how to live successfully and their total skepticism as to the place of man in the scheme of things. The contradiction becomes most obvious in questions of ethics. If man is really the measure and if success is the criterion, it is difficult to see why a particular man should not commit any number of crimes as long as he can get away with them. And when the sophists openly boasted that with the aid of their specialized technique it was possible "to make the worse cause appear the better," people were bound, while accepting the fact, to wonder what had happened to the old ideas of "justice," "truth," etc., which these modern thinkers seemed to be dismissing as the outworn and meaningless conceptions of poets and mythographers. Is there, or need there be, any relationship at all between power and justice? Fifth-century literature is forever harping on this problem, and, as the influence of the sophists grows and the events of history take place, the problem becomes more pressing. It is stated with a peculiar and terrifying force by Thucydides in his *Melian Dialogue,* though one should add that the problem is present to Thucydides throughout his *History.* Another aspect of it concerns the relation between "law" and "human nature." In his descriptions of the revolution at Corcyra and of the effects of the plague at Athens Thucydides observes, what others have noted since, that in times when the restraint of law and the conventions of morality are removed, human nature can become something almost indescribably vile and savage. Yet the same human nature, in its well-organized political form, can deserve the splendid words which the same author puts into the mouth of Pericles as he surveys the greatness, the energy, the versatility, intelligence and charity of Athenian civilization.

Socrates, like Thucydides, was "in love with" Athens. Like him he was thoroughly well acquainted with the "new learning." He too had seen and known Athens at her greatest and at her lowest. He too was concerned with the moral problem of the time. It was a problem which bears some resemblance to that of our own days. The optimism, the belief in "progress," the faith in the value of a "scientific" approach to life seemed somehow to have let down the believers. The tremendous achievements of the intellect, the triumph of democracy, the wide spreading of education had not, as it appeared, made men better; indeed it could be claimed that they had made men worse. Socrates, unlike some of our modern prophets, concluded that what was required was not less but more education, not a retreat from the intellect but a more thorough and, in a sense, impassioned use of it.

Socrates' effect on philosophy was as revolutionary as

had been that of Thales and the Ionians. It is difficult to describe this effect in a few sentences and indeed it is impossible to say what it was in particular which made this Athenian a figure of such importance. Socrates was not the first to apply abstract reasoning to the problems of conduct and of society. As we have seen, he lived in an age when this was all the fashion. Nor did he invent "dialectic." He merely employed the method of Zeno in a different way. Nor was he the first to assert the dignity and value of the philosophic life. Pythagoras and Empedocles had already done this, and Pythagoras seems also to have inspired among his disciples the same veneration as Socrates did. Yet still, and in spite of the notorious difficulty in discovering from the accounts of Plato and of Xenophon what was "the true Socrates," it is evident that in him we are confronted with a character quite unlike any that had previously appeared. He is extraordinary through being ordinary, universal through being Athenian, religious through a method of skepticism, wise through a profession of ignorance. Yet in his character, his conduct and his opinions there are no contradictions. He is all of a piece. His personality is always imposing and one feels that even so great an artist as Plato could not, even if he had wished to do so, have distorted it. It is a personality which has impressed itself on posterity as has the personality of no other philosopher. Even the physical appearance is familiar to us. We envisage a snub-nosed man of very great physical toughness and strength, a sight that would be forbidding if it were not for the remarkable charm, cordiality and sense of humor which lit up both his face and his conversation. He was quite indifferent to luxury, danger in war, snobbism or moral intimidation in peace. He was far from indifferent to his friends, to his city and to the laws of that city even when they had unjustly condemned him to death. Both in his own day and afterwards he has been represented as a saint and as a menace to society. He wrote, so far as we know, nothing.

And when we attempt to estimate his importance in the history of Greek philosophy, we are continually forced to observe that the real importance is in the personality itself rather than in any easily definable doctrine or logical method. It was the personality which impressed such diverse characters as Plato and Xenophon, and which since then has aroused the fervent adoration of Erasmus and the hatred of Nietzche.

As for his method of thought and the doctrines which he propounded, they are, when looked at from one point of view, characterized by the most thoroughgoing intellectualism; looked at from another point of view, they appear almost as elements in a religious faith.

It seems certain that Socrates himself considered that he had what we should call a "vocation" and even that, at a definite period of his life, towards the beginning of middle age, he had an experience which can be described almost as a "conversion." In his youth he had been a physicist and was associated with Archelaus, a pupil of Anaxagoras. It is noteworthy that in the *Clouds* of Aristophanes he is caricatured as a crack-brained scientist rather than as a moral reformer or as a subversive influence. Some time shortly before the outbreak of the Peloponnesian War, when he was approaching the age of forty, a friend of his inquired of the Delphic oracle who was the wisest man alive. The oracle replied that no one was wiser than Socrates. Why the oracle should have paid this compliment to an obscure Athenian who, up to this time, seems to have done nothing remarkable remains a complete mystery. It appears that Socrates himself was as astonished as anyone else by the God's reply. But he took the reply seriously and undoubtedly believed in his divine mission. He decided, with characteristic "irony," that his only claim to wisdom was that, unlike others, he was profoundly conscious of his own ignorance, and he regarded it as his duty to reveal to others, by means of his own particular method of cross-examination, exactly how ignorant they really were. Not unnaturally he made enemies as well as friends.

His cross-examination was a development and clarification of the dialectic of Zeno. First he would take the "hypothesis" of the person under examination—a conventional definition, say, of courage or of justice—and, by testing it with the aid of examples taken from real life, would prove it to be inadequate or self-contradictory. The process would lead to another "hypothesis" which would be examined in its turn and, as a rule, also rejected. So far, the method can be described as negative. But its aim is very positive indeed. With charm, with irony, but with a quite tremendous intensity of emotion and of thought Socrates is really trying to find out what "courage" or "justice" is. He will test and, often, reject any answer that is proposed; but he is not engaging in "eristics"; he believes that there is an answer and he believes too that it is of the utmost importance to find it. Aristotle declares that Socrates is important and original for two reasons: the definition of general concepts and the use of the inductive method. This is true, but only part of the truth. There is also the religious fervor of his faith—a faith in the existence of an intellectual and moral order and in the possibility of discovering it. It is from this faith that proceed his paradoxical teachings that "Virtue is knowledge" and that "No one does wrong [makes a mistake] voluntarily." He means, presumably, that *if* we were able to see "the good" clearly, it would be impossible for us not to choose it in preference to "the bad" and he is, of course, realist enough to know that most people do not see "the good" with the necessary clarity. Hence, to him, the necessity of further and further inquiry, of a training (an *askesis*) of the mind as thorough as any ever taken up for the body by an Olympic athlete. Those who, as a result of this training, really "know" can neither make a mistake nor want to do so.

Intellectualism could scarcely go further. Nor, on the other hand, could faith. To us the creed, if not the method, may appear that of a visionary; yet everything we know of the real Socrates must make us certain that "visionary" is not a word that could be applied to him. He is most firmly rooted as a citizen of a particular state at a particular time. He never left Athens except to fight as an infantryman in her foreign campaigns. His mission is specifically to the Athenians and the moral philosophy of which he is the inventor is, very largely, a political philosophy. There is a sense in which he, like the sophists of whom he so greatly disapproved, made man the measure of all things. He seems to have given up his early interest in physics, though there was a time when he was momentarily impressed by Anaxagoras' idea of *Nous* as the cause of everything. This seemed to him to make sense; but he was dismayed when he discovered that Anaxagoras only used *Nous* as an explanation when no more "scientific" one occurred to him. What he himself was looking for was not the original "stuff" out of which everything was made, not an explanation of motion, not even a solution of the controversy between the One and the Many; it was rather some general insight which would show or suggest how all things (and in particular the nature of man in society) had been, were, or could be arranged "for the best." This underlying faith of his was indeed something new. Supported or inspired by this faith, he was able in his critical activities to be at once more devastating and more constructive than the sophists. There was no conventional idea which he was not prepared to "test"; and, since to an Athenian of this age all human life was political, democracy was one of the ideas which he examined. In fact, he was working towards a higher and more efficient concept of the state; but he was condemned by his fellow-citizens in 399 B.C. for corrupting the youth. And, as we have seen, his religious view of life—a view which was to be developed by Plato and Aristotle and which has affected the whole subsequent history of metaphysics—was of a much loftier nature than anything which had preceded it. He was accused of, and condemned for, "not believing in the gods in which the city believes" and, in a sense, his accusers were quite right. To the end he remained paradoxical. He had been condemned, he knew, unjustly; but he revered the laws of his city and, when offered an opportunity of escape, refused to take it. His conduct was that of a citizen most exceptionally loyal to his city. Yet he had indicated the existence of a "law" more genuine than that of any political organization.

In the following extracts from Plato's dialogue *Gorgias** we have a clear example of Socrates' opposition to the "realism" then in the air, to which some sophists gave countenance or even open support. The tough-minded Callicles is speaking:

CALLICLES: . . . For the truth is, Socrates, that you, who pretend to be engaged in the pursuit of truth, are appealing now to the popular and vulgar notions of right, which are not natural, but only conventional. Convention and nature are generally at variance with one another: and hence, if a person is too modest to say what he thinks, he is compelled to contradict himself; and you, in your ingenuity perceiving the advantage to be thereby gained, slyly ask of him who is arguing conventionally a question which is to be determined by the rule of nature; and if he is talking of the rule of nature, you slip away to custom; as you did in this very discussion about doing and suffering injustice. When Polus was speaking of the conventionally dishonourable, you assailed him from the point of view of nature; for by the rule of nature, to suffer injustice is the greater disgrace because the greater evil; but conventionally, to do evil is the more disgraceful. For the suffering of injustice is not the part of a man, but of a slave, who indeed had better die than live; since when he is wronged and trampled upon, he is unable to help himself, or any other about whom he cares. The reason, as I conceive, is that the makers of laws are the majority who are weak; and they make laws and distribute praises and censures with a view to themselves and to their own interests; and they terrify the stronger sort of men, and those who are able to get the better of them, in order that they may not get the better of them; and they say, that dishonesty is shameful and unjust; meaning, by the word injustice, the desire of a man to have more than his neighbours; for knowing their own inferiority, I suspect that they are too glad of equality. And therefore the endeavour to have more than the many, is conventionally said to be shameful and unjust, and is called injustice, whereas nature herself inti-

* 483-522 (with omissions), translated by Benjamin Jowett, 2nd edition. Oxford: The Clarendon Press, III pp. 359-60, 368-69, 385-89.

mates that it is just for the better to have more than the worse, the powerful more than the weaker; and in many ways she shows, among men as well as among animals, and indeed among whole cities and races, that justice consists in the superior ruling over and having more than the inferior. For on what principle of justice did Xerxes invade Hellas, or his father the Scythians? (not to speak of numberless other examples). These are the men who act according to ature; yes, by Heaven, and according to the law of nature·ᴗᴗ, perhaps, according to that artificial law, which we forge and impose upon our fellows, of whom we take the best and strongest from their youth upwards, and tame them like young lions—charming them with the sound of the voice, and saying to them, that with equality they must be content, and that the equal is the honourable and the just. But if there were a man who had sufficient force, he would shake off and break through, and escape from all this; he would trample under foot all our formulas and spells and charms, and all our laws, sinning against nature; the slave would rise in rebellion and be lord over us, and the light of natural justice would shine forth. And this I take to be the sentiment of Pindar, in the poem in which he says, that

Law is the king of all, mortals as well as immortals;

this, as he says,

Makes might to be right, and does violence with high hand.

. . . I plainly assert, that he who would truly live ought to allow his desires to wax to the uttermost, and not to chastise them; but when they have grown to their greatest he should have courage and intelligence to minister to them and to satisfy all his longings. And this I affirm to be natural justice and nobility. To this the many cannot attain; and they blame the strong man because they are ashamed of their own weakness, which they desire to conceal, and hence they say that intemperance is base. As I was saying before, they enslave the nobler natures, and being unable to satisfy their pleasures, they praise temperance and justice out of cowardice. For if a man had been originally the son of a king, or had a nature capable of acquiring an empire or a tyranny or exclusive power, what could be more truly base or evil than temperance—to a man like him, I say, who might freely be enjoying every good, and has no one to hinder him, and yet has admitted custom and reason and the opinion of other men to be lords over him?—must not he be in a miserable plight whom the reputation of justice and temperance hinders from giving more to his friends than to his enemies, even though he be a ruler in his city? Nay, Socrates, for you profess to be a votary of the truth, and the truth is this:—that luxury and intemperance and licence, if they are duly supported, are happiness and virtue—all the rest is a mere bauble, custom contrary to nature, fond inventions of men nothing worth.

SOCRATES: There is a noble freedom, Callicles, in your way of approaching the argument; for what you say is what the rest of the world think, but are unwilling to say. And I must beg of you to persevere, that the true rule of human life may become manifest. Tell me, then:—you say, do you not, that in the rightly-developed man the passions ought not to be controlled, but that we should let them grow to the utmost and somehow or other satisfy them, and that this is virtue?

CALLICLES: Yes; that is what I say.

(Continuing the argument, Socrates obliges Callicles to distinguish between what is pleasant and what is good. Is it not true that, where physical health is concerned, what we desire is not always good? If our bodies are diseased, should not some of our desires be checked? Callicles, rudely and reluctantly, agrees that this is so.)

SOCRATES: And does not the same argument hold of the soul, my good sir? While she is in a bad state and is senseless and intemperate and unjust and unholy, her desires ought to be controlled, and she ought to be prevented from doing anything which does not tend to her own improvement.

CALLICLES: Yes.

SOCRATES: And that will be for her true interests?

CALLICLES: To be sure.

SOCRATES: And controlling her desires is chastising her?

CALLICLES: Yes.

SOCRATES: Then control or chastisement is better for the

soul than intemperance or the absence of control, which you were just now preferring?

CALLICLES: I do not understand you, Socrates, and I wish that you would ask some one who does.

SOCRATES: Here is a gentleman who cannot endure to be improved or corrected, as the argument would say.

CALLICLES: I do not heed a word of what you are saying, and have only answered hitherto out of civility to Gorgias.

SOCRATES: What are we to do, then? Shall we break off in the middle?

CALLICLES: That I leave for you to determine.

SOCRATES: Well, but people say that "a tale should have a head and not break off in the middle," and I should not like to have the argument wandering about without a head; please then to go on a little longer, and put the head on.

CALLICLES: How tyrannical you are, Socrates! I wish that you and your arguments would rest, or that you would get some one else to argue with you.

SOCRATES: But who else is willing?—I want to finish the argument.

CALLICLES: Cannot you finish without my help, either talking straight on, or questioning and answering yourself?

SOCRATES: Must I then say with Epicharmus, "two men spoke before, but now one shall be enough"? I suppose that there is absolutely no help. And if I am to carry on the enquiry by myself, I will first of all remark that not only I but all of us should have an ambition to know what is true and what is false in this matter, for the discovery of the truth is a common good. And now I will proceed to argue according to my own notion. But if any of you think that I arrive at conclusions which are untrue you must interpose and refute me, for I do not speak from any knowledge of what I am saying; I am an enquirer like yourselves, and therefore, if my opponent says anything which is of force, I shall be the first to agree with him. I am speaking on the supposition that the argument ought to be completed; but if you think otherwise let us leave off and go our ways.

GORGIAS: I think, Socrates, that we should not go our ways until you have completed the argument; and this appears to me to be the wish of the rest of the company; I myself should very much like to hear what more you have to say.

SOCRATES: I too, Gorgias, should have liked to continue the argument with Callicles; but since you, Callicles, are unwilling to continue, I hope that you will listen and interrupt me if I seem to you to be in error. And if you refute me, I shall not be angry with you as you are with me, but I shall inscribe you as the greatest of benefactors on the tablets of my soul.

CALLICLES: My good friend, never mind me, but get on.

SOCRATES: Listen to me, then, while I recapitulate the argument:—Is the pleasant the same as the good? Not the same. Callicles and I are agreed about that. And is the pleasant to be pursued for the sake of the good? or the good for the sake of the pleasant? The pleasant is to be pursued for the sake of the good. And that is pleasant at the presence of which we are pleased, and that is good at the presence of which we are good? To be sure. And we are good, and all good things whatever are good when some virtue is present in us or them? That, Callicles, is my conviction. But the virtue of each thing, whether body or soul, instrument or creature, when given to them in the best way comes to them not by chance but as the result of the order and truth and art which are imparted to them: Am I not right? I maintain that I am. And is not the virtue of each thing dependent on order or arrangement? Yes, I say. And that which makes a thing good is the proper order inhering in each thing? That is my view. And is not the soul which has an order of her own better than that which has no order of her own? Certainly. And the soul which has order is orderly? Of course. And that which is orderly is temperate? Assuredly. And the temperate soul is good? No other answer can I give, Callicles dear; have you any?

CALLICLES: Go on, my good fellow.

SOCRATES: Then I shall proceed to add, that if the temperate soul is the good soul, the soul which is in the opposite condition, that is, the foolish and intemperate, is the bad soul. Very true.

And will not the temperate man do what is proper, both in relation to the gods and to men;—for he would not be temperate if he did not? Certainly he will do what is proper. In his relation to other men he will do what is just; and in his relation to the gods he will do what is holy; and he who does what is just and holy cannot be other than just and holy? Very true.

And he must be courageous, for the duty of a temperate man is not to follow or to avoid what he ought not, but what he ought, whether things or men or pleasures or pains, and patiently to endure when he ought; and therefore, Callicles, the temperate man, being, as we have described, also just and courageous and holy, cannot be other than a perfectly good man, nor can the good man do otherwise than well and perfectly whatever he does; and he who does well must of necessity be happy and blessed, and the evil man who does evil, miserable: now this latter is he whom you were applauding—the intemperate who is the opposite of the temperate. Such is my position which I assert to be true, and if I am right, then I affirm that he who desires to be happy must pursue and practise temperance and run away from intemperance as fast as his legs will carry him: he had better order his life so as not to need punishment; but if either he or any of his friends, whether private individual or city, are in need of punishment, then justice must be done and he must suffer punishment, if he would be happy. This appears to me to be the aim which a man ought to have, and towards which he ought to direct all the energies both of himself and of the state, acting so that he may have temperance and justice present with him and be happy, not suffering his lusts to be unrestrained, and in the never-ending desire to satisfy them leading a robber's life. Such an one is the friend neither of God nor man, for he is incapable of communion, and he who is incapable of communion is also incapable of friendship. And philosophers tell us, Callicles, that communion and friendship and orderliness and temperance and justice bind together heaven and earth and gods and men, and that this universe is therefore called Cosmos or order, not disorder or misrule, my friend. But although you are a philosopher you seem to me never to have observed that geometrical equality is mighty, both among gods and men; you think that you ought to cultivate inequality or excess, and do not care about geometry.—Well then, either the principle that the happy are made happy by the possession of justice and temperance, and the miserable miserable by the possession of vice, must be refuted, or, if it is granted, what will be the consequences? All the consequences which I drew before, Callicles, and about which you asked me whether I was in earnest when I said that a man ought to accuse himself and his son and his friend if he did anything wrong, and that to this end he should use his rhetoric—all those consequences are true. And that which you thought that Polus was led to admit out of modesty is true, viz. that, to do injustice, if more disgraceful than to suffer, is in that degree worse; and the other position, which, according to Polus, Gorgias admitted out of modesty, that he who would truly be a rhetorician ought to be just and have a knowledge of justice, has also turned out to be true. And now, let us proceed in the next place to consider whether you are right in throwing in my teeth that I am unable to help myself or any of my friends or kinsmen, or to save them in the extremity of danger, or that I am like an outlaw to whom any one may do what he likes,—he may box my ears, which was a brave saying of yours; or he may take away my goods or banish me, or even do his worst and kill me; and this, as you say, is the height of disgrace. My answer to you is one which has been already often repeated, but may as well be repeated once more. I tell you, Callicles, that to be boxed on the ears wrongfully is not the worst evil which can befall a man, nor to have my face and purse cut open, but that to smite and slay me and mine wrongfully is far more disgraceful and more evil; aye, and to despoil and enslave and pillage, or in any way at all to wrong me and mine, is far more disgraceful and evil to the doer of the wrong than to me who am the sufferer. . . . Do not repeat the old story—that he who likes will kill me and get my money; for then I shall have to repeat the old answer, that he will be a bad man and will kill the good, and that money will be of no use to him, but that he will wrongly use that which he wrongly took, and if wrongly, basely, and if basely, hurtfully.

CALLICLES: How confident you are, Socrates, that you will never come to harm! you seem to think that you are living in another country, and can never be brought into a court of justice, as you very likely may be brought by some miserable and mean person.

SOCRATES: Then I must indeed be a fool, Callicles, if I do not know that in the Athenian State any man may suffer anything. And if I am brought to trial and incur the dangers of which you speak, he will be a villain who brings me to trial—of that I am very sure, for no good man would accuse the innocent. Nor shall I be surprised if I am put to death. Shall I tell you why I anticipate this?

CALLICLES: By all means.

SOCRATES: I think that I am the only or almost the only

Athenian living who practises the true art of politics; I am the only politician of my time. Now, seeing that when I speak I speak not with any view of pleasing, and that I look to what is best and not to what is most pleasant, having no mind to use those arts and graces which you recommend, I shall have nothing to say in the justice court. And you might argue with me, as I was arguing with Polus:—I shall be tried just as a physician would be tried in a court of little boys at the indictment of the cook. What would he reply in such a case, if some one were to accuse him, saying, "O my boys, many evil things has this man done to you: he is the death of you, especially of the younger ones among you, cutting and burning and starving and suffocating you, until you know not what to do; he gives you the bitterest potions, and compels you to hunger and thirst. How unlike the variety of meats and sweets on which I feasted you!" What do you suppose that the physician would reply when he found himself in such a predicament? If he told the truth he could only say: "All this, my boys, I did for your health," and then would there not just be a clamour among a jury like that? How they would cry out!

CALLICLES: I dare say.

SOCRATES: Would he not be utterly at a loss for a reply?

CALLICLES: He certainly would.

SOCRATES: And I too shall be treated in the same way, as I well know, if I am brought before the court. For I shall not be able to rehearse to the people the pleasures which I have procured for them, and which, although I am not disposed to envy either the procurers or enjoyers of them, are deemed by them to be benefits and advantages. And if any one says that I corrupt young men, and perplex their minds, or that I speak evil of old men, and use bitter words towards them, whether in private or public, it is useless for me to reply, as I truly might:—"All this I do for the sake of justice, and with a view to your interest, my judges, and of that only." And therefore there is no saying what may happen to me.

CALLICLES: And do you think, Socrates, that a man who is thus defenceless is in a good position?

SOCRATES: Yes, Callicles, if he have that defence, which you have often admitted that he should have; if he be his own defence, and have never said or done anything wrong, either in respect of gods or men; for that has often been acknowledged by us to be the best sort of defence. And if any one could convict me of inability to defend myself or others after this sort, I should blush for shame, whether I was convicted before many, or before a few, or by myself alone; and if I died because I have no powers of flattery or rhetoric, I am very sure that you would not find me repining at death. For no man but an utter fool and coward is afraid of death itself, but he is afraid of doing wrong. For to go to the world below having one's soul full of injustice is the last and worst of all evils.

CHAPTER III

Plato and Aristotle:
The Historical Background

When Socrates was executed in 399 B.C. he was about seventy years of age. Plato, the friend and pupil to whose genius and devotion we owe so much of our knowledge of Socrates, was then about thirty. The history of Greece in their lifetimes had been both brilliant and disastrous.

At about the time when Socrates was born the enormous threat to Greece of the vast Persian empire had passed away. At the beginning of the century the Ionian cities of Asia Minor, Thales' birthplace among them, had been ruthlessly punished for revolt against the satraps of Darius. The assistance given to the rebels by Athens and Eretria, while powerless to save them, was enough to expose Greece itself to the Persian vengeance. But at Marathon in 490, at Salamis ten years later, and again at Plataea in 479, the Greeks had triumphed against the huge armies and navies of Darius and his successor Xerxes, and in doing so had established, not only their own independence, but a heroic legend that worked as an inspiration to the magnificent achievements of the following years. Athens in particular, on which had fallen the major burden of the Persian Wars, rose not only to the height of her political power, but to the height of that achievement in literature and the arts by which she has earned "the undying gratitude of mankind."* Throughout the early years of Socrates, Athens, at the head of the Confederacy of Delos, was an imperial power; and by the initiative of her great democratic statesman Pericles, the

* H. A. L. Fisher, *A History of Europe.* London: Eyre & Spottiswoode; Boston: Houghton Mifflin Company, 1935, I, p. 29.

city itself was so adorned as to be a worthy visible symbol of its own pre-eminence, and indeed of the ascendancy of all Greeks over "the barbarians." Work on the Parthenon began in 447.

But by the time that Plato was born Athens was again at war. From about 435 she had come into conflict, perhaps inevitably, with Sparta, her powerful rival, and the Lacedaemonian Confederacy; and in 431 began the Peloponnesian War. Its course was costly, and for many years inconclusive. Athens, a sea power, could strike no decisive blow against the Spartan armies; while they, though they could invade and ravage Athenian territory, could neither capture the strongly fortified city nor prevent sea-borne supplies from entering it freely. But after the death of Pericles in 429 the Athenian leadership was less prudent and more bellicose, and an attempt in 421 to bring the conflict to an end failed for lack of the will on either side to keep the peace. The real turning point came in 413. In that year the Spartans occupied Decelea in Attica, thus denying to Athens the resources of her own territory, and in the autumn her ambitious expedition to Sicily ended in total defeat in the harbor of Syracuse. Thereafter her allies began to fall away; her own internal politics fell into confusion; and at last, her sea power broken at the battle of Aegospotami, Athens herself was blockaded, occupied and garrisoned by the Spartans. This was in 404, the twenty-eighth year of the war.

The effects of this protracted struggle were in many ways disastrous. The mere destruction, the sheer waste of manpower and resources, was serious enough—far worse, it seems certain, in proportion to the numbers involved, than that suffered by any country in either of the two great wars of our century. But more serious still, perhaps, was that other effect which Thucydides stressed: the decline, particularly steep in once splendid Athens, in the quality and temper of political life. In the course of the struggle men had become familiar with a new ruthlessness, with a newly anarchic employment of power, and with a new disrespect for established usage and tradition. Plato, no doubt owing in part to the influence of Socrates, seems never himself to have been inclined towards the skeptical, even cynical, "realism" that was so much in the air in his youth, and that was indeed preached by many of the sophists. But the wretched course of Athenian politics in his early years, culminating (in his view) as it did in the execution of his beloved Socrates, affected him profoundly nevertheless. It seems in fact to have made him a philosopher. His family was one of the most illustrious in Athens, and therefore had been, inevitably, prominent in politics; and Plato's own early ambitions were also political. But gradually he had become disenchanted. "Whereas at first," he wrote afterwards, "I had been full of enthusiasm for public work, now I could only look on and watch everything whirling round me this way and that. . . . In the end I came to the conclusion that all the cities of the present age are badly governed." And so he drew back from the political arena, in the hope of finding in "true philosophy" some basis for the conduct of affairs that might eliminate the confusion and gross error that he saw around him. It is clear too that, when he turned to consider the theory of political life, he had lost all faith in the system of democracy. He seems to have regarded it simply as grossly inefficient, as calculated merely to endow with authority and power those who happened to gain the ear of the ignorant populace, and who most probably themselves would be ignorant and incompetent men; and it must be said that the post-Periclean democracy of Athens appeared to bear out this opinion to the letter. In theory then, and in practice in two interventions in the affairs of Sicily, Plato inclined to the idea of a despotism, not so much benevolent as philosophically enlightened, a government of the expert, but of the expert in metaphysics. His ideal was the authoritarian rule of the "philosopher-king." But he saw little hope of his ideal being realized in Greece, and in the end his hopes for Sicily were also disappointed. Athens, after 404 B.C., was quite unable to regain either her old political position or her political vitality. The Spartan pre-eminence as a result of her victory in the war was both misused and brief. And the succeeding supremacy of Thebes was also brief and precarious. The politics of Syracuse, not seriously influenced by Plato's intervention, followed a depressing course of intrigue and violence.

The association between Aristotle and Plato dates probably from 368-67 B.C., when Aristotle, at the age of eighteen, came to join Plato's Academy in Athens. He was a native of Stagira in northern Greece. His father had been employed as a doctor at the Macedonian court, and but for his premature death it seems likely that Aristotle would have followed him in that profession. But in fact he remained in the Academy for twenty years, leaving it only when Plato died in 348. A brief migration to Assos, on the coast of Asia Minor, where an important branch of the Academy had been established, ended abruptly when his patron Hermeias was detected by the Persians in treasonable negotiations with Philip of Macedon; and after a few years spent apparently in Lesbos Aristotle was summoned himself to the Macedonian court, to be tutor to the heir and future emperor, Alexander.

This was in about 342 B.C., and by that time it was already apparent that the balance of power in the Greek world had changed. The old city-states, the political units to which Plato and Aristotle had been accustomed, and beyond which even their political thinking did not go, were in fact no longer a match for the kingdom of Macedonia. Even in combination—and their combinations were at all times highly precarious—they were outweighed by the resources and by the armies developed and deployed by the sagacious and enterprising Philip; and this was made terribly clear in 338, when at Chaeronea a joint army of Athens and Thebes met decisive defeat at the hands of the Macedonians. But Philip's design was not in fact the subjection of Greece. Regarding himself (though he was only half-accepted) as a Greek, his ultimate aim was to lead all the forces of Greece against the Persian empire. His plans for this enterprise were far advanced when, in 336, he was assassinated. Their execution fell to his heir, Aristotle's pupil, the great Alexander.

At about this time Aristotle returned to Athens. The head of Plato's Academy was now one Xenocrates of

Chalcedon, with whose somewhat mystical mode of philosophy Aristotle was not in sympathy. He therefore set up a school of his own, which became known as the Peripatos—"the covered walk"—and its inmates as the Peripatetics. This school, which was a center of highly organized scientific research as well as of philosophical inquiry, flourished greatly. But the sudden death of Alexander at the age of thirty-two was the occasion for an impetuous revolution in Athens, in which Aristotle, because of his close Macedonian associations, became an object of attack. He was accused, even more absurdly than Socrates had been, of "impiety"; but unlike Socrates, he lost no time in making his escape. He retired to the town of Chalcis in Euboea, where he died in the following year at the age of sixty-three.

The lifetimes of Plato and Aristotle thus span a period of just over a hundred years, in which the history of Greece, on the whole, makes depressing reading. During and after the long-drawn disaster of the Peloponnesian War, Greece could not recover the glories of the old wars against the Persians. Her victories and defeats were internecine, almost suicidal. And it seems in retrospect obvious enough that her amalgam of brilliant but contentious political entities was destined quite inevitably to be overborne by some centralized power, as it was by the northern state of Macedonia. It would be, however, a grave mistake to suppose that Greece in this period was somehow decadent, and even more so to suppose that the Greeks themselves felt this to be so. It is easy to exaggerate the extent to which her city-states had been formerly self-sufficient and independent; some form of "hegemony" or near-empire had long been familiar; and it is easy to exaggerate also the extent to which the rise of Macedonia altered the picture. As has been said, the Greek cities were not brought into subjection. In any case military and political power was by no means all that a Greek desired for his city; he thought as much, or more, of its educative and civilizing influence upon its citizens and others. It is accordingly not really absurd that both Plato and Aristotle, in their political and ethical thinking, should have continued to assume as the ideal basis of both the stable political structure of a city-state. In spite of the long tale of disasters in the history of Greece, such states still existed. This was the great age of political oratory, and the orators dealt with live issues in still living communities. In some cases, Rhodes for example, particular cities achieved in this period their highest prosperity. And in any case the city-state, the restricted community living together, could still be regarded as the ideal setting for the pursuit of the good life. It was not in these years, but in the course of those that came after, that a real sense of breakdown and of utter insecurity became widespread. To Plato and Aristotle, Isocrates and Demosthenes, the conditions of public and political life in Greece appeared, if not always good, at least always remediable. They had not lost hope.

CHAPTER IV

Plato

Plato in philosophy was a genuine innovator on a scale to which succeeding centuries offer no parallel. It may appear that, for many hundreds of years, the influence of Aristotle was more conspicuous and profound, but there is a sense in which this was not so: for Aristotle himself was, and usually spoke of himself as being, a Platonist— he owed far more, certainly, to Plato than Plato owed even to Socrates, whose influence upon him, though powerful, was limited in its scope. The range of Plato's own work was so immense that it is really impossible for an account of it to be both adequate and brief. There is not really to be found, among his numerous dialogues, any single "system" or set of doctrines that could be put forward as a final characterization of his position, and besides this Plato himself gives us to understand that his published writings do not embody all, or even the most important, of the doctrines that were actually taught in the Academy. A man's best thought, he seems to say, is likely to be, and even ought to be, reserved for living discussion in a limited circle of his followers and friends.

The best that can be done, then, for our present purpose is to identify in his writings certain recurrent or developing themes, with which it was characteristic of Plato to play, among an amazing range and richness of other interests, variations upon one or two central concerns.

We have seen already that the procedure of Socrates —the procedure by which, with constructive fervor and positive intent, he attacked the half-truths and muddled clichés of conventional thought—was a species of what has been called "dialectic." This notion of dialectic, or "dialectical method," runs through very many of dialogues. But in the course of time it underwent much change and elaboration.

In the earliest dialogues—*Charmides* for instance, or *Laches*—not only is Socrates the leading dramatic character; he is also represented, as in later dialogues he is not, as proceeding in a manner that is quite clearly "Socratic." At this time, not long after the execution of Socrates, his influence on Plato's writings was still very strong; and indeed it is likely that many of the earlier dialogues were written specifically to record the contents and character of actual discussions with Socrates, who himself had left no writings behind him. Here, accordingly, "dialectic" is the dialectic of Socrates. The object of the inquiry is to establish a *definition*—of "temperance" in *Charmides,* of "courage" in *Laches*—and the procedure is to test (and overthrow) successive attempts and amended attempts at definition submitted by Socrates' more or less unwary interlocutors. Socrates' interest in definitions is attested by Aristotle; and here we see him in pursuit of definitions of (as it happens) certain ethical notions, refuting by a dexterous use of counter-examples the suggestions in which conventional unclarity found too ready expression.

Now there is a point which inevitably crops up in such discussions, reflection on which led Plato away from Socrates. A common mistake in attempting to frame a definition is to generalize too boldly from some particular *instance* of what is to be defined—to observe, for example, that religious people often go to church, and thence to conclude that religion can be *defined* as "churchgoing." Socrates doubtless was aware of this sort of mistake, and would have insisted that a distinction be drawn between the thing itself, and this or that particular instance of it —between courage, say, and this or that case of courageous conduct. But it appears that Plato—and not, apparently, Socrates—came to put upon this sort of distinction a special interpretation: he came to think that, *apart* from all the things and occurrences which make up the world of ordinary life, there must *exist* another realm of entities of a quite different sort—a realm of timeless, "intelligible" things of which "sensible" phenomena are merely the transitory instances, and of which definitions are, as it were, true descriptions. To these supposed things he gave the name Ideas, or Forms; and the resulting "Theory of Ideas"—which was in fact never one single theory nor finally worked out—was for very many years the heart of controversy in the Academy, and in the eyes of others the hallmark of Plato and his pupils.

The question at what precise stage, and to what extent, Plato came to think of his Forms as actually existing in a supersensible realm (not merely, that is, as instantiated in *this* world) is still a matter for some dispute. But this at least is clear: in quite early dialogues Plato speaks of ordinary objects as *copies* (always imperfect copies) of Forms, a way of speaking which plainly carries the implication that Forms and ordinary things have their separate existence and status.

The range of problems in the treatment of which Forms now appear is wide enough to show clearly why the theory was thought to be so important. We may mention some. It seems that Plato in his youth had been much impressed by the Heraclitean doctrine of "the flux," the view that in this world nothing is permanent or stable or at different times the same, and he had asked himself how, if this were so, knowledge was possible. What could be known to be true, if all things were perpetually changing? But now, it seemed, he was able to say that, though perhaps our ordinary world was a fleeting Heraclitean "river," yet there were Forms that did not change but existed in timeless perfection. Would these, then, not be the objects of true knowledge? Again, both on his own account and under the influence of Pythagoras, Plato was deeply interested in mathematics, which meant, at that time, predominantly geometry. Now when geometers spoke of the properties of "the square" or "the circle," to what were they referring? Not to their diagrams, nor to other particular squares or circles, for these were always imperfect. Must they not, then, be speaking of the Forms of "circle" or "square," non-sensible things having none of the imperfections found in their everyday "copies"?

A more ambitious employment of the theory occurs in the central books of Plato's most celebrated dialogue, *The Republic*. Here Forms are appealed to not only in the definition of knowledge, but in the definition of philosophy itself; in particular they introduce a new conception of "dialectical method." Plato is thinking here of the education of his "philosopher-kings," those possible rulers in whom his political pessimism had led him to look for the way out from the confusions of his age. He holds, first of all, that it is an essential first step to go beyond the assumptions, the "opinions," of everyday life. For all these, and for the character of the shifting, "unreal" world of daily experience, an "explanation" must be found in that real, timeless, and perfect realm in which Forms exist. But here he adds that Forms themselves are hierarchically ordered. Apprehension of some, those, for instance, of the mathematician, still leaves room for a question; some further "explanation" is called for. And in a famous passage he avers that the *Form of the Good* is the single and sufficient goal of dialectical inquiry. It is here, and here only, that the constant search after *reasons* can find a satisfactory terminus. If once a man could clearly and fully apprehend the Form of the Good, then he would see exactly *why* all else should be as it is. He speaks almost, at times, as if the Form of the Good were actually the *creator* and controller of all other things, and in that sense essential to their explanation. But he does not profess, either here or in any other dialogue, to have attained for himself this ultimate and sufficient insight; and though he says here that its achievement is the purpose of "dialectic," the essential purpose of the philosopher, he says little in detail—perhaps he had little to say—of the actual method by which that purpose is to be pursued.

All this, it may be thought, has much of the character of a visionary mysticism. But Plato, for all the intensity of his imagination, was a true philosopher, never satisfied with half-formulations or unargued assertion. It seems quite clear that he never regarded the Theory of Ideas as a final solution, but rather as a fertile topic for further inquiry. In later years he revised, according to Aristotle's testimony, the account of mathematics to which that theory had led him. The definition of knowledge he actually reconsidered in a dialogue, *Theaetetus,* which makes no mention of the theory whatever. And constantly he returned, in his *Parmenides* and elsewhere, to the grave difficulties involved in his "objectification" of the Forms—to the problems of how such objects, if objects they were, could be related to the objects of the ordinary world, and to each other. Although his theory was for many years at the center of the Academy's researches, it was never allowed to put an end to inquiry; "dialectic" in Socrates' sense always continued, and no doctrine was deemed to be exempt from scrutiny and objection.

Plato's own conception of dialectic underwent one further transformation which must briefly be described. His new idea, foreshadowed in the *Phaedrus* quite soon after the composition of the *Republic,* is perhaps best stated in the later *Philebus.* Plato there says: "There neither is nor ever will be a better than my own favorite way, which has nevertheless often deserted me and left me helpless in the hour of need. . . . It is the parent of all the discoveries in the arts. . . . We ought, in every inquiry, to begin by laying down one Form of that which is the object of inquiry; this unity we shall find in everything. Having found it, we may next proceed to look for two, if there be two, or, if not, then for three or some other number, subdividing each of these units, until at last the unity with which we began is seen not only to be one and many and an infinity of things, but also a definite number; we must not attribute infinity to the many until the entire number of the species intermediate between unity and infinity has been discovered. . . ."* This, he now holds, is the proper procedure of dialectic.

It may seem that the idea behind these rather strange words is an unexciting one: essentially, Plato seems to be proposing a program of definition *per genus et differentiam,* a mere method of orderly classification. It must be remembered, however, that the logical insight expressed

---

* W. D. Ross, *Plato's Theory of Ideas,* London and New York: Oxford University Press, 1951, p. 240.

in this procedure was then wholly new. Moreover, Plato believed in the possibility of discovering (or constructing) by resolute use of this method a kind of map of the world of Forms, or perhaps rather a kind of genealogical table in which all would appear with their proper degrees of subordination. He may have thought at one time of the Good as the highest *genus,* as it were the ancestor of all the rest. Later (his interest shifting from ethics and politics to logic) he considered the claims of Existence, Sameness, and Difference. Still later the Form of Unity was given pride of place. But in fact, quite apart from the interest or lack of interest of Plato's own applications of this "dialectical method" in his inquiries into Forms and their interrelations, there proved to be great value in his idea for those who were embarking upon strictly scientific researches. All sciences, it has been said, must begin with classification. And the many studies in natural history which were organized by Aristotle owed much of their method to this latest development by Plato of "dialectic."

It would be impossible, while remaining within the scope of the present book, to give any adequate presentation in Plato's own words of the ideas roughly sketched out above; for that the reader must be referred elsewhere. However, some notion of the intensity with which his views were felt and expounded can be derived from his famous and haunting image of "the Cave"—from that passage in Book VII of the *Republic** in which he seeks to make the reader grasp the full significance of progressive philosophical enlightenment; unless, he implies, we can progress in this direction, we remain in the Cave, the home of illusion and error, with, accordingly, no notion of the good life for ourselves and others, and thence no hope of bringing order into a distracted world.

"Next, then," I said, "take the following parable of education and ignorance as a picture of the condition of our nature. Imagine mankind as dwelling in an underground cave with a

* *Republic,* 514-21, in *Great Dialogues of Plato,* translated by W. H. D. Rouse. New York: The New American Library, 1956, pp. 312-19. (Mentor Books.)

long entrance open to the light across the whole width of the cave; in this they have been from childhood, with necks and legs fettered, so they have to stay where they are. They cannot move their heads round because of the fetters, and they can only look forward, but light comes to them from fire burning behind them higher up at a distance. Between the fire and the prisoners is a road above their level, and along it imagine a low wall has been built, as puppet showmen have screens in front of their people over which they work their puppets."

"I see," he said.

"See, then, bearers carrying along this wall all sorts of articles which they hold projecting above the wall, statues of men and other living things,[1] made of stone or wood and all kinds of stuff, some of the bearers speaking and some silent, as you might expect."

"What a remarkable image," he said, "and what remarkable prisoners!"

"Just like ourselves," I said. "For, first of all, tell me this: What do you think such people would have seen of themselves and each other except their shadows, which the fire cast on the opposite wall of the cave?"

"I don't see how they could see anything else," said he, "if they were compelled to keep their heads unmoving all their lives!"

"Very well, what of the things being carried along? Would not this be the same?"

"Of course it would."

"Suppose the prisoners were able to talk together, don't you think that when they named the shadows which they saw passing they would believe they were naming things?"[2]

"Necessarily."

"Then if their prison had an echo from the opposite wall, whenever one of the passing bearers uttered a sound, would they not suppose that the passing shadow must be making the sound? Don't you think so?"

"Indeed I do," he said.

"If so," said I, "such persons would certainly believe that there were no realities except those shadows of handmade things."[3]

[1] Including models of trees, etc.
[2] Which they had never seen. They would say "tree" when it was only a shadow of the model of a tree.
[3] Shadows of artificial things, not even the shadow of a growing tree: another stage from reality.

"So it must be," said he.

"Now consider," said I, "what their release would be like, and their cure from these fetters and their folly; let us imagine whether it might naturally be something like this. One might be released, and compelled suddenly to stand up and turn his neck round, and to walk and look towards the firelight; all this would hurt him, and he would be too much dazzled to see distinctly those things whose shadows he had seen before. What do you think he would say, if someone told him that what he saw before was foolery, but now he saw more rightly, being a bit nearer reality and turned towards what was a little more real? What if he were shown each of the passing things, and compelled by questions to answer what each one was? Don't you think he would be puzzled, and believe what he saw before was more true than what was shown to him now?"

"Far more," he said.

"Then suppose he were compelled to look towards the real light, it would hurt his eyes, and he would escape by turning them away to the things which he was able to look at, and these he would believe to be clearer than what was being shown to him."

"Just so," said he.

"Suppose, now," said I, "that someone should drag him thence by force, up the rough ascent, the steep way up, and never stop until he could drag him out into the light of the sun, would he not be distressed and furious at being dragged; and when he came into the light, the brilliance would fill his eyes and he would not be able to see even one of the things now called real?"[1]

"That he would not," said he, "all of a sudden."

"He would have to get used to it, surely, I think, if he is to see the things above. First he would most easily look at shadows, after that images of mankind and the rest in water, lastly the things themselves. After this he would find it easier to survey by night the heavens themselves and all that is in them, gazing at the light of the stars and moon, rather than by day the sun and the sun's light."

"Of course."

"Last of all, I suppose, the sun; he could look on the sun itself by itself in its own place, and see what it is like, not reflections of it in water or as it appears in some alien setting."

"Necessarily," said he.

"And only after all this he might reason about it, how this

[1] To the next stage of knowledge: the real thing, not the artificial puppet.

is he who provides seasons and years, and is set over all there is in the visible region, and he is in a manner the cause of all things which they saw."

"Yes, it is clear," said he, "that after all that, he would come to this last."

"Very good. Let him be reminded of his first habitation, and what was wisdom in that place, and of his fellow-prisoners there; don't you think he would bless himself for the change, and pity them?"

"Yes, indeed."

"And if there were honours and praises among them and prizes for the one who saw the passing things most sharply and remembered best which of them used to come before and which after and which together, and from these was best able to prophesy accordingly what was going to come—do you believe he would set his desire on that, and envy those who were honoured men or potentates among them? Would he not feel as Homer says,[1] and heartily desire rather to be serf of some landless man on earth and to endure anything in the world, rather than to opine as they did and to live in that way?"

"Yes indeed," said he, "he would rather accept anything than live like that."

"Then again," I said, "just consider; if such a one should go down again and sit on his old seat, would he not get his eyes full of darkness coming in suddenly out of the sun?"

"Very much so," said he.

"And if he should have to compete with those who had been always prisoners, by laying down the law about those shadows while he was blinking before his eyes were settled down—and it would take a good long time to get used to things—wouldn't they all laugh at him and say he had spoiled his eyesight by going up there, and it was not worth-while so much as to try to go up? And would they not kill anyone who tried to release them and take them up, if they could somehow lay hands on him and kill him?"[2]

"That they would!" said he.

"Then we must apply this image, my dear Glaucon," said I, "to all we have been saying. The world of our sight is like the habitation in prison, the firelight there to the sunlight here, the ascent and the view of the upper world is the rising of the soul into the world of mind; put it so and you will not be far from my own surmise, since that is what you want to hear; but

[1] *Odyssey* xi. 489.
[2] Plato probably alludes to the death of Socrates.

God knows if it is really true. At least, what apears to me is, that in the world of the known, last of all,[1] is the idea of the good, and with what toil to be seen! And seen, this must be inferred to be the cause of all right and beautiful things for all, which gives birth to light and the king of light in the world of sight, and, in the world of mind, herself the queen produces truth and reason; and she must be seen by one who is to act with reason publicly or privately."

"I believe as you do," he said, "in so far as I am able."

"Then believe also, as I do," said I, "and do not be surprised, that those who come thither are not willing to have part in the affairs of men, but their souls ever strive to remain above; for that surely may be expected if our parable fits the case."

"Quite so," he said.

"Well then," said I, "do you think it surprising if one leaving divine contemplations and passing to the evils of men is awkward and appears to be a great fool, while he is still blinking—not yet accustomed to the darkness around him, but compelled to struggle in law courts or elsewhere about shadows of justice, or the images which make the shadows, and to quarrel about notions of justice in those who have never seen justice itself?"

"Not surprising at all," said he.

"But any man of sense," I said, "would remember that the eyes are doubly confused from two different causes, both in passing from light to darkness and from darkness to light; and believing that the same things happen with regard to the soul also, whenever he sees a soul confused and unable to discern anything he would not just laugh carelessly; he would examine whether it had come out of a more brilliant life, and if it were darkened by the strangeness; or whether it had come out of greater ignorance into a more brilliant light, and if it were dazzled with the brighter illumination. Then only would he congratulate the one soul upon its happy experience and way of life, and pity the other; but if he must laugh, his laugh would be a less downright laugh than his laughter at the soul which came out of the light above."

"That is fairly put," said he.

"Then if this is true," I said, "our belief about these matters must be this, that the nature of education is not really such as some of its professors say it is; as you know, they say that there is not understanding in the soul, but they put it in, as if they were putting sight into blind eyes."

[1] The end of our search.

"They do say so," said he.

"But our reasoning indicates," I said, "that this power is already in the soul of each, and is the instrument by which each learns; thus if the eye could not see without being turned with the whole body from the dark towards the light, so this instrument must be turned round with the whole soul away from the world of becoming until it is able to endure the sight of being and the most brilliant light of being: and this we say is the good, don't we?"

"Yes."

"Then this instrument," said I, "must have its own art, for the circumturning or conversion, to show how the turn can be most easily and successfully made; not an art of putting sight into an eye, which we say has it already, but since the instrument has not been turned aright and does not look where it ought to look—that's what must be managed."

"So it seems," he said.

"Now most of the virtues which are said to belong to the soul are really something near to those of the body; for in fact they are not already there, but they are put later into it by habits and practices; but the virtue of understanding everything really belongs to something certainly more divine, as it seems, for it never loses its power, but becomes useful and helpful or, again, useless and harmful, by the direction in which it is turned. Have you not noticed men who are called worthless but clever, and how keen and sharp is the sight of their petty soul, and how it sees through the things towards which it is turned? Its sight is clear enough, but it is compelled to be the servant of vice, so that the clearer it sees the more evil it does."

"Certainly," said he.

"Yet if this part of such a nature," said I, "had been hammered at from childhood, and all those leaden weights of the world of becoming knocked off—the weights, I mean, which grow into the soul from gorging and gluttony and such pleasures, and twist the soul's eye downwards—if, I say, it had shaken these off and been turned round towards what is real and true, that same instrument of those same men would have seen those higher things most clearly, just as now it sees those towards which it is turned."

"Quite likely," said he.

"Very well," said I, "isn't it equally likely, indeed, necessary, after what has been said, that men uneducated and without experience of truth could never properly supervise a city, nor

AL ×-×× 68

Miss Parris

Becky -

Miss
Sentz please
call

can those who are allowed to spend all their lives in education right to the end? The first have no single object in life, which they must always aim at in doing everything they do, public or private; the second will never do anything if they can help it, believing they have already found mansions abroad in the Islands of the Blest."

"True," said he.

"Then it is the task of us founders," I said, "to compel the best natures to attain that learning which we said was the greatest, both to see the good, and to ascend that ascent; and when they have ascended and properly seen, we must never allow them what is allowed now."

"What is that, pray?" he asked.

"To stay there," I said, "and not be willing to descend again to those prisoners, and to share their troubles and their honours, whether they are worth having or not."

"What!" said he, "are we to wrong them and make them live badly, when they might live better?"

"You have forgotten again, my friend," said I, "that the law is not concerned how any one class in a city is to prosper above the rest; it tries to contrive prosperity in the city as a whole, fitting the citizens into a pattern by persuasion and compulsion, making them give of their help to one another wherever each class is able to help the community. The law itself creates men like this in the city, not in order to allow each one to turn by any way he likes, but in order to use them itself to the full for binding the city together."

"True," said he, "I did forget."

"Notice then, Glaucon," I said, "we shall not wrong the philosophers who grow up among us, but we shall treat them fairly when we compel them to add to their duties the care and guardianship of the other people. We shall tell them that those who grow up philosophers in other cities have reason in taking no part in public labours there; for they grow up there of themselves, though none of the city governments wants them; a wild growth has its rights, it owes nurture to no one, and need not trouble to pay anyone for its food. But you we have engendered, like king bees[1] in hives, as leaders and kings over yourselves and the rest of the city; you have been better and more perfectly educated than the others, and are better able to share in both ways of life. Down you must go then, in turn, to the habitation of the others, and accustom

[1] Both the Greeks and Romans spoke always of "king," not "queen," of a hive.

yourselves to their darkness; for when you have grown accustomed you will see a thousand times better than those who live there, and you will know what the images are and what they are images of, because you have seen the realities behind just and beautiful and good things. And so our city will be managed wide awake for us and for you, not in a dream, as most are now, by people fighting together for shadows, and quarrelling to be rulers, as if that were a great good. But the truth is more or less that the city where those who are to rule are least anxious to be rulers is of necessity best managed and has least faction in it; while the city which gets rulers who want it most is worst managed."

"Certainly," said he.

"Then will our fosterlings disobey us when they hear this? Will they refuse to help, each group in its turn, in the labours of the city, and want to spend most of their time dwelling in the pure air?"

"Impossible," said he, "for we shall only be laying just commands on just men. No, but undoubtedly each man of them will go to the ruler's place as to a grim necessity, exactly the opposite of those who now rule in cities."

"For the truth is, my friend," I said, "that only if you can find for your future rulers a way of life better than ruling, is it possible for you to have a well-managed city; since in that city alone those will rule who are truly rich, not rich in gold, but in that which is necessary for a happy man, the riches of a good and wise life: but if beggared and hungry, for want of goods of their own, they hasten to public affairs, thinking that they must snatch goods for themselves from there, it is not possible. Then rule becomes a thing to be fought for; and a war of such a kind, being between citizens and within them, destroys both them and the rest of the city also."

"Most true," said he.

"Well, then," said I, "have you any other life despising political office except the life of true philosophy?"

"No, by heaven," said he.

"But again," said I, "they must not go awooing office like so many lovers! If they do, their rival lovers will fight them."

"Of course they will!"

"Then what persons will you compel to accept guardianship of the city other than those who are wisest in the things which enable a city to be best managed, who also have honours of another kind and a life better than the political life?"

"No others," he answered.

By way of further illustration of Plato's work, it has seemed best not to assemble a collection of disconnected fragments, but rather to present, of some single dialogue, a large enough proportion to give room for real argument to develop. For this purpose the *Meno* seems particularly suitable. It belongs to the earlier group of Plato's writings, and is more "Socratic" both in form and content than the later dialogues are. It lies close, however, to the heart of Plato's own interests; in many ways it is an ideal introduction to the *Republic,* in which the question raised here—What is virtue, and can it be taught?—is given an answer more positive than Plato could offer at this stage. It has the advantage, too, of being in itself perfectly clear, and therefore not in need of explanation and commentary; nor does it raise questions in those parts of Plato's philosophy, full discussion of which would be impossible in present limits.

Although there is no good reason to suppose that such a conversation as this between Menon and Socrates ever actually occurred, that supposition would not be impossible. We learn from Xenophon that Menon, of a distinguished Thessalian family, took part in the campaign of Cyrus the younger against his brother Artaxerxes in 401 B.C.; and he might have been in Athens in, say, the previous year—a few years, that is, before the death of Socrates, and indeed at a time when Plato too could have been present. Xenophon speaks of Menon very unfavorably; Plato represents him in this dialogue only as being somewhat impatient, and in particular as being too easily impressed by the sophists. It is a curious point that the later part of the dialogue brings Anytos into the conversation; for it was Anytos who, a few years later than the fictional date of the discussion, brought the charges which resulted in Socrates' execution. Plato was actually writing, of course, after this event; the sharp warning to Socrates with which Anytos departs is a dramatic device, not a piece of inspired foresight. But in view of this it is all the more striking that he should write of Anytos, as he does, with moderation, and even charity. Perhaps this implies that he bore against Anytos no personal resentment, feeling that, so long as the true basis of good conduct was undiscovered, individual wrongdoers were not too much to be blamed.

The dialogue[1] opens abruptly:

MENON: Can you tell me, Socrates—can virtue be taught? Or if not, does it come by practice? Or does it come neither by practice nor by teaching, but do people get it by nature, or in some other way?

SOCRATES: My dear Menon, the Thessalians have always had a good name in our nation—they were always admired as good horsemen and men with full purses. Now, it seems to me, we must add brains to the list. Your friend Aristippos is a very good example, and his townsmen from Larissa. Gorgias[2] is the man who set it all going. As soon as he got there, all the Aleuadai[3] were at his feet—your own bosom friend Aristippos was one—not to mention the rest of Thessaly. Here's a custom he taught you, at least—to answer generously and without fear if anyone asked you a question; quite natural, of course, when one knows the answer. Just what he did himself; he was a willing victim of the civilised world of Hellas[4]—any Hellene might ask him anything he liked, and every mortal soul got his answer!

But here, my dear Menon, it is just the opposite. There is a regular famine of brains here, and your part of the world seems to hold a monopoly in that article. At least, if you do ask anyone here a question like that, all you will get is a laugh and—"My good man, you must think I am inspired! Virtue? Can it be taught? Or how does it come? Do I know that? So far from knowing whether it can be taught or can't be taught, I don't know even the least little thing about virtue, I don't even know what virtue is!"

I'm in the same fix myself, Menon. I am as poor of the article as the rest of us, and I have to blame myself that I don't know the least little thing about virtue, and when I

---

[1] *Meno*, 70-74, 77-79, 86-95, 96-100, in *Great Dialogues of Plato*, translated by W. H. D. Rouse. New York: The New American Library, 1956, pp. 28 ff. (Mentor Books.)

[2] A celebrated Sophist from Leontini in Sicily; he taught rhetoric based upon impressive language. He visited Athens in 427 B. C., and travelled about Greece, lecturing.

[3] As it were, the leaders of society in Thessaly.

[4] Greece. The ancient Greeks called themselves Hellenes, and their country Hellas; it was later called Graecia by the Romans.

don't know what a thing is, how can I know its quality? Take Menon, for example: If someone doesn't know in the least who Menon is, how can he know whether Menon is handsome or rich or even a gentleman, or perhaps just the opposite? Do you think he can?

MENON: Not I. But look here, Socrates, don't *you* really know what virtue is? Are we to give that report of you in Larissa?

SOCRATES: Just so, my friend, and more—I never met anyone who did, so far as I know.

MENON: What! Did not you meet Gorgias when he was here?

SOCRATES: Oh, yes.

MENON: Didn't you think *he* knew?

SOCRATES: I have rather a poor memory, Menon, so I can't say at the moment whether I did think so. But perhaps he did know, or perhaps you know what he said: kindly remind me, then, what he did say. You say it yourself, if you like; for I suppose you think as he thought.

MENON: Oh, yes.

SOCRATES: Then let us leave him out of it, since he is not here; tell me yourself, in heaven's name, Menon, what do you say virtue is? Tell me, and don't grudge it; it will be the luckiest lie I ever told if it turns out that you know and Gorgias knew, and I went and said I never met anyone who did know.

MENON: That is nothing difficult, my dear Socrates. First, if you like, a man's virtue, that is easy; this is a man's virtue: to be able to manage public business, and in doing it to help friends and hurt enemies, and to take care to keep clear of such mischief himself. Or, if you like, a woman's virtue, there's no difficulty there: she must manage the house well, and keep the stores all safe, and obey her husband. And a child's virtue is different for boy and girl, and an older man's, a freeman's, if you like, or a slave's, if you like. There are a very large number of other virtues, so there is no difficulty in saying what virtue is; for according to each of our activities and ages each of us has his virtue for doing each sort of work, and in the same way, Socrates, I think, his vice.

SOCRATES: I seem to have been lucky indeed, my dear Menon, if I have been looking for one virtue and found a whole swarm of virtues in your store. However, let us take up this image, Menon, the swarm. If I asked you what a bee really is, and you answered that there are many different kinds of bees, what would you answer me if I asked you then: "Do you say there are many different kinds of bees, differing from each other in being bees more or less? Or do they differ in some other respect, for example in size, or beauty, and so forth?" Tell me, how would you answer that question?

MENON: I should say that they are not different at all one from another in beehood.

SOCRATES: Suppose I went on to ask: "Tell me this, then— what do you say exactly is that in which they all are the same, and not different?" Could you answer anything to that?

MENON: Oh, yes.

SOCRATES: Very well, now then for virtues. Even if there are many different kinds of them, they all have one something, the same in all, which makes them virtues. So if one is asked, "What is virtue?" one must have this clear in his view before he can answer the question. Do you understand what I mean?

MENON: I think I understand; but I do not yet grasp your question as I could wish.

SOCRATES: Do you think that virtue alone is like that, Menon—I mean one thing in a man and another in a woman, and so forth, or do you also say the same of health and size and strength? Do you think health is one thing in a man, and another in a woman? Or is the essence the same everywhere if it be health, whether it be in a man or in anything else whatever?

MENON: I think health is the same thing in both man and woman.

SOCRATES: And what of size and strength? If a woman is strong, is it the same essence and the same strength which will make her strong? By the same strength I mean this: the strength is not different in itself whether it be in a man or a woman. Do you think there is any difference?

MENON: Why, no.

SOCRATES: Yet virtue will differ in itself in a boy and in an old man, in a woman and in a man?

MENON: I can't help thinking, Socrates, that this is not quite like those other things.

SOCRATES: Very well: Did you not say that man's virtue is to manage public affairs well, and woman's to manage a home?

MENON: Yes, I did.

SOCRATES: Then is it possible to manage a state or a house

or anything well, without managing temperately [1] and justly?

MENON: Certainly not.

SOCRATES: If, then, they manage temperately and justly, they will manage with temperance and justice?

MENON: Necessarily.

SOCRATES: Then both need the same things, if they are to be good, both woman and man—justice and temperance.

MENON: So it seems.

SOCRATES: What of the boy and the old man? If they are reckless and unjust, could they ever be good?

MENON: Certainly not.

SOCRATES: But they must be temperate and just?

MENON: Yes.

SOCRATES: Then all men are good in the same way? For when they have the same things, they are good.

MENON: So it seems.

SOCRATES: Then I suppose if they had not the same virtue, they would not be good in the same way.

MENON: Certainly not.

SOCRATES: Since therefore the same virtue is in all, try to tell me, and try to remember, what Gorgias says it is, and what you say too.

MENON: What can it be but to be able to rule men? If you want something which is the same in all.

SOCRATES: That is just what I do want. But is it the same virtue in a boy, Menon, and a slave, for each of them to be able to rule his master? And do you think he that ruled would still be a slave?

MENON: No, Socrates, I certainly don't think that.

SOCRATES: For it isn't reasonable, my good fellow. But here is another thing to consider. You say, "able to rule": shall we not add to it justly, not unjustly?

MENON: I think so, yes; for justice is virtue, Socrates.

SOCRATES: Virtue, Menon, or *a* virtue?

MENON: What do you mean by that?

SOCRATES: The same as in anything else. For example, if you please, take roundness: this I would say is *a* figure, not simply thus—figure. I would say so because there are other figures.

MENON: What you said was quite right, since I agree that there are other virtues besides justice.

SOCRATES: What are they, tell me, just as I would tell you

[1] The Greek word translated "temperately" means rather "with soundness of mind."

other figures if you ask; then you tell me some other virtues.

MENON: Very well. Courage, I think, is a virtue and temperance and wisdom and high-mindedness and plenty more.

SOCRATES: Here we are again, Menon: We looked for one virtue and found many, although that was in another way; but the one that is in all these things we cannot find! . . .

MENON: Then, my dear Socrates, virtue seems to me to be, as the poet says, "to rejoice in what is handsome and to be able"; I agree with the poet, and I say virtue is to desire handsome things and to be able to provide them.

SOCRATES: Do you say that the man who desires handsome things is desirous of good things?

MENON: By all means.

SOCRATES: Do you imply that there are some that desire bad things, and others good? Don't you think, my dear fellow, that all desire good things?

MENON: No, I don't.

SOCRATES: But some desire bad things?

MENON: Yes.

SOCRATES: Thinking the bad things to be good, you mean, or even recognising that they are bad, still they desire them?

MENON: Both, I think.

SOCRATES: Do you really think, my dear Menon, that anyone, knowing the bad things to be bad, still desires them?

MENON: Certainly.

SOCRATES: What does he desire, do you say—to have them?

MENON: To have them; what else?

SOCRATES: Thinking that the bad things benefit him that has them, or knowing that they injure whoever gets them?

MENON: Some thinking that the bad things benefit, some also knowing that they injure.

SOCRATES: Do those who think that the bad things benefit know that the bad things are bad?

MENON: I don't think that at all.

SOCRATES: Then it is plain that those who desire bad things are those who don't know what they are, but they desire what they thought were good whereas they really are bad; so those who do not know what they are, but think they are good, clearly desire the good. Is not that so?

MENON: It really seems like it.

SOCRATES: Very well. Those who desire the bad things, as you say, but yet think that bad things injure whoever gets them, know, I suppose, that they themselves will be injured by them?

MENON: They must.

SOCRATES: But do not these believe that those who are injured are miserable in so far as they are injured?

MENON: They must believe that too.

SOCRATES: Miserable means wretched?

MENON: So I think.

SOCRATES: Well, is there anyone who wishes to be miserable and wretched?

MENON: I think not, Socrates.

SOCRATES: Then nobody desires bad things, my dear Menon, nobody, unless he wishes to be like that. For what is the depth of misery other than to desire bad things and to get them?

MENON: It really seems that is the truth, Socrates, and no one desires what is bad.

SOCRATES: You said just now, didn't you, that virtue is to desire good things and to be able to provide them.

MENON: Yes, I did.

SOCRATES: Well, one part of what you said, the desiring, is in all, and in this respect one man is no better than another.

MENON: It seems so.

SOCRATES: It is clear, then, that if one is better than another, he must be better in the ability.

MENON: Certainly.

SOCRATES: Then according to your argument virtue is the power to get good things.

MENON: My dear Socrates, the whole thing, I must admit, seems to be exactly as you take it.

SOCRATES: Now let us see whether your last is true—perhaps you might be right. You say virtue is to be able to provide the good?

MENON: Quite so.

SOCRATES: Don't you call good such things as health and wealth?

MENON: Yes, and to possess gold and silver and public honour and appointments.

SOCRATES: Don't you say some other things are good besides these?

MENON: No, at least, I mean all such things as those.

SOCRATES: Very well; to provide gold and silver is virtue, according to Menon, the family friend of the Great King.[1] Do you add to your providing, my dear Menon, the qualification "fairly and justly"? Or does that make no difference to you,

[1] The King of Persia, the owner of fabulous riches.

and if a man provides them unjustly, you call it virtue all the same?

MENON: Oh dear me no, Socrates.

SOCRATES: It is vice then.

MENON: Dear me, yes, of course.

SOCRATES: It is necessary then, as it seems, to add to this getting, justice or temperance or piety or some other bit of virtue; or else it will not be virtue, although it provides good things.

MENON: Why, how could it be virtue without these?

SOCRATES: And not to get gold and silver when that is not just, neither for yourself nor anyone, is not this not-getting also virtue?

MENON: It looks like it.

SOCRATES: Then the getting of such good things would not be virtue any more than the not-getting; but as it seems, getting with justice would be virtue, and getting without such qualifications, vice.

MENON: I think it must be as you put it.

SOCRATES: Now we said a little while ago that each of them is a bit of virtue, justice and temperance and all things like that.

MENON: Yes.

SOCRATES: Then are you making fun of me, Menon?

MENON: How so, Socrates?

SOCRATES: Because I begged you just now not to break virtue into bits, or give me virtue as a handful of small change, and I gave you specimens to show how you ought to answer; and you simply paid no attention—now you tell me virtue is to be able to get good things with justice, and justice, you say, is a bit of virtue!

MENON: Yes, that is what I say.

SOCRATES: It follows, then, from what you agree, that to do whatever we do along with a bit of virtue is virtue; for you say justice is a bit of virtue, and so with each of those bits. Well, why do I say this? Because when I begged you to tell me what whole virtue is, instead of telling me that (far from it!) you say that every action is virtue if it be done with a bit of virtue, just as if you had explained what virtue is as a whole and I should know it at once even if you chopped your coin up into farthings. Then I must put the very same question from the beginning, as it seems: My dear friend Menon, what is virtue, if a little bit of virtue would make any action virtue? For that is as much as saying, whenever anyone says it, that all action with justice is virtue. Don't you think yourself that I must put the same question again, or do you believe that we can know what a bit of virtue is, when we do not know virtue itself? . . .

MENON: By all means. However, my dear friend, I should very much like to consider and to hear what I began by asking, whether we ought to tackle what virtue is as being something which can be taught, or as if men get it by nature or in some other way.

SOCRATES: But if I were your master, Menon, as well as master of myself, we should not consider beforehand whether virtue can be taught or not until we had tried to find out first what virtue really is. But since you make no attempt to master yourself—I suppose you want to be a free man—but you do attempt to master me, and you do master me! I will give way to you—for what else am I to do?—and it seems we must consider what qualities a thing has when we don't know yet what it is. Please relax at least one little tittle of your mastery, and give way so far that we may use a hypothesis to work from, in considering whether it can come by teaching or in some other way. I mean by hypothesis what the geometricians often envisage, a standing ground to start from; when they are asked, for instance, about a space, "Is it possible to inscribe this triangular space in this circle?" They will say, "I don't know yet whether it can be done, but I think I have, one may say, a useful hypothesis to start from, such as this: If the space is such that when you apply it to the given line[1] of the circle, it is deficient by a space of the same size as that which has been applied, one thing appears to follow, and if this be impossible, another.[2] I wish, then, to make a hypothesis before telling you what will happen about the inscribing of it in the circle, whether that be possible or not."

There now, let us take virtue in that way. Since we don't know what it is or what it is like, let us make our hypothesis or ground to stand on, and then consider whether it can be taught or not. We proceed as follows: If virtue is a quality among the things which are about the soul, would virtue be teachable, or not? First, if it is like or unlike knowledge, can it be taught or not, or as we said just now, can it be remembered—we need not worry which name we use—but can it be taught? Or is it

---

[1] Diameter.

[2] Mr. Ivor Thomas is thanked for help here. The matter is explained by him in his *Greek Mathematical Works*, vol. 1, p. 395ff. (Loeb Classical Library.)

plain to everyone that only one thing is taught to men, and that is knowledge?

MENON: So it seems to me at least.

SOCRATES: Then if virtue is a knowledge, it is plain that it could be taught.

MENON: Of course.

SOCRATES: We have soon done with that—if it is such, it can be taught, if not such, not.

MENON: Certainly.

SOCRATES: Now we have to consider, as it seems, whether virtue is a knowledge or something distinct from knowledge.

MENON: Agreed, that must be considered next.

SOCRATES: Very well. Don't we say that virtue is a good thing? This hypothesis holds for us, that it is good?

MENON: We do say so.

SOCRATES: Then if there is something good, and yet separate from knowledge, possibly virtue would not be a knowledge, but if there is no good which knowledge does not contain, it would be a right notion to suspect that it is a knowledge.

MENON: That is true.

SOCRATES: Further, by virtue we are good?

MENON: Yes.

SOCRATES: And if good, helpful; for all good things are helpful. Are they not?

MENON: Yes.

SOCRATES: And virtue, therefore, is helpful?

MENON: That must follow from what we have agreed.

SOCRATES: Let us consider then, taking up one by one, what sorts of things are helpful to us. Health, we say, and strength, and good looks, and wealth, of course; these and things like these we say are helpful, eh?

MENON: Yes.

SOCRATES: And these same things we say do harm sometimes also; do you agree with that?

MENON: I do.

SOCRATES: Consider then what leads each of these when it is helpful to us, and what leads each when it does harm. Are they not helpful when led by right use, and harmful when they are not?

MENON: Certainly.

SOCRATES: Let us pass on then, and consider the things that concern the soul. You speak of temperance and justice and courage and cleverness at learning and memory and high-mindedness, and all such things?

MENON: Yes.

SOCRATES: Look now; such of these as seem to you to be not knowledge but different from knowledge, are they not sometimes harmful and sometimes helpful? For example courage, if courage is not intelligence but something like boldness; is it not true that when a man is bold without sense, he is harmed, but when with sense, he is helped?

MENON: Yes.

SOCRATES: Is it not the same with temperance and cleverness at learning? When things learnt are accompanied by sense and are fitted in their proper places they are helpful; without sense, harmful?

MENON: Very much so.

SOCRATES: Then, in short, all the stirrings and endurings of the soul, when wisdom leads, come to happiness in the end, but when senselessness leads, to the opposite?

MENON: So it seems.

SOCRATES: Then if virtue is one of the things in the soul, and if it must necessarily be helpful, it must be wisdom: since quite by themselves all the things about the soul are neither helpful nor harmful, but they become helpful or harmful by the addition of wisdom or senselessness.

According to this argument, virtue, since it is helpful, must be some kind of wisdom.

MENON: I think so.

SOCRATES: Very well then, come now to the other things we mentioned a while since, wealth and so forth, and said they were sometimes good and sometimes harmful. When wisdom led any soul it made the things of the soul helpful, didn't it, and senselessness made them harmful: so also with these, the soul makes them helpful when it uses them rightly and leads them rightly, but harmful when not rightly?

MENON: Certainly.

SOCRATES: The sensible soul leads them rightly, the senseless wrongly?

MENON: That is true.

SOCRATES: Then cannot we say this as a general rule: In man everything else depends on the soul; but the things of the soul itself depend on wisdom, if it is to be good; and so by this argument the helpful would be wisdom—and we say virtue is helpful.

MENON: We do.

SOCRATES: Then we say virtue is wisdom, either in whole or in part?

MENON: I think what we say is well said, Socrates.

SOCRATES: Then if this is right, nature would not make men good.

MENON: I think not.

SOCRATES: Here is another thing surely: If good men were good by nature, we should have persons who could distinguish those young ones who were good in their nature, and we might take them over as they were indicated and keep them safe in the acropolis, and hallmark them more carefully than fine gold, that no one might corrupt them, but that when they grew up they should be useful to their cities.

MENON: Quite likely that, Socrates.

SOCRATES: Then since the good are not good by nature, is it by learning?

MENON: I really think that must be so; and it is plain, my dear Socrates, according to the hypothesis, that if virtue is knowledge, it can be taught.

SOCRATES: Yes, by Zeus, perhaps, but what if we were wrong in admitting that?

MENON: Well, it did seem just then to be a right conclusion.

SOCRATES: But what if we ought not to have agreed that it was right enough for then only, but for now also and all future time, if it is to be sound?

MENON: Why, what now? What makes you dissatisfied and distrustful? Do you think virtue is not knowledge?

SOCRATES: I will tell you Menon. It can be taught if it is knowledge; I do not wish to dispute the truth of that statement. But I have my doubts whether it is knowledge; pray consider if there is any reason in that. Just look here: If a thing can be taught—anything, not virtue only—must there not be both teachers and learners of it?

MENON: Yes, I think so.

SOCRATES: On the contrary, again, if there are neither teachers nor learners, we might fairly assume the thing cannot be taught?

MENON: That is true; but don't you think there are teachers of virtue?

SOCRATES: I have in truth often tried to find if there were teachers of it, but, do what I will, I can find none. Yet there are many on the same search, and especially those whom I believe to be best skilled in the matter. (*Enter* ANYTOS) Why look here, my dear Menon, in the nick of time here is Anytos, he has taken a seat beside us. Let us ask him to share in our search; it would be reasonable to give him a share. For in the first pace, Anytos has a wealthy father, the wise Anthemion, who became rich not by a stroke of luck or by a gift, like Ismenias the Theban who got "the fortune of a Polycrates" the other day,[1] but he got his by his own wisdom and care. In the next place, his father has a good name generally in the city; he is by no means overbearing and pompous and disagreeable, but a decent and mannerly man; and then he brought up our Anytos well, and educated him well, as the public opinion is—at least, they choose him for the highest offices. It is right to ask the help of such men when we are looking for teachers of virtue, if there are any or not, and who they are. Now then, Anytos, please help us, help me and your family friend Menon here, to find out who should be teachers of this subject. Consider it thus: If we wished Menon here to be a good physician, to whom should we send him to be his teachers? To the physicians, I suppose?

ANYTOS: Certainly.

SOCRATES: And what if we wanted him to be a good shoemaker, we should send him to the shoemakers?

ANYTOS: Yes.

SOCRATES: And so with everything else?

ANYTOS: Certainly.

SOCRATES: Something else, again, I ask you to tell me about these same things. We should be right in sending him to the physicians, we say, if we wanted him to be a physician. When we say this, do we mean that we should be sensible, if we sent him to those who profess the art, rather than to those who do not, and who also exact a fee for this very thing and declare themselves teachers, for anyone who wants to come and learn? If we looked to such things and sent him accordingly, should we not be doing right?

ANYTOS: Yes.

SOCRATES: Then the same about pipe-playing[2] and the rest. If we want to make anyone a piper, it is great folly to be unwilling to send him to men who undertake to teach the art, and exact a fee for it; and instead to make trouble for others by letting him seek to learn from people who neither pretend to be teachers nor have a single pupil in the art which we want the person we send to learn from them. Don't you think that is plain unreason?

---

[1] A proverb from the life of Polycrates, tyrant of Samos. This Theban had helped Anytos and the other banished Athenians the year before the supposed date of this dialogue.

[2] The pipe was a wind instrument, blown at the end like an oboe.

ANYTOS: Yes, by Zeus. I do, even stupidity.

SOCRATES: You are right. Now you can join me in consulting together about our friend Menon here. The fact is, Anytos, he has been telling me this long time that he desires the wisdom and virtue by which men manage houses and cities well and honour their parents, and know how to entertain fellow-citizens and strangers and to speed them on their way, as a good man ought to do. Then consider whom we should properly send him to for this virtue. Is it not clear from what has just been said that we should send him to those who profess to be teachers of virtue, and declare themselves to be public teachers for any of the Hellenes who wish to learn, with a proper fee fixed to be paid for this?

ANYTOS: And who are these, my dear Socrates?

SOCRATES: *You* too know, I suppose, that these are the men who are called Sophists.

ANYTOS: O Heracles! Hush, my dear Socrates! May none of my relations or friends, here or abroad, fall into such madness as to go to these persons and be tainted! These men are the manifest canker and destruction of those they have to do with.

SOCRATES: What's that, Anytos? These are the only men professing to know how to do us good, yet they differ so much from the rest that they not only do not help us as the others do, when one puts oneself into their hands, but on the contrary corrupt us? And for this they actually ask pay, and make no secret of it? I, for one, cannot believe you. For I know one man, Protagoras, who has earned more money from this wisdom than Pheidias did for all those magnificent works of his, or any ten other statue-makers. This is a miracle! Those who cobble old shoes or patch up old clothes could not hide it for thirty days if they gave back shoes and clothes worse than they got them, for if they did that they would soon starve to death: but Protagoras, it seems, hid it from all Hellas, and corrupted those who had to do with him, and sent them away worse than he got them, for more than forty years!—for I think he was nearly seventy when he died, after forty years in his art—and in all that time to this day his great name has lasted! And not only Protagoras, but very many others, some born before his time and others living still. Are we to suppose, according to what you say, that they knew they were deceiving and tainting the young, or did they deceive themselves? And shall we claim that these were madmen, when some call them wisest of all mankind?

ANYTOS: Anything but madmen, Socrates; the young men are much madder who pay them money; and madder still those, their relations, who entrust young people to them; maddest of all, the cities which allow them to come in and do not kick them out—whether he is a foreigner or native who attempts to do such a thing.

SOCRATES: Why, Anytos, have you ever been wronged at all by Sophists? What makes you so hard on them?

ANYTOS: Good God, I have never had anything to do with one, and I would never allow anyone else of my family to have to do with them.

SOCRATES: Then you are quite without experience of these men?

ANYTOS: And I hope I may remain so.

SOCRATES: Astonishing! Then how could you know anything about this matter, whether there is anything good or bad in it, if you are quite without experience of it?

ANYTOS: Easily. At least I know who these are; whether I have experience of them or not.

SOCRATES: Perhaps you are a prophet, Anytos; since how indeed otherwise you could know about them, from what you say yourself, I should wonder. But we were not trying to find out who those are that Menon might go to and become a scoundrel—let them be Sophists if you like—but those others, please tell us and do good to this, your family friend, by showing him some to whom he should go in all this great city, who could make him of some account in that virtue which I described just now.

ANYTOS: Why didn't *you* show him?

SOCRATES: Well, I did say whom I thought to be teachers of these things, but it turns out I made a mess of it, so you say; and perhaps there is something in what you maintain. Now pray take your turn, and tell him which of the Athenians he should try. Tell us a name, of anyone you like.

ANYTOS: Why ask for[1] the name of one man? Any well-bred gentleman[2] of Athens he might meet will make him better than Sophists can, every single one of them, if he will do as he is told.

SOCRATES: Did these well-bred gentlemen become like that by luck? Did they learn from no one, and can they nevertheless teach other people what they themselves never learnt?

[1] Literally, "Why must you hear."
[2] Literally, Any of "the beautiful and good"; a usual term for "gentleman."

ANYTOS: I suppose they learnt from their fathers, who were also gentlemen before them; or do not you think there have been plenty of fine men in our city?

SOCRATES: I think, Anytos, that there are plenty of men here good at politics, and that there have been plenty before no less than now; but have they been also good teachers of their virtue? For this is what our discussion is really about—not if there are or have been good men here, but if virtue can be taught—that is what we have been considering for so long. And the point we are considering is just this: whether the good men of these times and of former times knew how to hand on to another that virtue in which they were good, or whether it cannot be handed on from one man to another, or received by one man from another—that is what we have been all this while trying to find out, I and Menon. Well then, consider it thus, in your own way of discussing: Would you not say Themistocles[1] was a good man?

ANYTOS: Indeed I should, none better.

SOCRATES: And also a good teacher of his own virtue, if ever anyone was?

ANYTOS: That is what I think, of course if he wished.

SOCRATES: But don't you think he would have wished others to be fine gentlemen, especially, I take it, his own son? Or do you think he grudged it to him, and on purpose did not pass on the virtue in which he was good? I suppose you have heard that Themistocles had his son Cleophantos taught to be a good horseman. At least, he could remain standing upright on horseback, and cast a javelin upright on horseback, and do many other wonderful feats which the great man had him taught, and he made him clever in all that could be got from good teachers. Haven't you heard this from older men?

ANYTOS: Oh yes, I have heard that.

SOCRATES: Then no one could have blamed his son for lack of good natural gifts.

ANYTOS: Perhaps not.

SOCRATES: What do you say to this, then: that Cleophantos became a good and wise man in the same things as his father Themistocles, did you ever hear that from young or old?

ANYTOS: No, indeed.

SOCRATES: Are we to believe, then, that he wished to educate his son in these things, but not to make the boy better than his neighbours in that wisdom in which he was himself

[1] Who during the wars with Persia laid the foundations of the navy—and of the greatness—of Athens.

teachers nor learners of any given thing, this cannot be taught.

MENON: We have.

SOCRATES: No teachers of virtue appear, then?

MENON: No.

SOCRATES: And if no teachers, no learners?

MENON: So it seems.

SOCRATES: Then virtue could not be taught?

MENON: It looks like it, if our enquiry has been right. So I am wondering now, Socrates, whether there are no good men at all, or what could be the way in which the good men who exist come into being.

SOCRATES: We are really a paltry pair, you and I, Menon; Gorgias has not educated you enough, nor Prodicos me. Then the best thing is to turn our minds on ourselves, and try to find out someone to make us better by hook or by crook. In saying this I have my eye on our recent enquiry, where we were fools enough to miss something; it is not only when knowledge guides mankind that things are done rightly and well; and perhaps that is why we failed to understand in what way the good men come into being.

MENON: What do you mean by that, Socrates?

SOCRATES: This: That the good men must be useful; we admitted, and rightly, that this could not be otherwise.

MENON: Yes.

SOCRATES: Yes, and that they will be useful if they guide our business rightly, we admitted also: was that correct?

MENON: Yes.

SOCRATES: But that it is not possible to guide rightly unless one knows, to have admitted that looks like a blunder.

MENON: What do you mean?

SOCRATES: I will tell you. If someone knows the way to Larissa, or where you will, and goes there and guides others, will he not guide rightly and well?

MENON: Certainly.

SOCRATES: Well, what of one who has never been there, and does not know the way; but if he has a right opinion as to the way, won't he also guide rightly?

MENON: Certainly.

SOCRATES: And so long as he has a right opinion about that of which the other has knowledge, he will be quite as good a guide as the one who knows, although he does not know, but only thinks, what is true.

MENON: Quite as good.

SOCRATES: Then true opinion is no worse guide than wisdom, for rightness of action; and this is what we failed to see just now while we were enquiring what sort of a thing virtue is. We said then that wisdom alone guides to right action; but, really, true opinion does the same.

MENON: So it seems.

SOCRATES: Then right opinion is no less useful than knowledge.

MENON: Yes, it is less useful; for he who has knowledge would always be right, he who has right opinion, only sometimes.

SOCRATES: What! Would not he that has right opinion always be right so long as he had right opinion?

MENON: Oh yes, necessarily, I think. This being so, I am surprised, Socrates, why knowledge is ever more valued than right opinion, and why they are two different things.

SOCRATES: Do you know why you wonder, or shall I tell you?

MENON: Oh, tell me, please.

SOCRATES: Because you have not observed the statues of Daidalos.[1] But perhaps you have none in your part of the world.

MENON: What are you driving at?

SOCRATES: They must be fastened up, if you want to keep them; or else they are off and away.[2]

MENON: What of that?

SOCRATES: If left loose there is not much value in owning one of his works—like a runaway slave; it doesn't stay; but chained up it is worth a great deal; for they are fine works of art. What am I driving at? Why, at the true opinions. For the true opinions, as long as they stay, are splendid and do all the good in the world; but they will not stay long—off and away they run out of the soul of mankind, so they are not worth much until you fasten them up with the reasoning of cause and effect. But this, my dear Menon, is remembering, as we agreed before. When they are fastened up, first they become knowledge, secondly they remain; and that is why knowledge is valued more than right opinion, and differs from right opinion by this bond.[3]

[1] Daidalos (*Daedalus*), the mythical sculptor and craftsman; the ancient Greeks attributed to him the masterpieces whose origins they did not know.
[2] A common saying.
[3] "Opinion in good men is knowledge in the making."—Milton, *Areopagitica*.

MENON: I do declare, Socrates, you have a good comparison there.

SOCRATES: Well, I speak by conjecture, not as one who knows; but to say that right opinion is different from knowledge, that, I believe, is no conjecture in me at all. That I would say I know; there are few things I would say that of, but this I would certainly put down as one of those I know.

MENON: You are quite right in saying this, Socrates.

SOCRATES: Now then, is this not right: True opinion guiding achieves the work of each action no less than knowledge?

MENON: Yes, I think that also is true.

SOCRATES: Then right opinion is nothing inferior to knowledge, and will be no less useful for actions; and the man who has right opinion is not inferior to the man who has knowledge.

MENON: Yes.

SOCRATES: Again, the good man we have agreed to be useful.

MENON: Yes.

SOCRATES: Since, then, not only by knowledge would men be good and useful to their cities (if they were so) but also by right opinion, and since neither knowledge nor true opinion comes to mankind by nature, being acquired[1]—or do you think that either of them does come by nature, perhaps?

MENON: No, not I.

SOCRATES: Therefore they come not by nature, neither could the good be so by nature.

MENON: Not at all.

SOCRATES: Since not by nature, we enquired next whether it could be taught.

MENON: Yes.

SOCRATES: Well, it seemed that it could be taught if virtue was wisdom.

MENON: Yes.

SOCRATES: And if it could be taught, it would be wisdom.

MENON: Certainly.

SOCRATES: And if there were teachers, it could be taught, if no teachers, it could not?

MENON: Just so.

SOCRATES: Further, we agreed that there were no teachers of it?

MENON: That is true.

SOCRATES: We agreed, then, that it could not be taught, and that it was not wisdom?

[1] The text of Plato is uncertain here.

MENON: Certainly.

SOCRATES: But, however, we agree that it is good?

MENON: Yes.

SOCRATES: And that which guides rightly is useful and good?

MENON: Certainly.

SOCRATES: Again, only these two things guide rightly, right opinion and knowledge; and if a man has these, he guides rightly—for things which happen rightly from some chance do not come about by human guidance: but in all things in which a man is a guide towards what is right, these two do it, true opinion and knowledge.

MENON: I think so.

SOCRATES: Well, since it cannot be taught, no longer is virtue knowledge.

MENON: It seems not.

SOCRATES: Then of two good and useful things one has been thrown away, and knowledge would not be guide in political action.

MENON: I think not.

SOCRATES: Then it was not by wisdom, or because they are wise, that such men guided the cities, men such as Themistocles and those whom Anytos told us of; for which reason, you see, they could not make others like themselves, because not knowledge made them what they were.

MENON: It seems likely to be as you say, Socrates.

SOCRATES: Then if it were not knowledge, right opinion is left, you see. This is what politicians use when they keep a state upright; they have no more to do with understanding than oracle-chanters and diviners, for these in ecstasy tell the truth often enough, but they know nothing of what they say.

MENON: That is how things really are.

SOCRATES: Then it is fair, Menon, to call those men divine, who are often right in what they say and do, even in grand matters, but have no sense while they do it.

MENON: Certainly.

SOCRATES: Then we should be right in calling these we just mentioned divine, oracle-chanters and prophets and the poets or creative artists, all of them; most of all, the politicians, we should say they are divine and ecstatic, being inspired and possessed by the god when they are often right while they say grand things although they know nothing of what they say.

MENON: Certainly.

SOCRATES: And the women, too, Menon, call good men

divine; and the Laconians[1] when they praise a good man say, "A divine man that!"

MENON: Yes, and they appear to be quite right, my dear Socrates, although our friend Anytos may perhaps be angry with you for saying it.

SOCRATES: I don't care. We will have a talk with him[2] by and by, Menon. But if we have ordered all our enquiry well and argued well, virtue is seen as coming neither by nature nor by teaching; but by divine allotment incomprehensively[3] to those to whom it comes—unless there were some politician so outstanding as to be able to make another man a politician. And if there were one, he might almost be said to be among the living such as Homer says of Teiresias among the dead, for Homer says of him that he alone of those in Hades has his mind, the others are flittering shades.[4] In the same way also here on earth such a man would be, in respect of virtue, as something real amongst shadows.

MENON: Excellently said, I think, Socrates.

SOCRATES: Then from this our reasoning, Menon, virtue is shown as coming to us, whenever it comes, by divine dispensation; but we shall only know the truth about this clearly when, before enquiring in what way virtue comes to mankind, we first try to search out what virtue is in itself.

But now it is time for me to go; and your part is to persuade your friend Anytos to believe just what you believe about it, that he may be more gentle; for if you can persuade him, you will do a service to the people of Athens also.

---

[1] The Spartans.
[2] Anytos was one of the accusers in his trial for life.
[3] Literally, "without mind."
[4] *Odyssey*, x. 494.

CHAPTER V

Aristotle

The prestige which Aristotle enjoyed after his death was greater, and more enduring, than perhaps that of any other thinker has ever been. So great was it that, centuries later, appeal to his authority was often made, and often accepted, as perfectly conclusive in philosophical argument and even, with far less reason, in questions of natural science. This was in many ways unfortunate. Eventually, when, about the sixteenth century and later, new beginnings were made in many fields of human inquiry, it became the mark of a progressive thinker to ignore or abuse the man with whose authority so much in preceding centuries had been so closely associated. At all times, too, his admirers were inclined to treat his works as constituting a rigid and final system, consistent, undeveloping, to be defended sentence by sentence. It is only quite recently that it has become orthodox to recognize, what after all would naturally be expected, that Aristotle in the course of his life sometimes changed his opinions. In particular the work of Werner Jaeger has put forward the picture of him as gradually tending away from his Platonic beginnings to a very different mode of thought that was more naturally his own.

It must be remembered that for no less than twenty years Aristotle was actually a member of Plato's school at Athens. In this period he wrote dialogues in the Platonic manner, which have not come down to us. It is quite probable that these, which surviving fragments show to have been elegant literary productions, were in some respects critical of Academic doctrine, but still they were certainly in the Platonic mode. But the bulk of Aristotle's work which we now possess consists of writings not published during his lifetime, not in dialogue form, not highly finished, and often very far from Platonic. These manuscript treatises and lecture notes were collected and arranged after his death, and appear to have had some limited circulation until, in the first century B.C., Andronicus, then the head of the Peripatetic school, produced an edition on which all our surviving texts are based. In the meantime Aristotle's published works were increasingly neglected, until at last they were finally lost, and with them, unfortunately, the best reminder of Aristotle's purely Platonic beginnings.

Speaking in very general terms indeed—and here we cannot possibly hope to do otherwise—we may say that the point on which Aristotle came to differ most fundamentally from Plato was that of the *separation,* always conspicuous in Plato, between the ordinary world and its contents, and a supposed other world of "intelligible" entities. The divergence here was, perhaps, as much a matter of temperament as strictly of argument. There was in Plato a powerfully imaginative, almost fantastic, streak which inclined him always towards bold flights of speculation and away from the humdrum details of the everyday world. This aspect of his doctrines was that chiefly emphasized by his immediate successors, and this fact, combined with the progressive emancipation of Aristotle's own thinking, led to a widening breach between Aristotle and Platonism. About Aristotle there was nothing otherworldly. In ethics, in science, in politics, even in theology, the problems that concerned him related to man's place in *this* world, his understanding of it, the life he should live in the conditions here actually obtaining. The Platonic inclination to condemn this world as "unreal" by comparison with the world of Forms would have seemed to him fantastic, implying a kind of deliberate rejection of all that to man is most familiar, most solid, most important. Thus, broadly speaking, he sought to substitute in metaphysics, for Plato's distinction between this "unreal" world and another, a distinction between two aspects of this one real world. He was inclined to agree that Forms, timeless and unchanging, were the proper objects of the highest knowledge. But he regarded them not as independently existing entities quite separate from the things of this world, but as features of the things of this world, inseparable from them. We can indeed distinguish, he held, between Form and Matter; but actually existing objects must have both. The stuff that, say, a statue is made of can be distinguished from the particular form that it has; it might have had, and may come to have in the future, some other form. But it cannot exist with no form at all. And still less could the form that it now has be supposed to exist, independently of any matter having that form. Forms are *in* things; they cannot be detached from things. And against the supposition of such a detachment Aristotle repeatedly deploys arguments, some of which had indeed been first raised by Plato himself, but to which no acceptable answer had ever been found. Socrates, Aristotle would say, was right in attaching the importance that he did to exact definition; and Plato was right in holding that definition is "of the Form"; but any Form thus defined is the form that some matter has, and not itself a separately existing individual thing.

A very large part of Aristotle's surviving work deals with questions that might nowadays be classified as scientific. He devoted much time, particularly in his later years, to the organization of systematic, co-operative research, consisting largely in an accumulation of facts about the natural world of a sort that had not previously been attempted. But rather differently from this, he also paid great attention to what might be called the conceptual side of science—to the general categories, forms of classification, and types of explanation that should provide the framework for factual research. At this point the influence of Plato upon Aristotle was very strong; and unfortunately Aristotle's own influence upon his successors was predominantly bad. His preferred type of explanation proved unfertile.

Plato held, and in his *Phaedo* attributes to Socrates also, the view that true explanation must be *teleological,* in terms of purpose. "Is my sitting here in prison," Socrates asks, "explained by the fact that I have bones and joints and flexible muscles, all of which together enable me to sit here?" No, surely. These factors may render him *able* to sit in prison, but they do not explain *why* he is sitting there. To explain this one must mention his decision to remain, his purpose of total obedience to the laws of Athens even though they should work to his disadvantage. One must not confuse, Plato says, the antecedent conditions which are necessary for a given event, and the true cause which really explains why it occurs. The best explanation, the only real explanation, consists in mentioning the end or purpose to be achieved. This view was enthusiastically adopted by Aristotle. One might well wish to object that Plato's conclusion in its general form involves the assumption that what is true of human behavior is true also of mere physical events—human behavior can be explained in terms of purposes, for human beings really do have and act from purposes, but the same surely cannot be said of plants, or seas, or the stars. But Aristotle deliberately overrules this objection. He says in the *Physics*, "As in intelligent action, so in nature. Intelligent action is for the sake of an end, therefore the nature of things also is so." In this passage (quoted below) he seems to have been led to this conclusion through a false opposition of purpose and *chance*. If, he implies, we deny that natural happenings occur with a purpose, we shall have to say that they occur by chance. But "we do not ascribe to chance the frequency of rain in winter"; fire does not burn by chance, nor is each sunrise a happy coincidence. "Therefore action for an end is present in things which come to be and are by nature." However, the conclusion does not follow. Certainly the rising of the sun is not a mere coincidence; but what this means is simply that it is part of the order of nature, a regularly occurring "natural" phenomenon; we are not in the least obliged to assume any purpose or end. To do so is in fact to extend into the physical world a way of thinking that suits the special case of human, and perhaps a few other, living beings.

The great defect in the approach which Aristotle thus adopted consists in the fact that it *seems* to yield satisfactory results, which however mark no real advance in our knowledge at all. That flames tend to rise upwards can be verbally "explained" by saying that their end or "aim" is to reach a higher place; that plants grow can be similarly explained by the supposition that they aim at achieving the full-grown state. But it is clear that these explanations are really nothing more than rephrasings of the very fact to be explained: fire rises because it naturally does so, plants grow because they grow. Genuine advances in scientific understanding have in fact always taken the form that Plato and Aristotle explicitly disapproved—that is, the discovery of antecedent conditions upon which a certain result is found to follow. And the scientific propagandists of the Renaissance, attempting to encourage practical research into causes in this sense, reserved their most withering criticism and contempt for Aristotle's damaging wrong step at this important point.

It is sometimes held that Aristotle's pioneering work in logic has been equally damaging. This, however, is certainly unfair. It is true that his investigation and classification of certain types of deductive argument was so powerfully done that for centuries it was thought to be both final and complete; but this prejudice among his successors was not Aristotle's fault. And on the whole what he achieved has withstood amazingly the test of time. A few years ago many modern logicians, engaged in researches quite different from those of Aristotle, were apt to insinuate that their results were not only different from, but inconsistent with, his—that in the light of modern logic he was seen to have been often *mistaken*. But this was not so. His inquiries can now be seen to have been *limited* —he restricted his attention very narrowly to syllogistic forms—but new extensions of logic do not conflict with his limited findings. In many ways his work in logic was more powerfully creative than anything else that he did; and probably, even if in succeeding centuries it was glorified too much and in some ways debased, the discipline which it provided for at least two thousand years was on balance enormously beneficial to the history of thought. Here again, though, he was a target for much abuse at the Renaissance, since his interest in *deduction*—inevitable in a formal logician—made his work of no help to those whose interests lay in the non-deductive procedures of scientific discovery. His logical writings came to be known as the *Organum,* "the instrument." Francis Bacon's *Novum Organum* offered, at the start of the seventeenth century, a deliberate challenge to the Aristotelian tradition, which had, he unkindly asserted, "done more harm than good."

I have thought it best to include in this book, from Aristotle's writings, a fairly long extract from his best-known ethical work, the *Nicomachean Ethics.* Too much of the rest of his work is so difficult, so unfamiliar, or in other ways so obscure that it would scarcely be intelligible without an impossibly detailed commentary. But this objection does not apply to his moral philosophy, which is on the whole, though closely argued, very lucidly written, and the general tone of which is often startlingly contemporary. This makes it all the more necessary to bear in mind a few points at which Aristotle's ideas do differ from ours.

First (though this is partly a mere difficulty in translation from the Greek) it has to be remembered that, when Aristotle talks about "happiness," he does not mean exactly what we might naturally expect, though "happiness" is perhaps the most convenient near-synonym in English. To achieve *eudaimonia* is, for Aristotle, rather to succeed in living "the good life," than to achieve that more or less transitory state of mind and mood that we often think of as "being happy." To be *eudaimon* certainly includes being happy, but it implies also more than this—that the condition achieved is a stable, long-term affair, and also that it is attained by the right means, by proper conduct. It follows from this that Aristotle is not a *hedonist;* he does not regard the attainment of happiness, considered as a state of feeling—still less, the attainment of pleasure—as in itself a sufficient justification for any action or course of action. The *eudaimon* man is he who orders his life *well,* not he who, by hook or by crook, secures pleasure or happiness.

This point to a large extent mitigates the oddity of another—namely, that Aristotle seems not to believe in the desirability, perhaps not even in the possibility, of genuine altruism. Deliberation by me as to how I should act is always represented by him as, in the last analysis, consideration of means to *eudaimonia* for myself. The resulting theory is, I think, genuinely egoistic. However, since the attainment of my own *eudaimonia* requires me to act well in my relations with others, Aristotle certainly gives here no countenance to *selfishness;* for selfishness implies, what Aristotle disallows, pursuit of my own interests without regard for the interests of other people.

It should be noticed also that Aristotle, unlike Plato, and in very sharp contrast with his immediate successors, regards *eudaimonia* as a public affair. The good life, in his view, implies good conduct in relation to others, and in public life, and at least a reasonable degree also of worldly success. Plato had been inclined to think of *eudaimonia* as strictly an inner, psychological condition; in post-Aristotelian philosophy it was to be consistently represented as invulnerable to the impact of all external affairs. But Aristotle takes the, surely, more ordinary view that to live well includes living with reasonable material success, and conducting one's self well in one's dealings with other people. Nor does he for a moment suppose that this is impossible, too difficult, or too dangerous to adopt as one's aim.

A more subtle point is this: There is a sense in which Aristotle does not employ at all our concept of "morality." Here again one is apt to be misled by difficulties of translation. The Greek word *arete* in this context is usually rendered as "virtue," and we naturally think of virtue as a moral affair. But this implies a restriction that is not present in the Greek. "Moral virtues" in Aristotle are simply good qualities of character displayed in right conduct; and *any* good qualities of character may be so called—good manners, affability, wit, proper dignity of bearing, as well as honesty, truthfulness, temperance, or charity. It is not, of course, that Aristotle does not discuss what we should regard as moral questions; it is only that he does not specially distinguish them from other questions of what is good in conduct and character, and indeed he has not the linguistic means of doing so. This absence of our modern, limited concept of morality seems characteristic of the ancient world in general. In Cicero for instance, writing three centuries later, we again find no distinction drawn between moral and nonmoral questions about human character, no sharp distinction between good manners, "good form," and good morals.

Finally, we should observe that Aristotle was no reformer. With his insistence upon the avoidance of all extremes, and his constant reference to "what is ordinarily said," he appears as being concerned to codify and elucidate the ordinary judgments of enlightened, educated men; he had no desire to propagate any radically new moral attitudes. For this reason some, who are accustomed to the expression by moralists of views more lofty than those most applied in practice, find Aristotle's tone somewhat low and unedifying. Others complain that he has nothing to say of extreme situations, of desperate predicaments. But I think it may be found that he often states, with masterly clarity, what civilized men are in fact disposed to think and do, in the ordinary conditions in which civilized life is to be lived.

The *Nicomachean Ethics** begins as follows:

I. Every art and every investigation, and likewise every practical pursuit or undertaking, seems to aim at some good: hence it has been well said that the Good is that at which all things aim. (It is true that a certain variety is to be observed among the ends at which the arts and sciences aim: in some cases the activity of practising the art is itself the end, whereas in others the end is some product over and above the mere exercise of the art; and in the arts whose ends are certain things beside the practice of the arts themselves, these products are essentially superior in value to the activities.) But as there are numerous pursuits and arts and sciences, it follows that their ends are correspondingly numerous: for instance, the end of the science of medicine is health, that of the art of shipbuilding a vessel, that of strategy victory, that of domestic economy wealth. Now in cases where several such pursuits are subordinate to some single faculty—as bridle-making and

* Translated by H. Rackham. London: William Heinemann Ltd., 1926; Cambridge, Mass.: Harvard University Press, Book I, pp. 3-17, 25-69. (The Loeb Classical Library.)

the other trades concerned with horses' harness are subordinate to horsemanship, and this and every other military pursuit to the science of strategy, and similarly other arts to different arts again—in all these cases, I say, the ends of the master arts are things more to be desired than the ends of the arts subordinate to them; since the latter ends are only pursued for the sake of the former. (And it makes no difference whether the ends of the pursuits are the activities themselves or some other thing beside these, as in the case of the sciences mentioned.)

II. If therefore among the ends at which our actions aim there be one which we will for its own sake, while we will the others only for the sake of this, and if we do not choose everything for the sake of something else (which would obviously result in a process *ad infinitum,* so that all desire would be futile and vain), it is clear that this one ultimate End must be the Good, and indeed the Supreme Good. Will not then a knowledge of this Supreme Good be also of great practical importance for the conduct of life? Will it not better enable us to attain our proper object, like archers having a target to aim at? If this be so, we ought to make an attempt to comprehend at all events in outline what exactly this Supreme Good is, and of which of the sciences or faculties it is the object.

Now it would seem that this supreme End must be the object of the most authoritative of the sciences—some science which is pre-eminently a master-craft. But such is manifestly the science of Politics; for it is this that ordains which of the sciences are to exist in states, and what branches of knowledge the different classes of the citizens are to learn, and up to what point; and we observe that even the most highly esteemed of the faculties, such as strategy, domestic economy, oratory, are subordinate to the political science. Inasmuch then as the rest of the sciences are employed by this one, and as it moreover lays down laws as to what people shall do and what things they shall refrain from doing, the end of this science must include the ends of all the others. Therefore, the Good of man must be the end of the science of Politics. For even though it be the case that the Good is the same for the individual and for the state, nevertheless, the good of the state is manifestly a greater and more perfect good, both to attain and to preserve. To secure the good of one person only is better than nothing; but to secure the good of a nation or a state is a nobler and more divine achievement.

This then being its aim, our investigation is in a sense the study of Politics.

III. Now our treatment of this science will be adequate, if it achieves that amount of precision which belongs to its subject matter. The same exactness must not be expected in all departments of philosophy alike, any more than in all the products of the arts and crafts. The subjects studied by political science are Moral Nobility and Justice; but these conceptions involve much difference of opinion and uncertainty, so that they are sometimes believed to be mere conventions and to have no real existence in the nature of things. And a similar uncertainty surrounds the conception of the Good, because it frequently occurs that good things have harmful consequences: people have before now been ruined by wealth, and in other cases courage has cost men their lives. We must therefore be content if, in dealing with subjects and starting from premises thus uncertain, we succeed in presenting a rough outline of the truth: when our subjects and our premises are merely generalities, it is enough if we arrive at generally valid conclusions. Accordingly we may ask the student also to accept the various views we put forward in the same spirit; for it is the mark of an educated mind to expect that amount of exactness in each kind which the nature of the particular subject admits. It is equally unreasonable to accept merely probable conclusions from a mathematician, and to demand strict demonstration from an orator.

Again, each man judges correctly those matters with which he is acquainted; it is of these that he is a competent critic. To criticize a particular subject, therefore, a man must have been trained in that subject: to be a good critic generally, he must have had an all-round education. Hence the young are not fit to be students of Political Science. For they have no experience of life and conduct, and it is these that supply the premises and subject matter of this branch of philosophy. And moreover they are led by their feelings; so that they will study the subject to no purpose or advantage, since the end of this science is not knowledge but action. And it makes no difference whether they are young in years or immature in character: the defect is not a question of time, it is because their life and its various aims are guided by feeling; for to such persons their knowledge is of no use, any more than it is to persons of defective self-restraint. But Moral Science may be of great value to those who guide their desires and actions by principle.

Let so much suffice by way of introduction as to the student of the subject, the spirit in which our conclusions are to be received, and the object that we set before us.

IV. To resume, inasmuch as all studies and undertakings are directed to the attainment of some good, let us discuss what it is that we pronounce to be the aim of Politics, that is, what is the highest of all the goods that action can achieve. As far as the name goes, we may almost say that the great majority of mankind are agreed about this; for both the multitude and persons of refinement speak of it as Happiness, and conceive "the good life" or "doing well" to be the same thing as "being happy." But what constitutes happiness is a matter of dispute; and the popular account of it is not the same as that given by the philosophers. Ordinary people identify it with some obvious and visible good, such as pleasure or wealth or honour—some say one thing and some another, indeed very often the same man says different things at different times: when he falls sick he thinks health is happiness, when he is poor, wealth. At other times, feeling conscious of their own ignorance, men admire those who propound something grand and above their heads; and it has been held by some thinkers that beside the many good things we have mentioned, there exists another Good, that is good in itself, and stands to all those goods as the cause of their being good.

Now perhaps it would be a somewhat fruitless task to review all the different opinions that are held. It will suffice to examine those which are most widely accepted, or which seem to be supported by some measure of reason.

And we must not overlook the distinction between arguments that start from first principles and those that lead to first principles. This is a matter that was rightly raised by Plato, who used to enquire whether the true procedure is to start from or to lead up to one's first principles, as in a racecourse one may run from the judges to the far end of the track or the reverse. Now no doubt it is proper to start from the known. But "the known" has two meanings—"what is familiar to us," which is one thing, and "what is intelligible in itself," which is another. Perhaps then for us at all events it is proper to start from what is known to us. This is why in order to be a competent student of the Right and Just, and in short of the topics of Politics in general, the pupil is bound to have had a right moral upbringing. For the starting-point or first principle is the fact that a thing is so; if this be satisfactorily ascertained, there will be no need also to know the reason why it is so. And the man of good moral training knows first principles already, or can easily acquire them. As for the person who neither knows nor can learn, let him hear the words of Hesiod:

> Best is the man who can himself advise;
> He too is good who hearkens to the wise;
> But who, himself being witless, will not heed
> Another's wisdom, is a fool indeed.

But let us continue from the point where we digressed. To judge from the recognized types of Lives, the more or less reasoned conceptions of the Good or Happiness that prevail are the following. On the one hand the generality of men and the most vulgar identify the Good with pleasure, and accordingly look no higher than the Life of Enjoyment—for there are three specially prominent Lives, the one just mentioned, the Life of Politics, and thirdly, the Life of Contemplation. The generality of mankind then show themselves to be utterly slavish, by preferring what is only a life for cattle; but they get a hearing for their view as reasonable because many persons of high position share the feelings of Sardanapalus.*

Men of refinement, on the other hand, and men of action think that the Good is honour—for this may be said to be the end of the Life of Politics. But honour after all seems too superficial to be the Good for which we are seeking; since it appears to depend on those who confer it more than on him upon whom it is conferred, whereas we instinctively feel that the Good must be something proper to its possessor and not easy to be taken away from him. Moreover men's motive in pursuing honour seems to be to assure themselves of their own merit; at least they seek to be honoured by men of judgement and by people who know them, that is, they desire to be honoured on the ground of virtue. It is clear therefore that in the opinion at all events of men of action, virtue is a greater good than honour; and one might perhaps accordingly suppose that virtue rather than honour is the end of the Political Life. But even virtue proves on examination to be too incomplete to be the End; since it appears possible to possess it while you are asleep, or without putting it into practice throughout the whole of your life; and also for the virtuous

* A mythical, supposedly self-indulgent, Assyrian king.

man to suffer the greatest misery and misfortune—though no one would pronounce a man living a life of misery to be happy, unless for the sake of maintaining a paradox. But we need not pursue this subject, since it has been sufficiently treated in the ordinary discussions.

The third type of life is the Life of Contemplation, which we shall consider in the sequel.

The Life of Money-making is a hard kind of life; and clearly wealth is not the Good we are in search of, for it is only good as being useful, a means to something else. On this score indeed one might conceive the ends before mentioned to have a better claim, for they are approved for their own sakes. But even they do not really seem to be the Supreme Good; however, many arguments against them have been disseminated, so we may dismiss them. . . .

VII. We may now return to the Good which is the object of our search, and try to find out what exactly it can be. For good appears to be one thing in one pursuit or art and another in another: it is different in medicine from what it is in strategy, and so on with the rest of the arts. What definition of the Good then will hold true in all the arts? Perhaps we may define it as that for the sake of which everything else is done. This applies to something different in each different art—to health in the case of medicine, to victory in that of strategy, to a house in architecture, and to something else in each of the other arts; but in every pursuit or undertaking it describes the end of that pursuit or undertaking, since in all of them it is for the sake of the end that everything else is done. Hence if there be something which is the end of all the things done by human action, this will be the practicable Good—or if there be several such ends, the sum of these will be the Good. Thus by changing its ground the argument has reached the same result as before. We must attempt however to render this still more precise.

Now there do appear to be several ends at which our actions aim; but as we choose some of them—for instance wealth, or flutes, and instruments generally—as a means to something else, it is clear that not all of them are final ends; whereas the Supreme Good seems to be something final or perfect. Consequently if there be some one thing which alone is a final end, this thing—or if there be several final ends, the one among them which is the most final—will be the Good which we are seeking. In speaking of degrees of finality, we mean that a thing pursued as an end in itself is more final than one pursued as a means to something else, and that a thing never chosen as a means to anything else is more final than things chosen both as ends in themselves and as means to that thing; and accordingly a thing chosen always as an end and never as a means we call absolutely final. Now happiness above all else appears to be absolutely final in this sense, since we always choose it for its own sake and never as a means to something else; whereas honour, pleasure, intelligence, and excellence in its various forms, we choose indeed for their own sakes (since we should be glad to have each of them although no extraneous advantage resulted from it), but we also choose them for the sake of happiness, in the belief that they will be a means to our securing it. But no one chooses happiness for the sake of honour, pleasure, etc., nor as a means to anything whatever other than itself.

The same conclusion also appears to follow from a consideration of the self-sufficiency of happiness—for it is felt that the final good must be a thing sufficient in itself. The term self-sufficient, however, we employ with reference not to oneself alone, living a life of isolation, but also to one's parents and children and wife, and one's friends and fellow citizens in general, since man is by nature a social being. On the other hand a limit has to be assumed in these relationships; for if the list be extended to one's ancestors and descendants and to the friends of one's friends, it will go on *ad infinitum*. But this is a point that must be considered later on; we take a self-sufficient thing to mean a thing which merely standing by itself alone renders life desirable and lacking in nothing, and such a thing we deem happiness to be. Moreover, we think happiness the most desirable of all good things without being itself reckoned as one among the rest; for if it were so reckoned, it is clear that we should consider it more desirable when even the smallest of other good things were combined with it, since this addition would result in a larger total of good, and of two goods the greater is always the more desirable.

Happiness, therefore, being found to be something final and self-sufficient, is the End at which all actions aim.

To say however that the Supreme Good is happiness will probably appear a truism; we still require a more explicit account of what constitutes happiness. Perhaps then we may arrive at this by ascertaining what is man's function. For the goodness or efficiency of a flute-player or sculptor or craftsman of any sort, and in general of anybody who has some function or business to perform, is thought to reside in that function; and similarly it may be held that the good of man resides in the function of man, if he has a function.

Are we then to suppose that, while the carpenter and the shoemaker have definite functions or businesses belonging to them, man as such has none, and is not designed by nature to fulfil any function? Must we not rather assume that, just as the eye, the hand, the foot and each of the various members of the body manifestly has a certain function of its own, so a human being also has a certain function over and above all the functions of his particular members? What then precisely can this function be? The mere act of living appears to be shared even by plants, whereas we are looking for the function peculiar to man; we must therefore set aside the vital activity of nutrition and growth. Next in the scale will come some form of sentient life; but this too appears to be shared by horses, oxen, and animals generally. There remains therefore what may be called the practical life of the rational part of man. (This part has two divisions, one rational as obedient to principle, the other as possessing principle and exercising intelligence.) Rational life again has two meanings; let us assume that we are here concerned with the active exercise of the rational faculty, since this seems to be the more proper sense of the term. If then the function of man is the active exercise of the soul's faculties in conformity with rational principle, or at all events not in dissociation from rational principle, and if we acknowledge the function of an individual and of a good individual of the same class (for instance, a harper and a good harper, and so generally with all classes) to be generically the same, the qualification of the latter's superiority in excellence being added to the function in his case (I mean that if the function of a harper is to play the harp, that of a good harper is to play the harp well): if this is so, and if we declare that the function of man is a certain form of life, and define that form of life as the exercise of the soul's faculties and activities in association with rational principle, and say that the function of a good man is to perform these activities well and rightly, and if a function is well performed when it is performed in accordance with its own proper excellence—if then all this be so, the Good of man proves to be the active exercise of his soul's faculties in conformity with excellence or virtue, or if there be several human excellences or virtues, in conformity with the best and most perfect among them.

Moreover, to be happy takes a complete lifetime. For one swallow does not make summer, nor does one fine day; and similarly one day or a brief period of happiness does not make a man supremely blessed and happy.

Let this account then serve to describe the Good in outline —for no doubt the proper procedure is to begin by making a rough sketch, and to fill it in afterwards. If a work has been well laid down in outline, to carry it on and complete it in detail may be supposed to be within the capacity of anybody; and in this working out of details Time seems to be a good inventor or at all events coadjutor. This indeed is how advances in the arts have actually come about, since anyone can fill in the gaps. Also the warning given above must not be forgotten; we must not look for equal exactness in all departments of study, but only such as belongs to the subject matter of each, and in such a degree as is appropriate to the particular line of enquiry. A carpenter and a geometrician both try to find a right angle, but in different ways; the former is content with that approximation to it which satisfies the purpose of his work; the latter, being a student of truth, seeks to find its essence or essential attributes. We should therefore proceed in the same manner in other subjects also, and not allow side issues to outbalance the main task in hand.

Nor again must we in all matters alike demand an explanation of the reason why things are what they are; in some cases it is enough if the fact that they are so is satisfactorily established. This is the case with first principles; and the fact is the primary thing—it *is* a first principle. And different principles are learnt in different ways—some by induction, others by intuition, others again by some form of habituation; so we must endeavour to arrive at the principles of each kind in their natural manner, and must also be careful to define them correctly, since they are of great importance for the subsequent course of the enquiry. The beginning is admittedly more than half of the whole, and throws light at once on many of the questions under investigation.

VIII. Accordingly we must examine our first principle not only as a logical conclusion deduced from certain premises but also in the light of the current opinions on the subject. For if a proposition be true, all the facts harmonize with it, but if it is false, it is quickly seen to be discordant with them.

Now things good have been divided into three classes, external goods on the one hand, and goods of the soul and of the body on the other; and of these three kinds of goods, those of the soul are commonly said to be the highest, and good in the fullest degree. But our actions, that is, the soul's active exercise of its functions, must be placed in the class of things of the soul; hence so far as this opinion goes—and it is of long standing, and generally accepted by students of philosophy—it supports the correctness of our definition of Happiness.

It also shows it to be right in declaring the End to consist in certain actions or activities, for thus the End is included among goods of the soul, and not among external goods.

Again, our definition accords with the description of the happy man as one who "lives well" or "does well"; for it has virtually identified happiness with a form of good life or doing well.

And moreover all the various characteristics that are looked for in happiness are found to belong to the Good as we define it. Some people think happiness is goodness or virtue, others prudence, others a form of wisdom; others again say it is all of these things, or one of them, in combination with pleasure, or accompanied by pleasure as an indispensable adjunct; another school include external prosperity as a concomitant factor. Some of these views have been held by many people and from ancient times, others by a few distinguished men, and neither class is likely to be altogether mistaken; the probability is that their beliefs are at least partly, or indeed mainly, correct.

Now with those who pronounce happiness to be virtue, or some particular virtue, our definition is in agreement; for "activity in conformity with virtue" involves virtue. But no doubt it makes a great difference whether we conceive the Supreme Good to depend on possessing virtue or on displaying it—on disposition, or on the manifestation of a disposition in action. For a man may possess the disposition without its producing any good result, as for instance when he is asleep, or has ceased to function from some other cause; but virtue in active exercise cannot be inoperative—it will of necessity act, and act well. And just as at the Olympic games the wreaths of victory are not bestowed upon the handsomest and strongest persons present, but on men who enter for the competitions—since it is among these that the winners are found—so it is those who *act* rightly who carry off the prizes and good things of life.

And further, the life of active virtue is essentially pleasant.

For on the one hand, the feeling of pleasure is an experience of the soul. Also, when a man is described as "fond of" so-and-so, the thing in question gives him pleasure: for instance a horse gives pleasure to one fond of horses, a play to one fond of the theatre, and similarly just actions are pleasant to the lover of justice, and acts conforming with virtue generally to the lover of virtue. But whereas the mass of mankind take pleasure in things that conflict with one another, because they are not pleasant of their own nature, the lovers of what is noble take pleasure in things pleasant by nature. But lovers of the noble take pleasure in actions conforming with virtue. Therefore actions in conformity with virtue are pleasant essentially as well as pleasant to lovers of the right. Thus their life has no need of pleasure as a sort of additional appendage, but contains its pleasure in itself. For there is the further consideration that the man who does not enjoy doing noble actions is not a good man at all: no one would call a man just if he did not like acting justly, nor liberal if he did not like doing liberal things, and similarly with the other virtues. But if so, actions in conformity with virtue must be essentially pleasant.

But they are also of course both good and noble, and each in the highest degree, if the good man judges them rightly; and his judgement is as we have said. It follows therefore that happiness is at once the best, the noblest, and the pleasantest of things: these qualities are not separated as the inscription at Delos makes out—

> Justice is noblest, and health is best,
> But the heart's desire is the pleasantest—,

for the best activities possess them all; and it is the best activities, or one activity which is the best of all, in which according to our definition happiness consists.

Nevertheless it is manifest that happiness also requires external goods in addition, as we said; for it is impossible, or at least not easy, to play a noble part unless furnished with the necessary equipment. For many noble actions require instruments for their performance, in the shape of friends or wealth or political power; also there are certain external advantages, the lack of which sullies supreme felicity, such as good birth, satisfactory children, and personal beauty: a man of very ugly appearance or low birth, or childless and alone in the world, is not our idea of a happy man, and still less so perhaps is one who has children or friends that are worthless, or who has had good ones but lost them by death. As we said therefore, happiness does seem to require the addition of external prosperity, and this is why some people identify it with good fortune (though others identify it with virtue).

IX. It is this that gives rise to the question whether happiness is a thing that can be learnt, or acquired by training, or cultivated in some other manner, or whether it is bestowed by some divine dispensation or even by fortune. (1) Now if anything that men have is a gift of the gods, it is reasonable to suppose that happiness is divinely given—indeed of all man's possessions it is most likely to be so, inasmuch as it is the best of them all. This subject however may perhaps more properly belong to another branch of study. Still, even if happiness is not sent us from heaven, but is won by virtue and by some kind of study or practice, it seems to be one of the most divine things that exist. For the prize and end of virtue must clearly be supremely good—it must be something divine and blissful. (2) And also on our view it will admit of being widely diffused, since it can be attained through some process of study or effort by all persons whose capacity for virtue has not been stunted or maimed. (3) Again, if it is better to be happy as a result of one's own exertions than by the gift of fortune, it is reasonable to suppose that this is how happiness is won; inasmuch as in the world of nature things have a natural tendency to be ordered in the best possible way, and the same is true of the products of art, and of causation of any kind, and especially the highest. Whereas that the greatest and noblest of all things should be left to fortune would be too contrary to the fitness of things.

Light is also thrown on the question by our definition of happiness, which said that it is a certain kind of activity of the soul; whereas the remaining good things are either merely indispensable conditions of happiness, or are of the nature of auxiliary means, and useful instrumentally. This conclusion moreover agrees with what we laid down at the outset; for we stated that the Supreme Good was the end of the political science, but the principal care of this science is to produce a certain character in the citizens, namely to make them virtuous, and capable of performing noble actions.

We have good reasons therefore for not speaking of an ox or horse or any other animal as being happy, because none of these is able to participate in noble activities. For this cause also children cannot be happy, for they are not old enough to be capable of noble acts; when children are spoken of as happy, it is in compliment to their promise for the future. Happiness, as we said, requires both complete goodness and a complete lifetime. For many reverses and vicissitudes of all sorts occur in the course of life, and it is possible that the most prosperous man may encounter great disasters in his declining years, as the story is told of Priam in the epics; but no one calls a man happy who meets with misfortunes like Priam's, and comes to a miserable end.

X. Are we then to count no other human being happy either, as long as he is alive? Must we obey Solon's warning,* and "look to the end"? And if we are indeed to lay down this rule, can a man really be happy even after he is dead? Surely that is an extremely strange notion, especially for us who define happiness as a form of activity! While if on the other hand we refuse to speak of a dead man as happy, and Solon's words do not mean this, but that only when a man is dead can one safely call him blessed as being now beyond the reach of evil and misfortune, this also admits of some dispute; for it is believed that some evil and also some good can befall the dead, just as much as they can happen to the living without their being aware of it—for instance honours, and disgraces, and the prosperity and misfortunes of their children and their descendants in general. But here too there is a difficulty. For suppose a man to have lived in perfect happiness until old age, and to have come to a correspondingly happy end: he may still have many vicissitudes befall his descendants, some of whom may be good and meet with the fortune they deserve, and others the opposite; and moreover these descendants may clearly stand in every possible degree of remoteness from the ancestors in question. Now it would be a strange thing if the dead man also were to change with the fortunes of his family, and were to become a happy man at one time and then miserable at another; yet on the other hand it would also be strange if ancestors were not affected at all, even over a limited period, by the fortunes of their descendants.

But let us go back to our former difficulty, for perhaps it will throw light on the question we are now examining. If we are to look to the end, and congratulate a man when dead not as actually being blessed, but because he has been blessed

* To Croesus, the proverbially rich King of Lydia.

in the past, surely it is strange if at the actual time when a man is happy that fact cannot be truly predicated of him, because we are unwilling to call the living happy owing to the vicissitudes of fortune, and owing to our conception of happiness as something permanent and not readily subject to change, whereas the wheel of fortune often turns full circle in the same person's experience. For it is clear that if we are to be guided by fortune, we shall often have to call the same man first happy and then miserable; we shall make out the happy man to be a sort of "chameleon, or a house built on the sand."

But perhaps it is quite wrong to be guided in our judgement by the changes of fortune, since true prosperity and adversity do not depend on fortune's favours, although, as we said, our life does require these in addition; but it is the active exercise of our faculties in conformity with virtue that causes happiness, and the opposite activities its opposite.

And the difficulty just discussed is a further confirmation of our definition; since none of man's functions possess the quality of permanence so fully as the activities in conformity with virtue: they appear to be more lasting even than our knowledge of particular sciences. And among these activities themselves those which are highest in the scale of values are the more lasting, because they most fully and continuously occupy the lives of the supremely happy: for this appears to be the reason why they are not easily forgotten.

The happy man therefore will possess that element of stability which we demand, and will remain happy all his life; since he will be always or at least most often employed in doing and contemplating the things that are in conformity with virtue. And he will bear changes of fortune most nobly, and with perfect propriety in every way, being as he is "good in very truth" and "four-square without reproach."

But the accidents of fortune are many and vary in degree of magnitude; and although small pieces of good luck, as also of misfortune, clearly do not change the whole course of life, yet great and repeated successes will render life more blissful, since both of their own nature they help to embellish happiness, and also they can be nobly and virtuously utilized; while great and frequent reverses can crush and mar our bliss both by the pain they cause and by the hindrance they offer to many activities. Yet nevertheless even in adversity nobility shines through, when a man endures repeated and severe misfortune with patience, not owing to insensibility but from generosity and greatness of soul. And if, as we said, a man's life is determined by his activities, no supremely happy man can ever become miserable. For he will never do hateful or base actions, since we hold that the truly good and wise man will bear all kinds of fortune in a seemly way, and will always act in the noblest manner that the circumstances allow; even as a good general makes the most effective use of the forces at his disposal, and a good shoemaker makes the finest shoe possible out of the leather supplied him, and so on with all the other crafts and professions. And this being so, the happy man can never become miserable; though it is true he will not be supremely blessed if he encounters the misfortunes of a Priam. Nor yet assuredly will he be variable and liable to change; for he will not be dislodged from his happiness easily, nor by ordinary misfortunes, but only by severe and frequent disasters, nor will he recover from such disasters and become happy again quickly, but only, if at all, after a long term of years, in which he has had time to compass high distinctions and achievements.

May not we then confidently pronounce that man happy who realizes complete virtue in action, and is adequately furnished with external goods, not for any casual period but throughout a complete lifetime? Or should we add, that he must also be destined to go on living in the same manner, and to die accordingly, because the future is hidden from us, and we conceive happiness as an end, something utterly and absolutely final and complete? If this is so, we shall pronounce those of the living who possess and are destined to go on possessing the good things we have specified to be supremely blessed, though on the human scale of bliss.

So much for a discussion of this question.

XI. That the happiness of the dead is not influenced at all by the fortunes of their descendants and their friends in general seems too heartless a doctrine, and contrary to accepted beliefs. But the accidents of life are many and diverse, and vary in the degree in which they affect us. To distinguish between them in detail would clearly be a long and indeed endless undertaking, and a general treatment in outline may perhaps be enough. Even our own misfortunes, then, though in some cases they exercise considerable weight and influence upon the course of our lives, in other cases seem comparatively unimportant; and the same is true of the misfortune of our friends of all degrees. Also it makes a great difference whether any calamity happens during one's lifetime or when one is dead, much more so than it does in a tragedy whether the crimes and horrors are assumed to have taken place beforehand or are enacted on the stage. We ought therefore to take this difference also into account, and still more perhaps the doubt that exists whether the dead really participate in good or evil at all. For the above considerations seem to show that even if any good or evil does penetrate to them, the effect is only small and trifling, either intrinsically or in relation to them, or if not trifling, at all events not of such magnitude and kind as to make the unhappy happy or to rob the happy of their blessedness.

It does then appear that the dead are influenced in some measure by the good fortune of their friends, and likewise by their misfortunes, but that the effect is not of such a kind or degree as to render the happy unhappy or *vice versa*.

XII. These questions being settled, let us consider whether happiness is one of the things we praise or rather one of those that we honour; for it is at all events clear that it is not a mere potentiality.

Now it appears that a thing which we praise is always praised because it has a certain quality and stands in a certain relation to something. For we praise just men and brave men, in fact good men and virtue generally, because of their actions and the results they produce; and also we praise those who are strong of body, swift of foot and the like on account of their possessing certain natural qualities, and standing in a certain relation to something good and excellent. The point is also illustrated by our feeling about praises addressed to the gods: it strikes us as absurd that the gods should be referred to our standards, and this is what praising them amounts to, since praise, as we said, involves a reference of its object to something else. But if praise belongs to what is relative, it is clear that the best things do not merit praise, but something greater and better: as indeed is generally recognized, since we speak of the gods as blessed and happy, and also "blessed" is the term that we apply to the most godlike men; and similarly with good things—no one praises happiness as one praises justice, but we call it "a blessing," deeming it something higher and more divine than things we praise.

Indeed it seems that Eudoxus took a good line in advocating the claims of pleasure to the prize of highest excellence, when he held that the fact that pleasure, though a good, is not praised, is an indication that it is superior to the things we praise, as God and the Good are, because they are the standards to which everything else is referred.

For praise belongs to virtue, since it is this that makes men capable of accomplishing noble deeds, while encomia* are for deeds accomplished, whether bodily feats or achievements of the mind. However, to develop this subject is perhaps rather the business of those who have made a study of encomia. For our purpose we may draw the conclusion from the foregoing remarks, that happiness is a thing honoured and perfect. This seems to be borne out by the fact that it is a first principle or starting-point, since all other things that all men do are done for its sake; and that which is the first principle and cause of things good we agree to be something honourable and divine.

XIII. But inasmuch as happiness is a certain activity of soul in conformity with perfect virtue, it is necessary to examine the nature of virtue. For this will probably assist us in our investigation of the nature of happiness. Also, the true statesman seems to be one who has made a special study of virtue, since his aim is to make the citizens good and law-abiding men—witness the lawgivers of Crete and Sparta, and the other great legislators of history; but if the study of virtue falls within the province of Political Science, it is clear that in investigating virtue we shall be keeping to the plan which we laid down at the outset.

Now the virtue that we have to consider is clearly human virtue, since the good or happiness which we set out to seek is human good and human happiness. But human virtue means in our view excellence of soul, not excellence of body; indeed our definition of happiness is an activity of the soul. Now if this is so, clearly it behooves the statesman to have some acquaintance with psychology, just as the physician who is to heal the eye or the other parts of the body must know their anatomy. Indeed a foundation of science is even more requisite for the statesman, inasmuch as politics is a higher and more honourable art than medicine; but physicians of the better class devote much attention to the study of the human body. The student of politics therefore as well as the psychologist must study the nature of the soul, though he will do so as an

* Laudatory orations, distinguished by Aristotle in his *Rhetoric* as one of the three branches of oratory.

aid to politics, and only so far as is requisite for the objects of enquiry that he has in view: to pursue the subject in further detail would doubtless be more laborious than is necessary for his purpose.

Now on the subject of psychology some of the teaching current in extraneous discourses is satisfactory, and may be adopted here: namely that the soul consists of two parts, one irrational and the other capable of reason. (Whether these two parts are really distinct in the sense that the parts of the body or of any other divisible whole are distinct, or whether though distinguishable in thought as two they are inseparable in reality, like the convex and concave sides of a curve, is a question of no importance for the matter in hand.) Of the irrational part of the soul again one division appears to be common to all living things, and of a vegetative nature: I refer to the part that causes nutrition and growth; for we must assume that a vital faculty of this nature exists in all things that assimilate nourishment, including embryos—the same faculty being present also in the fully-developed organism (this is more reasonable than to assume a different nutritive faculty in the latter). The excellence of this faculty therefore appears to be common to all animate things and not peculiar to man; for it is believed that this faculty or part of the soul is most active during sleep, but when they are asleep you cannot tell a good man from a bad one (whence the saying that for half their lives there is no difference between the happy and the miserable). This is a natural result of the fact that sleep is a cessation of the soul from the functions on which its goodness or badness depend—except that in some small degree certain of the bodily processes may emerge into consciousness during sleep, and consequently the dreams of the good are better than those of ordinary men. We need not however pursue this subject further, but may omit from consideration the nutritive part of the soul, since it exhibits no specifically human excellence.

But there also appears to be another element in the soul, which, though irrational, yet in a manner participates in rational principle. In self-restrained and unrestrained people we approve their principle, or the rational part of their souls, because it urges them in the right way and exhorts them for their good; but their nature seems also to contain another element beside that of rational principle, which combats and resists that principle. Exactly the same thing may take place in the soul as occurs with the body in a case of paralysis: when the patient wills to move his limbs to the right they swerve to the left; and similarly in unrestrained persons their impulses run counter to their principle. But whereas in the body we see the erratic member, in the case of the soul we do not see it; nevertheless it cannot be doubted that in the soul also there is an element beside that of principle, which opposes and runs counter to principle (though in what sense the two are distinct does not concern us here). But this second element also seems, as we said, to participate in rational principle; at least in the self-restrained man it obeys the behest of principle—and no doubt in the temperate and brave man it is still more amenable, for all parts of his nature are in harmony with principle.

Thus we see that the irrational part, as well as the soul as a whole, is double. One division of it, the vegetative, does not share in rational principle at all; the other, the seat of the appetites and of desire in general, does in a sense participate in principle, as being amenable and obedient to it (in the sense in fact in which we speak of "paying heed" to one's father and friends, not in the sense of the term "rational" in mathematics). And that principle can in a manner appeal to the irrational part, is indicated by our practice of admonishing delinquents, and by our employment of rebuke and exhortation generally.

If on the other hand it be more correct to speak of the appetitive part of the soul also as rational, in that case it is the rational part which, as well as the whole soul, is divided into two, the one division having rational principle in the proper sense and in itself, the other in the sense in which a child listens to its father.

Now virtue also is differentiated in correspondence with this division of the soul. Some forms of virtue are called intellectual virtues, others moral virtues: Wisdom, Understanding, and Prudence are intellectual, Liberality and Temperance are moral virtues. When describing a man's moral character we do not say that he is wise or intelligent, but gentle or temperate; but a wise man also is praised for his disposition, and praiseworthy dispositions we term virtues.

I have added below a short chapter from Aristotle's *Physics,** which deals with the already mentioned issue of

* Translated by P. H. Wicksteed and F. M. Cornford. London: William Heinemann Ltd., 1930; Cambridge, Mass.: Harvard University Press, Book II, Chap. VII. (The Loeb Classical Library.)

teleology. Damagingly misguided though the argument may be, its orderly and dispassionate exposition provides a good example of Aristotle's style.

*   *   *   *   *

We must now consider why Nature is to be ranked among causes that are final, that is to say purposeful; and further we must consider what is meant by "necessity" when we are speaking of Nature. For thinkers are for ever referring things to necessity as a cause, and explaining that, since hot and cold and so forth are what they are, this or that exists or comes into being "of necessity"; for even if one or another of them alleges some other cause, such as "Sympathy and Antipathy" or "Mind," he straight away drops it again, after a mere acknowledgement.

So here the question arises whether we have any reason to regard Nature as making for any goal at all, or as seeking any one thing as preferable to any other. Why not say, it is asked, that Nature acts as Zeus drops the rain, not to make the corn grow, but of necessity (for the rising vapour must needs be condensed into water by the cold, and must then descend, and incidentally, when this happens, the corn grows), just as, when a man loses his corn on the threshing-floor, it did not rain on purpose to destroy the crop, but the result was merely incidental to the raining? So why should it not be the same with natural organs like the teeth? Why should it not be a coincidence that the front teeth come up with an edge, suited to dividing the food, and the back ones flat and good for grinding it, without there being any design in the matter? And so with all other organs that seem to embody a purpose. In cases where a coincidence brought about such a combination as might have been arranged on purpose, the creatures, it is urged, having been suitably formed by the operation of chance, survived; otherwise they perished, and still perish, as Empedocles says of his "man-faced oxen."

Such and suchlike are the arguments which may be urged in raising this problem; but it is impossible that this should really be the way of it. For all these phenomena and all natural things are either constant or normal, and this is contrary to the very meaning of luck or chance. No one assigns it to chance or to a remarkable coincidence if there is abundant rain in the winter, though he would if there were in the dog-days; and the other way about, if there were parching heat. Accordingly, if the only choice is to assign these occurrences either to coincidence or to purpose, and if in these cases chance coincidence is out of the question, then it must be purpose. But, as our opponents themselves would admit, these occurrences are all natural. There is purpose, then, in what is, and in what happens, in Nature.

Further, in any operation of human art, where there is an end to be achieved, the earlier and successive stages of the operation are performed for the purpose of realizing that end. Now, when a thing is produced by Nature, the earlier stages in every case lead up to the final development in the same way as in the operation of art, and *vice versa,* provided that no impediment balks the process. The operation is directed by a purpose; we may, therefore, infer that the natural process was guided by a purpose to the end that is realized. Thus, if a house were a natural product, the process would pass through the same stages that it in fact passes through when it is pro-duced by art; and if natural products could also be produced by art, they would move along the same line that the natural process actually takes. We may therefore say that the earlier stages are for the purpose of leading to the later. Indeed, as a general proposition, the arts either, on the basis of Nature, carry things further than Nature can, or they imitate Nature. If, then, artificial processes are purposeful, so are natural processes too; for the relation of antecedent to consequent is identical in art and in Nature.

This principle comes out most clearly when we consider the other animals. For their doings are not the outcome of art (design) or of previous research or deliberation; so that some raise the question whether the works of spiders and ants and so on should be attributed to intelligence or to some similar faculty. And then, descending step by step, we find that plants too produce organs subservient to their perfect development—leaves, for instance, to shelter the fruit. Hence, if it is by nature and also for a purpose that the swallow makes her and the spider his web, and that plants make leaves for t sake of the fruit and strike down (and not up) with their ro in order to get their nourishment, it is clear that causalit the kind we have described is at work in things that come or exist in the course of Nature.

Also, since the term "nature" is applied both to mater

to form, and since it is the latter that constitutes the goal, and all else is for the sake of that goal, it follows that the form is the final cause.

Now there are failures even in the arts (for writers make mistakes in writing and physicians administer the wrong dose); so that analogous failures in Nature may evidently be anticipated as possible. Thus, if in art there are cases in which the correct procedure serves a purpose, and attempts that fail are aimed at a purpose but miss it, we may take it to be the same in Nature, and monstrosities will be like failures of purpose in Nature. So if, in the primal combinations, such "ox-creatures" as could not reach an equilibrium and goal, should appear, it would be by the miscarriage of some principle, as monstrous births are actually produced now by abortive developments of sperm. Besides, the sperm must precede the formation of the animal, and Empedocles' "primal all-generative" is no other than such sperm.

In plants, too, though they are less elaborately articulated, there are manifest indications of purpose. Are we to suppose, then, that as there were "ox-creatures man-faced" so also there were "vine-growths olive-bearing"? Incongruous as such a thing seems, it ought to follow if we accept the principle in the case of animals. Moreover, it ought still to be a matter of chance what comes up when you sow this seed or that.

In general, the theory does away with the whole order of Nature, and indeed with Nature's self. For natural things are exactly those which do move continuously, in virtue of a principle inherent in themselves, towards a determined goal; and the final development which results from any one such principle is not identical for any two species, nor yet is it any random result; but in each there is always a tendency towards an identical result, if nothing interferes with the process. A desirable result and the means to it may also be produced by chance, as for instance we say it was "by luck" that the stranger came and ransomed the prisoner before he left, where he ransoming is done as if the man had come for that purpose, though in fact he did not. In this case the desirable result is incidental; for, as we have explained, chance is an incidental cause. But when the desirable result is effected invariably or normally, it is not an incidental or chance occurrence; and in the course of Nature the result always occurred either invariably or normally, if nothing hinders. It is absurd to suppose that there is no purpose because in

Nature we can never detect the moving power in the act of deliberation. Art, in fact, does not deliberate either, and if the shipbuilding art were incorporate in the timber, it would proceed by nature in the same way in which it now proceeds by art. If purpose, then, is inherent in art, so is it in Nature also. The best illustration is the case of a man being his own physician, for Nature is like that—agent and patient at once.

That Nature is a cause, then, and a goal-directed cause, is above dispute.

CHAPTER VI

Greece after Aristotle:
A Changing Spirit

At the death of Alexander the Great in 323 B.C. his
empire, acquired by conquests of astonishing rapidity, included his own kingdom of Macedonia, Egypt, and an enormous tract of Asiatic territory from the Mediterranean to
northern India. He left no heir, and had made no plans for
the succession, so that his death was followed almost inevitably by many years of confused struggle over what
were, in the end, the remnants of his domain. Aristotle
himself died in 322, so that his death may be taken to
mark the beginning of a period of extreme social and
political disturbance, the character of which he seems
quite to have failed to foresee, and which radically affected the course of philosophical thought.

From this time onwards the political importance of the
Greek city-states rapidly declined. The great issues were
now fought out on so large a scale that they counted for
little. Alexander himself had always regarded the Greek
cities as, theoretically at least, independent allies, and
some of his successors were willing to continue this policy
so long at least as it suited their interests to do so. But
at other times the cities passed, more or less helplessly,
through a bewildering variety of political conditions and
degrees of subjection, never losing, however, their fatal
propensity to warfare among themselves. By the end of the
century it had finally become clear that Alexander's empire could not survive as a unity, and by 275 it was in the
hands of three dynasties descended from three of his gen-

erals—the Antigonids in Macedonia, the Ptolemies in Egypt, the Seleucids in the East. These dynasties, frequently at war among themselves, remained as the chief counters on the political board until, towards the end of the third century B.C., the power of Rome intervened and gradually became predominant. After the peace of Apamea, made in 188 between Rome and the Seleucid Antiochus, no Greek state could pretend any longer to independence. In 148 B.C. Macedonia itself became a Roman province, and Greece a protectorate under close supervision.

But Greece in this period was subject, not only to political decline and the confusion of the wars of others, but also to very serious social stress. The unification, however brief, of most of the known world under Alexander led to a far freer mingling of races and nationalites, greater freedom of thought, and a general spirit of racial and religious toleration; trade rapidly expanded, and commerce and finance grew to a scale unimagined a very few years before. But although some classes, and many enterprising or fortunate individuals, certainly enjoyed great prosperity, it seems no less certain that the condition of the majority grew steadily worse. Rents for houses and land rose sharply, as did the price of food; but wages for labor rose less if they rose at all, and in some places seem even to have fallen. Thus the general prosperity of the period was, and was felt to be, highly precarious. In all parts of Greece, and in the Aegean islands, many people were living at the very edge of a subsistence level, and there was constant danger that political issues might turn into direct and violent conflicts of interest between the rich and the poor. Sparta in particular, in the second half of the third century B.C., underwent three successive violent social revolutions. The impression of personal insecurity was very general, and not without reason.

In this shifting, expanding, dangerous gambler's world, there seems to have grown up a widespread sense of a vacuum that philosophy could and should fill. Custom, the unreflecting acceptance of tradition, was now out of the question, for old customs had died, or grown hollow, and tradition was broken. Many were doubtless content to take their chance, to live as Fortune or the interests of the moment might decide; but many felt the need to preserve, or need to discover, some firm foundation amid so much uncertainty and confusion. At that time no religion had power or prestige enough to satisfy such a demand, and the result was an enormous popular interest in philosophy. It seems indeed that the popular image of a philosopher is still that which was formed in this Hellenistic period—the image of a bearded figure of eccentric manners and appearance, unworldly, moralistic, probably poor, perhaps even a vagrant, with a store of maxims on how to endure unmoved the tribulations of life. Philosophers—though some of course continued to preside over established schools—were the wandering friars of this turbulent period.

It was inevitable that, in these conditions, there should have occurred an almost immediate movement away from the recent tradition of Plato and Aristotle. Those philosophers were certainly too difficult, and in a sense too conventional, to satisfy the new popular demands. Their work was too full of intricate logical argument, it demanded too high a devotion to abstract thought, to provide a possible basis for any popular creed. And Aristotle in particular, in his writing on ethics and politics, had tended to take for granted as the background of his argument just those political conditions and conventions of conduct which, so soon after his death, had ceased to exist. He addressed himself to the ordinary well-educated citizen of the (now) old-fashioned Greek city-state; he had not, and probably would not have wished to claim that he had, any moral message for mankind in general in a period of chaos. He and Plato were philosophers for intellectuals; and for this reason, though their prestige and their fame remained unassailable, the philosophy of the new period was provided by others, and was quite different from theirs.

Perhaps the clearest indication of the changed atmosphere of philosophy can be found in the changing conception of "happiness," the goal of life, and consequently of the means proposed for achieving it. For one thing, this question came to be the dominant concern of philosophy, at the expense of those epistemological and metaphysical inquiries which, for Plato and Aristotle at least, had been no less important and absorbing. But also the topic itself was very differently treated. Aristotle, in his *Nicomachean Ethics,* had taken the conventional—one would almost like to say, the *sensible*—view that the well-being of the individual was determined in large part by the circumstances in which he lived, by the activities in which he engaged, by the achievements which could be counted to his credit. He would certainly have recommended an active, indeed a masterful, part in the public affairs of one's community. But it is clear that, if so, the well-being of the individual is dependent in part upon external affairs; and in the precarious post-Aristotelian world, it seems to have been felt that individual happiness, thus conceived, was itself intolerably precarious. Accordingly almost every later school agreed in the attempt to maintain that happiness, rightly conceived, must lie in the sole power of the individual himself. The attempt to maintain this, however understandable, led at times to an extremity of paradox. Even so, it seems to have been tacitly agreed that some conception of happiness *must* be worked out which would ensure that, at least in theory, it could be attained quite independently of shifting, perilous and uncontrollable circumstances. The resulting tendency was, strongly and persistently, towards some sort of philosophy of "non-attachment"—towards a kind of strategic withdrawal, as it were, from a world which no one now could believe, as Aristotle did, to be manageable by careful and enlightened individual effort.

The three chapters that follow will be concerned with the four main Hellenistic—that is, post-Aristotelian—schools or types of philosophy. Of these Stoicism and Epicureanism, often in markedly unfriendly rivalry with each other, were by far the most important and influential. The Cynics and Sceptics were seldom in the same way taken altogether seriously, though their individual spokesmen were sometimes impressive and appealed very strongly to certain temperaments. Epicureanism, Stoicism, and above all Cynicism were—the conditions in which they grew up demanded that they should be—primarily moral doctrines, philosophies of life, far more earnestly occupied with the actual predicament of man than with any merely theoretical questions; and they were concerned in particular to teach, in a world that was too often dangerous and deceptive, the secret of individual well-being. And even the Sceptics were apt to recommend their scepticism as offering a relief from anxiety—as a kind of restful acquiescence in the single conviction that no exclusive faith or doctrine whatever would ever be proved, so that all intellectual struggles must be ultimately vain. The pursuit of knowledge passed from Aristotle to the distinguished scientists of the Hellenistic age. The philosophers took up instead the pursuit of virtue, of happiness, or—in this at least they were all agreed—of security.

It will be as well to end this present chapter with a note on chronology. The theoretical basis for the practical doctrines of Epicureanism was not the original invention of Epicurus. It was a development of the Atomism of the pre-Socratic Leucippus, transmitted most powerfully through the writings of Democritus. This Democritus, with whom our study of Epicureanism begins, was Socrates' contemporary; his philosophy, however, is connected more intimately with that of his successors than of his contemporaries, and I have presented him here as essentially the forerunner of Epicurus. Epicurus himself flourished soon after the death of Aristotle, but by far the most extensive account of his philosophy in ancient literature was given, more than a century later again, by the poet Lucretius. Quotations from his work also will be found in the following chapter.

In chapters VIII and IX it will also be observed that Stoicism and Scepticism are represented by writings that date from a late stage of their history. Like Epicureanism, both schools flourished in Athens in the immediate post-Aristotelian days, Scepticism having its home in fact in what had been Plato's Academy. But both schools lived on for many years, till far into the age of the Roman Empire, and inevitably the most copious and consecutive written accounts survive from their later days. The original founders were teachers much more than they were writers, and for us their teachings must be discerned in the writings of others.

CHAPTER VII

Later Development of Atomism: Democritus and Epicurus

Because of his close connection with Leucippus, Democritus is sometimes classed among the pre-Socratics, and in fact it is probable that he began "philosophizing" before Socrates did. Nevertheless he belongs to the age of Socrates and the sophists rather than to the age of pure "inquiry." He was a fellow-citizen of the great sophist Protagoras, and, like Socrates, he was interested not only in nature but in man. Born about 460 B.C., he lived to the age of ninety. According to tradition he traveled widely, but spent most of his life in his native city of Abdera in Thrace, where he had a "school" of philosophy. His great learning earned him the nickname of "Wisdom," and in later times, presumably because of his ethical theory of "cheerfulness," he was known as "the laughing philosopher." His writings, only fragments of which survive, seem to have covered every branch of learning, including the "modern" subjects of ethics, psychology and logic. He was indeed the Aristotle of his age, and Aristotle himself often alludes to his views. Curiously enough, Plato never mentions him—an unfortunate oversight, since Democritus may be regarded as the founder of materialism.

Democritus took over from Leucippus the basic theory of atomism and elaborated it so as to form a system designed to answer not only the original question of Thales but many others as well—in particular, perhaps, the question "How do we know anything?". The ultimate realities are, of course, atoms and the void. The atoms are all of the same substance, indivisible, infinite in number and infinitely various in shape. Presumably in order to make an infinite variety of shape possible, Democritus adds that they are indefinite in size. Some atoms, he says, can be "very large." The Nothing, which, though unreal, exists, is also infinite and the objects of sense are formed by the constant movement, and "vibration" of atoms in the void. Democritus seems to assume that motion is an eternal characteristic of the atoms, something which depends on "Necessity." By "Necessity" he means nothing more or less than "the nature of things" or "natural law." It seems therefore somewhat unfair of Aristotle to blame the atomists for not producing a cause for this motion. To them the motion is the cause of everything.

Atoms, differing from each other only in shape and size, can be arranged or placed in an infinite variety of ways. Their motions too in the void can be infinitely various, as they collide, bounce off each other, or become entangled in more or less temporary complexes. Nothing else exists. Yet out of these colorless, insensitive, indivisible, unintelligent and (except possibly in the case of the "very large" atoms) imperceptible objects has been evolved the whole world of our thought, sense and experience. The differences which we observe—e.g., differences between the animate and the inanimate, between the colored and the colorless, soft and hard, hot and cold—proceed solely from the various shapes and arrangements of the atoms and the density or lack of density of their conglomerations. They can indeed proceed from nothing else. It is, it seems, for this reason that Democritus (or Leucippus or both) states that our only "legitimate" knowledge is of the atoms and the void. Other knowledge—the knowledge which comes to us through the senses—is "bastard." Not, by any means, that the evidence of the senses is to be rejected. It is expressly stated that "the phenomenon is true." But the truth behind phenomena—namely, the atoms and the void—is not accessible to the senses. They are a "legitimate" inference from the evidence of the senses and are quite certainly true, whereas in the

realm of phenomena opinions may be misplaced or mis-
directed, even though the particular phenomenon itself is
always true. This is an attitude that is far removed from
scepticism. We have certainly such fragments as "We know
nothing truly; for truth is in the depths," and "sweet is
by convention, hot by convention, cold by convention,
color by convention; in truth are atoms and the void." But
these sayings do not necessarily imply that sensation is
unreliable. The "conventions" are, after all, all that we
have to go by and it would seem that Democritus is em-
phasizing this fact rather than making a confession of
scepticism when he imagines the senses as addressing the
mind as follows: "Wretched mind, it was from us that you
received your beliefs and do you now attempt to overthrow
us? Your victory would mean your own downfall."

As for the mind itself, or soul (Democritus makes no
distinction between the two), it also is, of course, material.
It is assumed to be made of particularly round "fiery"
atoms which are distributed over the body. It is through
these atoms that we receive the impressions or "idols" of
exterior things. Everything is constantly throwing off
"idols" (a development of Empedocles' "effluences") and
these "idols" make contact with the soul atoms whether
through touch on the surface of the body or through eye,
ear, nose or tongue. So much for ordinary sensation. But
there is a particular kind of sensation which we call
thought. This sensation may be referred to the mind; for,
though the mind and the soul are "the same" in the sense
that they are composed of the same round atoms, there is a
particularly dense concentration of these atoms in the
breast. "Idols" cannot pass through this dense concentration without moving the soul- or mind-atoms. Hence
thought.

The theory is a complicated one. In a short summary it
is impossible to do justice to it. A full and excellent account
is to be found in Cyril Bailey's authoritative work, *The
Greek Atomists and Epicurus*.* Here, too, there is no space

* Oxford: The Clarendon Press; New York: Oxford University Press,
1928.

to attempt to describe Democritus' cosmogony, his theory of the coming into being of innumerable worlds by means of the action of a "whirl." It is clear however that the creation and dissolution of worlds as of everything else is the work of "Necessity." Where Democritus speaks of "chance" he merely means a mechanical cause which to us is unknown. Everything has a mechanical cause in the movements of the atoms in the void.

To us such a view of the universe seems to imply atheism in religion and determinism in morals; but, as we shall see most clearly in the case of Epicurus, these were not the conclusions reached by the Greek atomists. As for Democritus we lack the evidence to say precisely what were his views of the gods. He seems to have believed that certain "idols" of very great size (his obsession with the very large is remarkable) did appear to men. These were "difficult to be destroyed, but not indestructible." They were certainly mere products of the atoms and the void—parts of nature, rather than controllers or inspirers of it.

With regard to Democritus' ethical theory what surprises us most is that in spite of his mechanistic theory of reality he seems not to have been concerned at all with the problem of free will and determinism. He assumes free will to exist and proceeds to elaborate a doctrine of "cheerfulness" as being the aim of a good life. By "cheerfulness" he seems to mean the contented, balanced and undismayed attitude of a sensible and prudent Greek of his age. His "cheerfulness" is not the same as the "pleasure" of Epicurus; he accepts the ordinary conventions, such as the importance of the political life. Some of his precepts remind one of the system of Epicurus, but it is quite impossible to say of him, as one must say of Epicurus, that his ethical theory is logically connected with his general system of materialism.

Epicurus, writing more than a hundred years after Democritus (his dates are 342/1–271/70 B.C.) was nothing if not a systematizer. He is sometimes represented as a moralist who, needing a philosophical background to his ethical theories, took over the atomic theory of Democritus and Leucippus and simply tacked it on to his own program of the good life. Cyril Bailey in his study of Epicurus has convincingly shown that this view of the matter is thoroughly mistaken. Epicurus is one of the most consistent thinkers who has ever lived and, far from taking over uncritically the doctrine of Democritus, he made considerable alterations in it—usually, it is true, in order to bring it into a line with his own ethical theory. Thus he founded one of the two philosophical systems which, from the end of the fourth century B.C. almost until the triumph of Christianity, continued to dominate the minds of the educated. Both Stoicism and Epicureanism can be called "creeds" as well as "philosophies." They were designed not only to explain nature, as thinkers from Thales to Democritus had attempted to do, but to satisfy a modern kind of scepticism which had arisen, at least in part, as the result of historical events. Chief of these events, as was suggested above, was the decline and fall of the authority of Athens and the other Greek city-states. In the world of the successors of Alexander it was no longer possible to think like Socrates or even like Plato, for now there was a sense in which politics did not matter. "The city," both as a practical reality and as an ideal, had ceased to exist. The individual, freed from his dependence on the city, had in a way, perhaps, gained wider horizons; in another way he had become disoriented and was in danger of being lost in a world too big for him either to control or to understand. What he needed was assurance in the ordinary operations of life and it was this assurance which Epicurus attempted to give him. Epicurus has been described by Cyril Bailey as "the apostle of common sense." He commends the quiet life. Yet it would be wrong to suppose that his creed is lacking in intellectual acuteness or that it is a mere expression of quietism. Neither Julius Caesar nor his assassin, Cassius, was a quietist.

Epicurus himself protested rather too much about his originality. He speaks slightingly of Democritus and calls the Democritean philosopher Nausiphanes, under whom he studied in his youth, "the mollusc." In spite of his own enormous philosophical output (he is said to have been the author of three hundred rolls) he was contemptuous of the productions of others and of all education other than that which he himself could afford. His advice to his pupil Pythocles is "Blest youth, set sail in your bark and flee from every form of culture." Yet for thirty-six years he taught in the famous "Garden" in Athens and enjoyed the devoted affection of his pupils, both male and female (he was the first to allow women to become members of a school of philosophy). Most of his works have been lost, but we have a full and undoubtedly accurate account of his doctrine in the poem *On Nature* by the Roman poet Lucretius, a contemporary of Julius Caesar.

To Lucretius, Epicurus is the greatest benefactor that mankind has ever known. This is because he has freed man from fear—from fear of the gods and from fear of what may happen to one after death. He has done this noble work quite simply, by explaining everything. There is no longer any room for doubt or perplexity. The nature of things is known and can be explained to anyone who is intelligent enough to listen to the argument.

In fact the argument is often extremely complicated, but it is extraordinarily consistent. It is based on a thoroughgoing belief in sensation as the only basis of knowledge. There is no question of a distinction between appearance and reality. Appearance is reality. Nor is there any basic distinction such as we have noticed in Democritus between thought and sensation. Epicurus does not accept Democritus' view that "legitimate" knowledge is confined to atoms and the void and that our knowledge of the "secondary qualities" is "by convention." To him the only "legitimate" knowledge is sensation, thought itself being a kind of sensation. True that both the mind and the senses can be, as it were, directed. The senses can be concentrated in attention; the mind can form an opinion. But both processes are purely material. If we can find sensations which will corroborate an opinion, or at least will not witness against it, then the opinion is true; otherwise it is false. This certainly may be described as the logic of common sense and Epicurus, using great ingenuity in attempting to solve obvious difficulties, never departs from it. He will soon insist that the sun and moon are "about the same size" as they appear to us to be.

For the basis of his all-embracing system he adopted the theories of Leucippus and Democritus, but he made, in the interests of his common-sense, sensational view of things, important alterations in these theories. Atoms and the void are accepted as the ultimate realities. They are, indeed, imperceptible, but, so far from being "witnessed against" by our perceptions, they are confirmed by a number of analogies from sensation and they account for sensation itself, which is always the result of corporeal contact.

With regard to the atoms themselves Epicurus again takes up a more common-sense view than that of Democritus. He observes that weight is a property of sensible objects and so he adds weight to the primary properties of the atoms and makes weight the cause of their movement. Their natural tendency is, he assumes, to fall "downwards" in space. But a stream of particles moving in parallel straight lines at a uniform velocity obviously would continue in this state for all eternity. To account for atomic combinations Epicurus asserts that at any moment any atom may, for no known reason, deviate slightly from its course. As a result of this slight deviation it will come into collision with other atoms and so give rise to the whole complex of movement out of which all things are made. This particular theory of Epicurus is, of course, lamentable from the point of view of a scientist. Whereas Democritus had created a beautifully simple system in which atoms in motion in the void could be held to account for everything and no other "cause" need be looked for, Epicurus now introduces in "the slight swerve" a new element of causation which has the disadvantage of being absolutely unpredictable and unexplainable. Yet again Epicurus is, in his own way, consistent. He has observed that if the determinism of Democritus is to be thoroughly thought out, there is no place for free will. Yet free will is a fact of experience. Either, therefore, it must be accounted for by supposing that there is something or other in "the soul" which is not atomic, or else the atoms themselves must be assumed to have the power of "free" movement. The first alternative would be disastrous to the whole theory of materialism; therefore the second, which is confirmed by an analogy from sensation, must be true.

This doctrine of "the slight swerve" is the most interesting of the alterations made by Epicurus in the theory of Democritus. There are others as well. He dismisses, for example, the possibility that there can be "very large" atoms. If there were, we should be able to see them. Moreover it is very hard to think of something visible which is also indivisible. Epicurus also elaborates in great detail the views of Democritus on the soul, on compound bodies and on perception. His great influence, however, undoubtedly derives chiefly from his moral theories. Physics are an essential background to these, but the real aim remains freedom from fear and freedom from pain.

One is freed from fear of death when one realizes the truth about the corporeal structure of the soul and how it is impossible for it to exist after the death of the body. As for the gods, so far from causing us terror, they are most agreeable objects to contemplate. They certainly exist, as is shown by the "idols" which frequently visit men, particularly in sleep. But it can easily be demonstrated that they have nothing whatever to do with human affairs. They are far too happy to bother about us and they live, not in any recognizable heaven, but in the "spaces between the worlds." Once again the theory is worked out in detail and from the final basis of sensation. There is no space here to examine the theory. It is a strangely anthropomorphic one and was worked out very fully by disciples of Epicurus, one of whom declares that the gods, being perfectly happy beings, must enjoy the pleasures of conversation and must be assumed to converse together either in Greek or in a language "not far removed from Greek."

Once freed from these great fears, it remains to decide

how best to live our life. Here the fundamental principle is, according to Epicurus, simple and quite obvious. A moment's observation will show us that what men seek is pleasure and what they avoid is pain. There is no point in reasoning here. We are now dealing with the basis of all reasoning, with pure sensation. There is therefore no question at all that the "end" of life is pleasure and nothing else. Since the standard of "the good" is pleasure, no pleasure can be better or worse than another; it can only be greater or less. Again on the basis of sensation Epicurus comes to the conclusion that "the beginning and the root of all good is the pleasure of the stomach; even wisdom and culture must be referred back to this."

By so uncompromisingly following his first principles to their conclusions Epicurus certainly got himself a bad name. Yet the true Epicurean who followed the Master's precepts was very far from being an "epicure." The life of the profligate or the glutton was greatly frowned upon, not so much because such a life was "wrong" as because it was injudicious. An orgy of food and drink may produce most agreeable sensations, but it is, our frames being constituted as they are, liable to be followed by a hangover. Strict simplicity in diet is therefore recommended and was certainly enforced or accepted by the company of disciples who met in the Garden. So too with what are known as the virtues. There is no reason in the nature of things why a man should be good rather than bad—except the very good reason that he will experience more pleasure if he is good. A man's life is continuous and he will live it with least disturbance if he is content with simple pleasures, if he avoids passion, and if he does nothing which will occasion remorse. The final aim is not violent pleasures succeeded by correspondingly violent pains, but a condition of tranquillity or imperturbability. Means towards the attainment of this aim will be found in frugal living, in friendship, in the delights of conversation and even in the contemplation of the gods who, wisely, have nothing to do with humanity at all. We are recommended to avoid ambition, any form of public activity, marriage and the begetting of children. These are likely, in the long run, to cause us more pain than pleasure.

It is an egotistic creed, but it is an entirely consistent one. It can even be adjudged respectable, since Epicurus' own ideas of enlightened self-interest tend to observe the proprieties (except in so far as the begetting of children is concerned) and to support orderly and efficient government. One can go further still and claim for the system a kind of austerity like that of the Stoics. It was Epicurus and not a Stoic who proclaimed that the wise man could be happy even on the rack.

Yet it must be allowed that in ethics the Master's precepts do not quite harmonize with that common sense that is the general opinion of mankind (to which often he defers). Suppose a man to be gifted with a really remarkable digestion, we could not logically blame him for spending his whole life in eating and drinking. Suppose a man to be incapable of remorse and strong enough to evade punishment, there is no reason why he should not indulge himself in any kind of crime which is calculated to give him pleasure. More than two hundred years after the Master's death, when his ideas had become widely spread in Rome, we find on the one hand the ardent (even overardent) convert Lucretius and on the other hand such characters as Caesar and Cassius, whose notions of a quiet life were very different from those of Epicurus himself. This is certainly a sign of how wide was the appeal of materialism and of common sense. The appeal is equally wide today and many of us are, one would imagine, Epicureans without knowing it.

There has survived from antiquity a rather curious little "manual" of Epicureanism, which early became known as the *Principal Doctrines.** That it is the work of Epicurus himself has been disputed, but the balance of opinion now inclines to the view that it is. I have decided, therefore, to include it here, since its odd mixture of cautious good

* Translated by Cyril Bailey in *Epicurus, the Extant Remains.* Oxford: The Clarendon Press; New York: Oxford University Press, 1926, pp. 95-105.

sense with a certain inhumanity conveys excellently the flavor of this important philosophical view.

1. The blessed and immortal nature knows no trouble itself nor causes trouble to any other, so that it is never constrained by anger or favour. For all such things exist only in the weak.

2. Death is nothing to us: for that which is dissolved is without sensation; and that which lacks sensation is nothing to us.

3. The limit of quantity in pleasures is the removal of all that is painful. Wherever pleasure is present, as long as it is there, there is neither pain of body nor of mind, nor of both at once.

4. Pain does not last continuously in the flesh, but the acutest pain is there for a very short time, and even that which just exceeds the pleasure in the flesh does not continue for many days at once. But chronic illnesses permit a predominance of pleasure over pain in the flesh.

5. It is not possible to live pleasantly without living prudently and honourably and justly, nor again to live a life of prudence, honour, and justice without living pleasantly. And the man who does not possess the pleasant life, is not living prudently and honourably and justly, and the man who does not possess the virtuous life, cannot possibly live pleasantly.

6. To secure protection from men anything is a natural good, by which you may be able to attain this end.

7. Some men wished to become famous and conspicuous, thinking that they would thus win for themselves safety from other men. Wherefore if the life of such men is safe, they have obtained the good which nature craves; but if it is not safe, they do not possess that for which they strove at first by the instinct of nature.

8. No pleasure is a bad thing in itself: but the means which produce some pleasures bring with them disturbances many times greater than the pleasures.

9. If every pleasure could be intensified so that it lasted and influenced the whole organism or the most essential parts of our nature, pleasures would never differ from one another.

10. If the things that produce the pleasures of profligates could dispel the fears of the mind about the phenomena of the sky and death and its pains, and also teach the limits of desires and of pains, we should never have cause to blame them: for they would be filling themselves full with pleasures from

every source and never have pain of body or mind, which is the evil of life.

11. If we were not troubled by our suspicions of the phenomena of the sky and about death, fearing that it concerns us, and also by our failure to grasp the limits of pains and desires, we should have no need of natural science.

12. A man cannot dispel his fear about the most important matters if he does not know what is the nature of the universe but suspects the truth of some mythical story. So that without natural science it is not possible to attain our pleasures unalloyed.

13. There is no profit in securing protection in relation to men, if things above and things beneath the earth and indeed all in the boundless universe remain matters of suspicion.

14. The most unalloyed source of protection from men, which is secured to some extent by a certain force of expulsion, is in fact the immunity which results from a quiet life and the retirement from the world.

15. The wealth demanded by nature is both limited and easily procured; that demanded by idle imaginings stretches on to infinity.

16. In a few things chance hinders a wise man, but the greatest and most important matters reason has ordained and throughout the whole period of life does and will ordain.

17. The just man is most free from trouble, the unjust most full of trouble.

18. The pleasure in the flesh is not increased, when once the pain due to want is removed, but only varied: and the limit as regards pleasure in the mind is begotten by the reasoned understanding of these very pleasures and of the emotions akin to them, which used to cause the greatest fear to the mind.

19. Infinite time contains no greater pleasure than limited time, if one measures by reason the limits of pleasure.

20. The flesh perceives the limits of pleasure as unlimited and unlimited time is required to supply it. But the mind, having attained a reasoned understanding of the ultimate good of the flesh and its limits and having dissipated the fears concerning the time to come, supplies us with the complete life, and we have no further need of infinite time: but neither does the mind shun pleasure, nor, when circumstances begin to bring about the departure from life, does it approach its end as though it fell short in any way of the best life.

21. He who has learned the limits of life knows that that

which removes the pain due to want and makes the whole of life complete is easy to obtain; so that there is no need of actions which involve competition.

22. We must consider both the real purpose and all the evidence of direct perception, to which we always refer the conclusions of opinion; otherwise, all will be full of doubt and confusion.

23. If you fight against all sensations, you will have no standard by which to judge even those of them that you say are false.

24. If you reject any single sensation and fail to distinguish between the conclusion of opinion as to the appearance awaiting confirmation and that which is actually given by the sensation or feeling, or each intuitive apprehension of the mind, you will confound all other sensations as well with the same groundless opinion, so that you will reject every standard of judgement. And if among the mental images created by your opinion you accept both that which awaits confirmation and that which does not, you will not escape error, since you will have preserved the whole cause of doubt in every judgement between what is right and what is wrong.

25. If on each occasion instead of referring your actions to the end of nature, you turn to some other nearer standard when you are making a choice or an avoidance, your actions will not be consistent with your principles.

26. Of desires, all that do not lead to a sense of pain, if they are not satisfied, are not necessary, but involve a craving which is easily dispelled, when the object is hard to procure or they seem likely to produce harm.

27. Of all the things which wisdom acquires to produce the blessedness of the complete life, far the greatest is the possession of friendship.

28. The same conviction which has given us confidence that there is nothing terrible that lasts for ever or even for long, has also seen the protection of friendship most fully completed in the limited evils of this life.

29. Among desires some are natural and necessary, some natural but not necessary, and others neither natural nor necessary, but due to idle imagination.

30. Wherever in the case of desires which are physical, but do not lead to a sense of pain, if they are not fulfilled, the effort is intense, such pleasures are due to idle imagination,

and it is not owing to their own nature that they fail to be dispelled, but owing to the empty imaginings of the man.

31. The justice which arises from nature is a pledge of mutual advantage to restrain men from harming one another and save them from being harmed.

32. For all living things which have not been able to make compacts not to harm one another or be harmed, nothing ever is either just or unjust; and likewise too for all tribes of men which have been unable or unwilling to make compacts not to harm or be harmed.

33. Justice never is anything in itself, but in the dealings of men with one another in any place whatever and at any time it is a kind of compact not to harm or be harmed.

34. Injustice is not an evil in itself, but only in consequence of the fear which attaches to the apprehension of being unable to escape those appointed to punish such actions.

35. It is not possible for one who acts in secret contravention of the terms of the compact not to harm or be harmed, to be confident that he will escape detection, even if at present he escapes a thousand times. For up to the time of death it cannot be certain that he will indeed escape.

36. In its general aspect justice is the same for all, for it is a kind of mutual advantage in the dealings of men with one another, but with reference to the individual peculiarities of a country or any other circumstances the same thing does not turn out to be just for all.

37. Among actions which are sanctioned as just by law, that which is proved on examination to be of advantage in the requirements of men's dealings with one another, has the guarantee of justice, whether it is the same for all or not. But if a man makes a law and it does not turn out to lead to advantage in men's dealings with each other, then it no longer has the essential nature of justice. And even if the advantage in the matter of justice shifts from one side to the other, but for a while accords with the general concept, it is none the less just for that period in the eyes of those who do not confuse themselves with empty sounds but look to the actual facts.

38. Where, provided the circumstances have not been altered, actions which were considered just, have been shown not to accord with the general concept of actual practice, then they are not just. But where, when circumstances have changed, the same actions which were sanctioned as just no longer lead

to advantage, there they were just at the time when they were
of advantage for the dealings of fellow-citizens with one another; but subsequently they are no longer just, when no longer
of advantage.

39. The man who has best ordered the element of disquiet
arising from external circumstances has made those things
that he could akin to himself or at least not alien: but with
all to which he could not do even this, he has refrained from
mixing, and has expelled from his life all which it was of
advantage to treat thus.

40. As many as possess the power to procure complete
immunity from their neighbours, these also live most pleasantly
with one another, since they have the most certain pledge
of security, and after they have enjoyed the fullest intimacy,
they do not lament the previous departure of a dead friend,
as though he were to be pitied.

Our only full and consecutive treatment of the doctrine
of Epicurus is to be found in the poem of Lucretius, *De
Rerum Natura*. It has seemed best, therefore, in the following pages to include several extracts from this great
poem. It should be added that from a few extracts it is
impossible to give an adequate idea of the complexity of
argument and the fervor which sustain the whole work. I
have ventured to translate one passage into verse in the
hope that in this way the reader will be able to see more
clearly how fervent was the resigned faith of some, at least,
of the followers of Epicurus.

1. THERE IS NO CRITERION OF TRUTH EXCEPT THE SENSES*

If anyone thinks that nothing is known, he does not know
whether this proposition can be known either, since he admits
that he knows nothing. It seems, therefore, rather pointless
to argue at all with someone who is standing on his head.
Nevertheless, suppose I were to grant that he does know this,
then I shall go on to ask him this one question: since up to now
he has never seen any truth in things, how does he know the
difference between knowing and not knowing in particular

* Lucretius, Book IV, 460 ff.

instances? What was it that gave him the concept of the true and the false? What evidence was there for drawing a distinction between what is doubtful and what is certain? You will find that the concepts of the true come in the first place from the senses, and that the evidence of the senses cannot be overthrown. To do so one must find some other standard of greater authority, able of itself to convict falsehood by asserting truth. But what can be considered of greater authority than the senses? Shall we say that reason, based on a deceptive sense-impression, is strong enough to contradict the senses, when reason itself is wholly based on the senses? If the senses are not true, then how can there be any truth in reason either? Or can hearing challenge the evidence of sight, or touch that of hearing? Will the tongue's taste argue against the touch, will the nose prove it wrong, will the eyes bring a contrary verdict? The answer, I think, is "no." For each has its own particular function and its own power. It is therefore necessary to use a particular sense in order to decide what is soft, or what is cold or hot, and another particular sense to perceive the various colors of things and to see what is involved in color [i.e., shape.–R.W.] . . . It follows that one sense cannot prove another sense wrong. Nor can the same sense convict itself of falsehood, since we must always give equal credit to every sense impression. What at any time has appeared to be true to the senses, is true. And if reason does prove unable to explain the cause why objects which were square when close at hand seem to be rounded when looked at from a distance, nevertheless it is much better with one's faulty reason to give an inaccurate explanation of these shapes than at any point to lose one's grip on what is absolutely obvious, to break faith with what is our first authority for everything and to tear up the entire foundation on which life and existence rest. Not only would the whole structure of reason collapse; life itself too would immediately disintegrate unless you have the courage to believe in the senses. . . .

2. MATTER AND SPACE*

Therefore everything in existence is, fundamentally, made out of two things. There are bodies and there is the void in which these bodies have their places and through which they

* Lucretius, Book I, 419 ff.

move in different directions. For sensation which is common to everybody declares that body exists. And unless we hold fast to this original belief in sensation, we shall find that in matters beyond the reach of sensation we shall have no principle to which we can refer and by means of which we can arrive at rational conclusions. Next, if there were no such thing as space (which is what we mean by "the void") there would be nowhere in which the bodies could be situated and it would be quite impossible for them to move about in different directions. . . . There is nothing else—nothing which you could say was distinct both from body and from void and could be pronounced to be a third substance. For everything that is to exist must be something in itself; if it is capable of touching and being touched, however light and small the touch may be, it will, provided that it does exist, increase the quantity of body to some extent, whether great or small, and be an addition to the sum of things. If on the other hand it is intangible and unable to prevent any object in motion from passing through it at any point, then unquestionably it must be what we call the empty void. Then again, whatever is to exist in itself will either do something, or else must remain passive itself while other things act upon it, or else must be of the sort in which things can exist and actions can take place. But nothing can act or be acted upon without body and nothing can afford space except the void and the empty. Therefore apart from the void and bodies it is impossible for there to exist in the sum of things any residual third substance. Such a substance could never at any time come within the reach of our senses, nor could any man lay hold of it by any process of reasoning.

You will find that all things which we say exist are either properties or accidents of these two. A property is what is absolutely inseparable from the object so long as the object remains in existence; thus weight is a property of stone, heat of fire, liquidity of water, touch of all bodies, intangibility of the void. On the other hand, examples of what we may properly call accidents are slavery, poverty and riches, freedom, war, peace and all the other things which can be present or absent without disrupting the nature of whatever we are considering. . . .

Bodies can be divided into (i) the original atoms, (ii) compounds made up of these atoms. As for the original atoms, no power is able to destroy them. Their solid bodies will resist and outlast all assaults. And yet it seems hard to believe that there is anything in existence with such absolute solidity. Heaven's thunderbolt goes through the walls of houses; so does sound and the noise of voices. Iron becomes white-hot in fire, and stones often split apart when exposed to violent heat. By heat too the hardness of gold is first undermined and then dissolved, and the icy texture of bronze, conquered by flame, turns to liquid. Both warmth and penetrating cold ooze through silver; we have felt both of them when we hold the goblet in our hands and a draught of liquid is poured into it from above. Indeed it certainly appears that there is no solidity anywhere. Nevertheless, since true reason and the very nature of things force me to speak, I must ask for your attention until in a few verses I demonstrate the existence of things which have bodies that are absolutely solid and everlasting. These, in our teaching, are called the seeds of things and their first beginnings, out of which the whole sum of things in its present state has been formed.

3. THE ATOMIC SWERVE*

There is one other point on this subject which I want you to understand. While the atoms are being carried down in a straight line through the void by their own weight, at quite uncertain times and at uncertain intervals they swerve slightly out of their course—just enough for one to be able to say that there has been an alteration in their movement. For if they had not this characteristic of moving out of the direct line, they would all fall downwards like drops of rain through the depths of the void; no collision would take place, no one atom would strike upon another; and so nature would never have produced anything at all.

If by any chance anyone holds the view that heavier bodies, through being carried down more quickly in a straight line through the void, are able to fall from on top on lighter bodies and in this way produce impacts out of which the creative motion could arise, he is quite wrong and has strayed far from the path of true reason. When things fall downwards through water or through thin air, they must indeed accelerate the speed of their fall in proportion to their weights. This is because the corporeal structure of water and the nature of

* Lucretius, Book II, 216 ff.

air cannot put a check on each thing equally; the heavier a thing is, the quicker they are mastered and have to give way. The empty void on the other hand cannot possibly offer any resistance to any thing anywhere or at any time: as its whole nature demands, it must always give way. Therefore all bodies, whether their weights are equal or not, must be carried through the peaceful void at an equal speed. And so the heavier bodies will never be able to fall from above on the lighter ones or by themselves produce the blows which give rise to the various motions by which nature carries on her work. Therefore (I must emphasize this point again and again) it is necessary that the atoms swerve slightly; and the swerve must only be the slightest possible; otherwise it will look as though we are assuming oblique motions, a theory which is against the evidence of real facts. For this is something which we see set down plainly before our eyes: that, so far as can be perceived, weights falling straight down from above do not have it in their nature to move obliquely. On the other hand no one has such power of perception as to be able to state that there is absolutely no deviation at all from a perfectly straight course.

Then again, if we assume that all motion always goes on in a continuous chain with new motion always arising out of the old in an absolutely determined order; and if the atoms, by means of this swerve, do not initiate a kind of motion that can break through the decrees of fate so that cause may not follow cause to infinity, then how can we explain this free will which we find in living creatures all over the earth? What, I say, is the origin of this faculty of ours which we have wrested from the fates and by which each of us goes where his pleasure leads him, deviating in our motions just as the atoms do at no fixed times or places, but just as our mind takes us? For it is beyond doubt that in these matters it is a man's will that provides the initiative and from it the movements spread through the limbs. You have no doubt observed too that when the barriers are let down at a given moment on a race-course, the strong eager bodies of the horses still cannot burst out into the track as suddenly as their minds in themselves would like to do. This is because the total quantity of matter has to be stirred up together throughout the whole body so that it may then make the collective effort of following the desire of the mind. So you may see that the origin of motion is an act of the intelligence and that this proceeds in the first place from the will of the mind, from it to be passed on further through the whole body and through the limbs. This is not at all the same thing as when we move forward because we are forced to do so by the impulsion of the great strength or great effort of someone else; for in this case it is quite clear that all the matter in the entire body is being pushed forward and hurried along against our will, until the will, operating through the limbs, has regained control. Do you see, then, that, though some external force often drives people on and often compels them to be swept forward headlong against their wills, nevertheless there is something in our breast capable of fighting against this impulse and resisting it? And it is owing to the power of this authority inside ourselves that the whole quantity of matter is sometimes compelled to alter course throughout the body and limbs, and, though pushed forward in one direction, is brought under control and made to settle back again.

You must admit therefore that the same principle holds true of the atoms: that, apart from weight and the blows of one atom on another, there must be another cause for motion, from which comes this power that is born in us, since we see that nothing can be produced out of nothing. It is weight that prevents everything being caused by the blows of one atom on another, as it were by an external force; but it is the minute swerve in the atoms, taking place at no definite time or place, which keeps the mind itself from being governed by an internal necessity in all its actions, and from being as it were subdued by this necessity so as to be merely a passive subject.

4. THERE IS NOTHING TO FEAR AFTER DEATH*

So then Death to us is nothing: it does not matter,
since it is understood that the mind's nature is mortal.
And just as in time past we felt no pain or discomfort
when from every direction the Carthaginian armies
moved into battle, and under the high vault of the heavens
everything trembled and shook in the crash and outbreak of
    war,
no one knowing for sure to which side would go the dominion
over the whole world of men by land and by sea;
so, when we cease to be, when the break is made in that union

* Lucretius, BOOK III, 830 ff.

of body and soul from which combined we have our existence,
then for certain to us who no longer exist there is nothing,
nothing that ever could happen, nothing to cause a sensation,
no, not if earth with sea and sea with sky were confounded.
And even if mind and soul, when once withdrawn from the
    body,
do have the power to feel, still it is nothing to us,
since we are what we are simply because of the union
formed between body and soul and their intimate junction
    together.
And even if, after our death, time should reassemble the matter
out of which we are made and place it just as it now is,
giving the light of life back to us once again,
this thing too would make to us no manner of difference
once the chain of memory and self-recollection was broken.
Now we are not affected by what at some moment of past time
we once were; that ancient misery does not concern us.
For one has only to think of all time past, of its boundless
stretching away and of all the various movements of matter;
it will be easy then to believe that those very atoms
out of which we are now formed have often before been
placed in exactly the same order as now. Yet we cannot
grasp that state again; our minds have ceased to remember;
in between is set a stoppage of life; all the motions
have drifted away and lost contact with former sensations.
So, if we are to experience sadness and pain in the future
our true selves must exist at that time for such things to
    befall us.
Death, however, rules this quite out and prevents there from
    being
ever the person again who can feel this complex of suffering.
Therefore we know for sure that death can bring us no terrors,
that he who does not exist cannot be unhappy, nor can it
matter at all to a man if he has been born in some past age.
His life is severed by death, and death, not life, is immortal.

CHAPTER VIII

Stoicism

Of the post-Aristotelian schools of philosophy there can be little doubt that Stoicism was the most influential. W. W. Tarn goes so far as to say that "the philosophy of the Hellenistic world was the Stoa; all else was secondary. What we see, broadly speaking, as we look down the three centuries, is that Aristotle's school loses all importance, and Plato's, for a century and a half, becomes a parasite upon the Stoa in the sense that its life as a school of scepticism consists wholly in combating Stoic doctrine; Epicurus' school continues unchanged, but only attracts small minorities; but the Stoa . . . finally masters Scepticism, in fact though not in argument, and takes to itself enough of a revived Platonism to form that modified Stoicism or Eclecticism which was the distinguishing philosophy of the earlier Roman empire."* The length of its life as a more or less organized body of doctrine, the number of its distinguished adherents in later antiquity, and indeed the frequent recurrence in all periods of characteristically Stoic attitudes, all imply that Stoicism is able to satisfy some deep and constant human demand.

There is a sense, however, in which it was always based on a kind of desperate dogmatism. It is impossible to distinguish, behind the copious and systematic writings of Chrysippus of Soli, the original doctrine of the founder of the Stoa, Zeno of Citium (c. 334/3-262/1 B.C.); but it is clear at least that he relied heavily in his teaching on the power of brief, unqualified assertion, and on the force of his own example and personality. In each of the three

* W. W. Tarn, *Hellenistic Civilization*. London: E. Arnold & Company; New York: Longmans, Green & Co., 1927, p. 266.

divisions of Stoic doctrine—Logical, Physical and Ethical —there is much more of vehement affirmation than of argument.

The Stoic answer to the arguments of sceptics was, in effect, the bare assertion that cases occur in which all doubt is out of the question. The human mind is originally "like a clean tablet"; the "impressions" from which all thinking and all knowledge derive differ in "clearness"; but *some* are borne in upon us with such force and vividness that they (in a phrase that perhaps is Zeno's own) "take hold of us by the hair and drag us to assent." It is said that Zeno would illustrate the resulting "grasp" of the truth by clenching his fist.

The "physical" doctrine of the Stoics was no less positive. It was monistic; there was only one "substance," one *phusis,* underlying all phenomena whatever. It was materialistic; the gods, human minds, even emotions and the qualities of objects, were all "bodies," all corporeal or material things. But it was at the same time rationalistic; *phusis* is often referred to by the name of God, and often identified with Reason. Thus, though everything that exists is asserted to be material, everything that occurs is held to be directed by rational purpose. Most curiously of all, it was also held that the universe, which came into being out of "divine fire," was supposed, after a cycle of enormous length, to be reconsumed in a cosmic conflagration, thereafter to repeat identical cycles forever.

But the ethics was by far the most important part of Stoic doctrine. Its overriding objective was the attainment of peace. We are at peace, we may all agree, when we have what we want. But this state may be sought, either by attempting to get what we want, *or* by attempting to want what it is that we get. This second course (expressed here with deliberate paradox) is that which the Stoics pursued. It may even be that "want" is too strong a word; the Stoic view was rather that all that occurs should be *accepted* without, at least ideally, any stirring whatever of emotion or appetite. The only good was virtue, the only evil vice. Virtue and vice were held to consist, respectively, primarily in right and wrong disposition of the will. But the will (it was assumed) was wholly and unalterably under the control of the individual. Hence, it could be held that the attainment of the true good was wholly within the power of each individual. Everything else, everything that did not fall within the sphere of his absolute control, was to be regarded with indifference—pain and pleasure along with the rest.

Thus far, the doctrine seems unsatisfactory in two respects. First, it appears that very often "external" matters are denied to be either good or bad *only* because they are not under absolute control of the will—the idea that good and evil are within the sole power of the individual is employed, not as a reasoned conclusion from experience, but as an axiom dogmatically laid down before experience. Second, in mere acceptance of what occurs there would seem to be no motive for action—as if the desired Stoic condition of *apatheia* must simply be that which we call "apathy."

The first of these objections cannot really be answered. To one who maintained, for instance, that pain was bad, the Stoic could only reply that his peace of mind would be less liable to disturbance if he could regard it with absolute indifference. This was indeed an *effective* answer for those many who regarded peace of mind as desirable above everything; but it was not, however effective, rationally cogent. But to the second point the Stoics did pay considerable attention. They held that, though the "wise man" would *desire* nothing but the right disposition of his own will, yet he would *choose* some things in preference to others. He would choose to act "in accordance with Nature." This meant two things. First, he would justifiably seek the fulfillment of his simple, "natural" human instincts; and second, because (they held) mankind was "naturally" one family, he would seek to serve his fellowmen. Each man, in a figure which they frequently employed, was assigned by Nature to his particular rôle in the drama of existence, a rôle which set him in relation with other men; and it was "fitting" for him to play this part to the best of his ability—though strictly, except in so far as it affected his own virtue, he should be wholly indifferent as to the outcome. To the question *why* a man should act in accordance with Nature, it was answered that Nature is Reason—the same Reason which every man recognizes as the highest part of himself; to the further question what Reason required him to do, it was answered that he should play out the part that was assigned to him, whether the outcome was agreeable to him or not, remembering that everything but virtue is really indifferent, and that everything that occurs has its place in Nature's grand design.

It may be clear even from this brief account in what the great strength of Stoicism consisted. First, it held out the hope of inner tranquillity. By insisting on the absolute sufficiency of the good will and upon the ultimate worthlessness of all else, it seemed to point the way to an unshakeable security through any and all vicissitudes of fortune. But second, it did not preach a policy of feeble resignation. On the contrary, Nature demanded the most strict and punctilious discharge of the obligations of one's station in life. The life of the Stoic, though untroubled, was also to be strenuous. And third, it put forward the genuinely inspiring idea—by no means a natural one to the Greeks—of mankind as a single family, of each man as fundamentally a "citizen of the world," and only secondarily and by convention a member of this or that restricted community. Alexander, according to Plutarch, put this idea into practice in the government of his vast and heterogeneous empire; but it was formulated in philosophy by Zeno. It is relevant, no doubt, that Zeno himself was not Greek; he was, apparently, of Semitic extraction.

There is one major theoretical difficulty in the Stoic doctrine, which may seem to us to be comparatively obvious, but which apparently did not receive much notice from the Stoics themselves. It is that there is a fundamental incompatibility between their two main devices for achieving *apatheia*. On the one hand they argued that everything was determined by Nature, that all that occurs can be seen by the reflective mind to occur inevitably, and hence that acceptance of whatever occurs is the only rational attitude. Indignation, regret, fear, hope, anxiety—all these are foolish, unjustifiable feelings, for all rest on the false idea that the actual course of events could be, or could have been, other than what it is, has been, and will be. There is nothing for the wise man to do but to resign himself to what Nature may bring him. On the other hard they insisted no less vigorously on the absolute freedom of the individual will—as if this alone were exempt from the direction of Nature, unique in being solely in the power of each man himself. One striking effect of this conflict is seen clearly in both Epictetus and Marcus Aurelius. Each is tacitly inclined to make a special case of himself—to reproach and exhort himself, to assume full responsibility for his own conduct and character, to resolve to direct his actions differently in the future, and so on, while tending to regard others as nearly as possible as automata, undeserving of censure for their defects of character and conduct since it is, after all, "in their nature" to have those defects. The resulting position, in a sense, is morally admirable; it leads to a personal insistence on the highest standards of conduct, without censoriousness for the many others who fail to live up to them; but it is, intellectually, somewhat paradoxical and strained. It would have been characteristic of the Stoics to insist with vehemence that we *can* regard others as the puppets of Nature, and that we *cannot* regard ourselves in the very same way; and this may be true; but it states the problem without resolving it.

In the century following the death of Zeno, Stoic doctrine came to be modified in certain respects. The chief influence in this period was that of Panaetius of Rhodes, born early in the second century B.C., the philosopher through whom all Stoic ideas were transplanted to that Roman soil where they flourished so greatly. In some respects his amendments of the doctrine were advantageous. The earlier Stoics, influenced partly by their general reverence for "Nature" and partly by their predominantly moral concerns, had been disposed to believe that there might be much sense in astrology, and conversely disinclined to take pure science very seriously; they were, in effect, apt to be superstitious. Panaetius, however, was a determined rationalist, and Roman Stoicism thus, at least in its early days, shook off the disadvantage of being associated with undue credulity. More serious, however, was the abandonment by Panaetius of the doctrine of recurring cosmic conflagration; and in fact he appears to have greatly modified also the conception of the Stoic "wise man." He retained the idea of humanity as a single family, but in ethics laid emphasis on the virtues of co-operation rather than upon the old, harsher ideal of the attainment of personal *apatheia,* of unfeeling tranquillity. This movement away from the purity of Stoic doctrine was even more marked in his pupil Posidonius of Apamea, a great traveler, a learned historian, a born encyclopedist, but a collector of thoughts rather than a thinker. He constructed what Eduard Zeller has called "a great pantheistic system, in which the whole of empirical knowledge finds a place; but unfortunately not only knowledge but also the whole superstition of his time." He was essentially concerned with fitting ideas together, rather than with subjecting any of them to critical inspection. However, his influence in his time was very great; and he is noteworthy as being, perhaps, the last philosopher in the pure Greek tradition, untouched by Rome.

Epictetus, the Stoic whose works have survived most substantially, was Greek by birth, but he lived long in Rome as a slave, and later as a free man. He was born in about the middle of the first century A.D., but although he is thus much later in time than Panaetius or Posidonius, he adheres far more closely to the old Stoic tradition. He studied thoroughly the works of Chrysippus, and deliberately attempted to revive the early inspiration of Zeno. In some respects he even went further. Zeno, while insisting that "conformity with nature or reason," the right disposition of the will, was alone truly valuable, had been prepared to admit that among indifferent things some could properly be preferred to others. Health and wealth, for example, though by no means really good, were, other things being equal, preferable to illness or poverty. Epictetus makes no mention of this concession. In his view, to be master of one's fate through control of the will, and through the control or elimination of all feeling whatever, is the only rational goal. As so often, however, in Stoicism, this harshness of doctrine was combined in him with an admirable tolerance of the failings of others, and in his own case with a genuine good humor in spite of affliction. This tolerance, regrettably, did not extend to the Epicureans. Unable apparently to see how closely in practice the Epicurean rule of life resembled the Stoic, Epictetus persistently speaks of Epicurus as if he had been the sort of self-indulgent, irresponsible hedonist that popular opinion has too often taken him to be. It seems that the true Stoic found something repulsive in any admission, however guarded, of the value of pleasure—in any qualification, however cautious, of the stern, inescapable demands of duty. And in this the characteristic spirit of Rome seems to have been in natural alliance with Stoicism. Though Epicurus had his distinguished followers, Stoicism was far more widely known and more influential.

There follow some extracts from the *Discourses* of Epictetus, as vividly preserved for us by his pupil Arrian.

1. OF THE THINGS WHICH ARE UNDER OUR CONTROL AND NOT UNDER OUR CONTROL.*

Among the arts and faculties in general you will find none that is self-contemplative, and therefore none that is either self-approving or self-disapproving. How far does the art of grammar possess the power of contemplation? Only so far as to pass judgement upon what is written. How far the art of music? Only so far as to pass judgement upon the melody. Does either of them, then, contemplate itself? Not at all. But if you are writing to a friend and are at a loss as to what to write, the art of grammar will tell you; yet whether or no you are to write to your friend at all, the art of grammar will not tell. The same holds true of the art of music with regard to melodies; but whether you are at this moment to sing and play on the lyre, or neither sing nor play, it will not tell. What art or faculty, then, will tell? That one which contemplates both itself and everything else. And what is this? The reasoning

* Epictetus, *The Discourses*, translated by W. A. Oldfather. London: William Heinemann Ltd., 1926; Cambridge, Mass.: Harvard University Press, I, Book I, Chap. I, pp. 7–15. (The Loeb Classical Library.)

faculty; for this is the only one we have inherited which will take knowledge both of itself—what it is, and of what it is capable, and how valuable a gift it is to us—and likewise of all the other faculties. For what else is it that tells us gold is beautiful? For the gold itself does not tell us. Clearly it is the faculty which makes use of external impressions. What else judges with discernment the art of music, the art of grammar, the other arts and faculties, passing judgement upon their uses and pointing out the seasonable occasions for their use? Nothing else does.

As was fitting, therefore, the gods have put under our control only the most excellent faculty of all and that which dominates the rest, namely, the power to make correct use of external impressions, but all the others they have not put under our control. Was it indeed because they would not? I for one think that had they been able they would have entrusted us with the others also; but they were quite unable to do that. For since we are upon earth and trammelled by an earthy body and by earthy associates, how was it possible that, in respect of them, we should not be hampered by external things?

But what says Zeus? "Epictetus, had it been possible I should have made both this paltry body and this small estate of thine free and unhampered. But as it is—let it not escape thee—this body is not thine own, but only clay cunningly compounded. Yet since I could not give thee this, we have given thee a certain portion of ourself, this faculty of choice and refusal of desire and aversion, or, in a word, the faculty which makes use of external impressions; if thou care for this and place all that thou hast therein, thou shalt never be thwarted, never hampered, shalt not groan, shalt not blame, shalt not flatter any man. What then? Are these things small in thy sight?" "Far be it from me!" "Art thou, then, content with them?" "I pray the Gods I may be."

But now, although it is in our power to care for one thing only and devote ourselves to but one, we choose rather to care for many things, and to be tied fast to many, even to our body and our estate and brother and friend and child and slave. Wherefore, being tied fast to many things, we are burdened and dragged down by them. That is why, if the weather keeps us from sailing, we sit down and fidget and keep constantly peering about. "What wind is blowing?" we ask. Boreas. "What have we to do with it? When will Zephyrus blow?" When it pleases, good sir, or rather when Aeolus pleases. For God has not made you steward of the winds, but Aeolus. "What then?" We must make the best of what is under our control, and take the rest as its nature is. "How, then, is its nature?" As God wills.

"Must I, then, be the only one to be beheaded now?" Why, did you want everybody to be beheaded for your consolation? Are you not willing to stretch out your neck as did a certain Lateranus at Rome, when Nero ordered him to be beheaded? For he stretched out his neck and received the blow, but, as it was a feeble one, he shrank back for an instant, and then stretched out his neck again. Yes, and before that, when Epaphroditus, a freedman of Nero, approached a certain man and asked about the ground of his offence, he answered, "If I wish anything, I will speak to your master."

"What aid, then, must we have ready at hand in such circumstances?" Why, what else than the knowledge of what is mine, and what is not mine, and what is permitted me, and what is not permitted me? I must die: must I, then, die groaning too? I must be fettered: and wailing too? I must go into exile: does anyone, then, keep me from going with a smile and cheerful and serene? "Tell your secrets." I say not a word; for this is under my control. "But I will fetter you." What is that you say, man? fetter *me*? My leg you will fetter, but my moral purpose not even Zeus himself has power to overcome. "I will throw you into prison." My paltry body, rather! "I will behead you." Well, when did I ever tell you that mine was the only neck that could not be severed? These are the lessons that philosophers ought to rehearse, these they ought to write down daily, in these they ought to exercise themselves.

Thrasea used to say: "I would rather be killed to-day than banished to-morrow." What, then, did Rufus say to him? "If you choose death as the heavier of two misfortunes, what folly of choice! But if as the lighter, who has given you the choice? Are you not willing to practise contentment with what has been given you?"

Wherefore, what was it that Agrippinus used to remark? "I am not standing in my own way." Word was brought him, "Your case is being tried in the Senate."—"Good luck betide! But it is the fifth hour now" (he was in the habit of taking his exercise and then a cold bath at that hour); "let us be off and take our exercise." After he had finished his exercise someone came and told him, "You have been condemned."—"To exile," says he, "or to death?"—"To exile."—"What about my property?"—"It has not been confiscated."—"Well then, let us go to Aricia and take our lunch there." This is what it means to have rehearsed the lessons one ought to rehearse, to have set desire and aversion free from every hindrance and made them proof against chance. I must die. If forthwith, I die; and if a little later, I will take lunch now, since the hour for lunch has come, and afterwards I will die at the appointed time. How? As becomes the man who is giving back that which was another's.

2. OF CONTENTMENT.*

Concerning gods there are some who say that the divine does not so much as exist; and others, that it exists, indeed, but is inactive and indifferent, and takes forethought for nothing; and a third set, that it exists and takes forethought, though only for great and heavenly things and in no case for terrestrial things; and a fourth set, that it also takes forethought for things terrestrial and the affairs of men, but only in a general way, and not for the individual in particular; and a fifth set, to which Odysseus and Socrates belonged, who say

Nor when I move am I concealed from thee.

We must, therefore, first of all inquire about each of these statements, to see whether it is sound or not sound. For if gods do not exist, how can it be an end to follow the gods? And if they exist, indeed, but care for nothing, how even thus will that conclusion be sound? But if, indeed, they both exist and exercise care, yet there is no communication from them to men,—yes, and, by Zeus, to me personally,—how even in this case can our conclusion still be sound? The good and excellent man must, therefore, inquire into all these things, before he subordinates his own will to him who administers the universe, precisely as good citizens submit to the law of the state. And he that is being instructed ought to come to his instruction with this aim, "How may I follow the gods in everything, and how may I be acceptable to the divine administration, and how may I become free?" Since he is free for whom all things happen according to his moral purpose, and whom none can restrain. What then? Is freedom insanity?

* *Ibid.*, Chap. XII, pp. 89-97.

Far from it; for madness and freedom are not consistent with one another. "But I would have that which seems best to me happen in every case, no matter how it comes to seem so." You are mad; you are beside yourself. Do you not know that freedom is a noble and precious thing? But for me to desire at haphazard that those things should happen which have at haphazard seemed best to me, is dangerously near being, not merely not noble, but even in the highest degree shameful. For how do we act in writing? Do I desire to write the name "Dio" as I choose? No, but I am taught to desire to write it as it ought to be written. What do we do in music? The same. And what in general, where there is any art or science? The same; otherwise knowledge of anything would be useless, if it were accommodated to every individual's whims. Is it, then, only in this matter of freedom, the greatest and indeed the highest of all, that I am permitted to desire at haphazard? By no means, but instruction consists precisely in learning to desire each thing exactly as it happens. And how do they happen? As he that ordains them has ordained. And he has ordained that there be summer and winter, and abundance and dearth, and virtue and vice, and all such opposites, for the harmony of the whole, and he has given each of us a body, and members of the body, and property and companions.

Mindful, therefore, of this ordaining we should go to receive instruction, not in order to change the constitution of things,— for this is neither vouchsafed us nor is it better that it should be,—but in order that, things about us being as they are and as their nature is, we may, for our own part, keep our wills in harmony with what happens. For, look you, can we escape from men? And how is it possible? But can we, if they associate with us, change them? And who vouchsafes us that power? What alternative remains, then, or what method can we find for living with them? Some such method as that, while they will act as seems best to them, we shall none the less be in a state conformable to nature. But you are impatient and peevish, and if you are alone, you call it a solitude, but if you are in the company of men, you call them schemers and brigands, and you find fault even with your own parents and children and brothers and neighbours. But you ought, when staying alone, to call that peace and freedom, and to look upon yourself as like the gods; and when you are in the company of many, you ought not call that a mob, nor a tumult, nor a disgusting thing, but a feast and a festival, and so accept all things contentedly.

What, then, is the punishment of those who do not accept? To be just as they are. Is one peevish because he is alone? Let him be in solitude! Is he peevish with his parents? Let him be an evil son and grieve! Is he peevish with his children? Let him be a bad father! "Throw him into prison." What sort of prison? Where he now is. For he is there against his will, and where a man is against his will, that for him is a prison. Just as Socrates was not in prison, for he was there willingly. "Alas, that I should be lame in my leg!"* Slave, do you, then, because of one paltry leg blame the universe? Will you not make a free gift of it to the whole? Will you not relinquish it? Will you not gladly yield it to the giver? And will you be angry and peevish at the ordinances of Zeus, which he defined and ordained together with the Fates who spun in his presence the thread of your begetting? Do you not know how small a part you are compared with the whole? That is, as to the body; for as to the reason you are not inferior to the gods, nor less than they; for the greatness of the reason is not determined by length nor by height, but by the decisions of its will. . . .

3. To those who take up the teachings of the philosophers only to talk about them.†

. . . Observe yourselves thus in your actions and you will find out to what sect of the philosophers you belong. You will find that most of you are Epicureans, some few Peripatetics, but these without any backbone; for wherein do you in fact show that you consider virtue equal to all things else, or even superior? But as for a Stoic, show me one if you can! Where, or how? Nay, but you can show me thousands who recite the petty arguments of the Stoics. Yes, but do these same men recite the petty arguments of the Epicureans any less well? Do these men handle with the same precision the petty arguments of the Peripatetics also? Who, then, is a Stoic? As we call a statue "Pheidian" that has been fashioned according to the art of Pheidias, in that sense show me a man fashioned according to the judgements which he utters. Show me a man who though sick is happy, though in danger is happy, though dying is happy, though condemned to exile is happy, though

* Epictetus himself was a cripple.
† *Ibid.*, Book II, Chap. XIX, pp. 367-71.

in disrepute is happy. Show him! By the gods, I would fain see a Stoic! But you cannot show me a man completely so fashioned; then show me at least one who is becoming so fashioned, one who has begun to tend in that direction; do me this favour; do not begrudge an old man the sight of that spectacle which to this very day I have never seen. Do you fancy that you are going to show me the Zeus or the Athena of Pheidias, a creation of ivory and gold? Let one of you show me the soul of a man who wishes to be of one mind with God, and never again to blame either God or man, to fail in nothing that he would achieve, to fall into nothing that he would avoid, to be free from anger, envy and jealousy—but why use circumlocutions?—a man who has set his heart upon changing from a man into a god, and although he is still in this paltry body of death, does none the less have his purpose set upon fellowship with Zeus. Show him to me! But you cannot. Why, then, do you mock your own selves and cheat everybody else? And why do you put on a guise that is not your own and walk about as veritable thieves and robbers who have stolen these designations and properties that in no sense belong to you?

And so now I am your teacher, and you are being taught in my school. And my purpose is this—to make of you a perfect work, secure against restraint, compulsion, and hindrance, free, prosperous, happy, looking to God in everything both small and great; and you are here with the purpose of learning and practising all this. Why, then, do you not complete the work, if it is true that you on your part have the right kind of purpose and I on my part, in addition to the purpose, have the right kind of preparation? What is it that is lacking? When I see a craftsman who has material lying ready at hand, I look for the finished product. Here also, then, is the craftsman, and here is the material; what do we yet lack? Cannot the matter be taught? It can. Is it, then, not under our control? Nay, it is the only thing in the whole world that *is* under our control. Wealth is not under our control, nor health, nor fame, nor, in a word, anything else except the right use of external impressions. This alone is by nature secure against restraint and hindrance. Why, then, do you not finish the work? Tell me the reason. For it lies either in me, or in you, or in the nature of the thing. The thing itself is possible and is the only thing that is under our control. Consequently, then, the fault lies either in me, or in you, or, what is nearer the truth, in us both. What then? Would you like to have us at last begin to introduce here a purpose such as I have described? Let us let bygones be bygones. Only let us begin, and, take my word for it, you shall see.

4. OF FREEDOM.*

. . . What, then, is it which makes a man free from hindrance and his own master? For wealth does not do it, nor a consulship, nor a province, nor a kingdom, but something else has to be found. What, therefore, is it which makes a man free from hindrance and restraint in writing?—The knowledge of how to write.—And what in playing on the harp?—The knowledge of how to play on the harp.—So also in living, it is the knowledge of how to live. Now you have already heard this, as a general principle, but consider it also in its particular applications. Is it possible for the man who is aiming at some one of these things which are under the control of others to be free from hindrance?—No.—Is it possible for him to be free from restraint?—No.—Therefore, it is not possible for him to be free, either. Consider then: Have we nothing which is under our control and others under the control of others?—How do you mean?—When you want your body to be whole, is the matter under your control, or not?—It is not.—And when you want it to be well?—Nor that, either.—And to live or to die?—Nor that, either.—Therefore, your body is not your own possession, it is subject to everyone who is stronger than you are.—Granted.—And your farm, is it under your control to have it when you want, and as long as you want, and in the condition that you want?—No.—And your paltry slaves?—No.—And your clothes?—No.—And your paltry house?—No.— And your horses?—None of these things.—And if you wish by all means your children to live, or your wife, or your brother, or your friends, is the matter under your control?—No, nor that, either.

Have you, then, nothing subject to your authority, which is under your control and yours only, or do you have something of that sort?—I do not know.—Look, then, at the matter this way, and consider it. No one can make you assent to what is false, can he?—No one.—Well, then, in the region of assent you are free from hindrance and restraint.—Granted.—

*Ibid., II, Book IV, Chap. I, pp. 265-73.

Come, can anyone force you to choose something that you do not want?—He can; for when he threatens me with death or bonds, he compels me to choose.—If, however, you despise death and bonds, do you pay any further heed to him?—No.—Is it, then, an act of your own to despise death, or is it not your own act?—It is mine.—So it is your own act to choose, or is it not?—Granted that it is mine.—And to refuse something? This also is yours.—Yes, but suppose I choose to go for a walk and the other person hinders me?—What part of you will he hinder? Surely not your assent?—No; but my poor body.—Yes, as he would a stone.—Granted that, but I do not proceed to take my walk.—But who told you, "It is your own act to take a walk unhindered"? As for me, I told you that the only unhindered thing was the desire; but where there is a use of the body and its co-operation, you have heard long ago that nothing is your own.—Granted that also.—Can anyone force you to desire what you do not want?—No one.—Or to purpose or plan, or, in a word, to deal with the impressions that come to you?—No, nor that, either; but he will hinder me, when I set my desire upon something, from achieving what I desire.—If you desire something which is your own and not subject to hindrance, how will he hinder you?—Not at all.—Who, then, tells you that the man who sets his desire upon what is not his own is free from hindrance?

Shall I not, then, set my desire on health?—No, not at all, nor on anything else which is not your own. For that which is not in your power to acquire or to keep is none of yours. Keep far away from it not merely your hands, but above all your desire; otherwise, you have delivered yourself into slavery, you have bowed your neck to the burden, if you admire anything that is not your own, if you conceive a violent passion for anything that is in subjection to another and mortal.—Is not my hand my own?—It is a part of you, but by nature it is clay, subject to hindrance and compulsion, a slave to everything that is stronger than you are. And why do I name you the hand? You ought to treat your whole body like a poor loaded-down donkey, as long as it is possible, as long as it is allowed; and if it be commandeered and a soldier lay hold of it, let it go, do not resist nor grumble. If you do, you will get a beating and lose your little donkey just the same. But when this is the way in which you should act as regards the body, consider what is left for you to do about all the other things that are provided for the sake of the body. Since the body is a little donkey, the other things become little bridles for a little donkey, little pack-saddles, little shoes, and barley, and fodder. Let them go too, get rid of them more quickly and cheerfully than of the little donkey itself.

Once prepared and trained in this fashion to distinguish what is not your own from what is your own possession, the things which are subject to hindrance from those which are free from it, to regard these latter as your concern, and the former as no concern of yours, diligently to keep your desire fixed on the latter, and your aversion directed toward the former, then have you any longer anyone to fear?—No one.—Of course; what is there to be fearful about? About the things that are your own, wherein is the true nature of good and evil for you? And who has authority over these? Who can take them away, who can hinder them, any more than one can hinder God? But shall you be fearful about your body and your property? About the things that are not your own? About the things that are nothing to you? And what else have you been studying, from the very outset, but how to discriminate between what is your own and what is not your own, what is under your control and what is not under your control, what is subject to hindrance and what is free from it? For what purpose did you go to the philosophers? That you might no less than before be unfortunate and miserable? You will not, then, in that case, be free from fear and perturbation. And what has pain to do with you? For fear of things anticipated becomes pain when these things are present. And what will you any longer passionately seek? For you possess a harmonious and regulated desire for the things that are within the sphere of the moral purpose, as being excellent, and as being within your reach; and you desire nothing outside the sphere of the moral purpose, so as to give place to that other element of unreason, which pushes you along and is impetuous beyond all measure.

Marcus Aurelius is at once one of the most remarkable, and one of the most attractive, of the philosophers of antiquity. He is remarkable in that, while unswervingly devoted to philosophy, he was also Emperor of Rome at, perhaps, the height of its prosperity and power. The historian Gibbon says of him, somewhat disapprovingly, that he "condescended to give lessons on philosophy, in a more public manner than was perhaps consistent with the modesty of a sage or the dignity of an emperor." But Gibbon is also obliged to admit that "his life was the noblest commentary on the precepts of Zeno. He was severe to himself, indulgent to the imperfections of others, just and beneficent to all mankind." It was sometimes said of him that his only wrong action was the appointment of his son Commodus as his successor—an action that indeed proved disastrous, but was surely forgivable.

He was born in Rome in 121 A.D., and adopted at the age of seventeen by the Emperor Antoninus Pius. His early studies were in law and rhetoric; but under the influence of Junius Rusticus, Prefect of Rome and an admirer of Epictetus, he gradually abandoned these pursuits in favor of philosophy, and the cultivation of his style in Latin in favor of plain, undecorated Greek. His reign was not without its misfortunes. In 166 the armies returning from war in Parthia and Armenia brought into Italy a disastrous bubonic plague; in the same year an invasion of Italy by German barbarians had to be repelled; and indeed the last ten years of his reign were spent in almost incessant campaigns on the northern frontiers, with an insurrection in the East, in 175, to be put down also. It appears from the manuscript of the *Meditations* that much of his writing was done in the adverse conditions of northern warfare; and it was in one of his northern camps that the Emperor died, when not yet sixty, in 180 A.D.

He was perhaps not wholly orthodox in his Stoicism. His writings suggest at least that he was by temperament both more human, and more ascetic, than the Stoic "wise man" was really required to be. The first book of his *Meditations* consists of a detailed catalogue of those from whom he had learned, and to whom he felt indebted; and in this, particularly perhaps in the tribute to his adoptive father Antoninus, it is difficult to believe that all emotional engagement is strictly suppressed. Again, though the Stoic sage should certainly have regarded the material trappings of civilization as of no significance, Marcus Aurelius seems to have been inclined to go further than this, to regard them as actually repulsive. It is as if he would have liked, not merely to be independent of worldly goods, but positively to reject them. A link may be discerned here between the later and the very earliest stages of Stoicism; for Zeno, before he came forward as a teacher on his own account, had been most strongly attracted at Athens by the Cynic doctrines, in which all the adornments of civilization were most violently condemned. However, both Marcus' asceticism of temperament and his frequent concessions to ordinary human feeling have probably increased the very large number of his later admirers. Perhaps the most interesting feature in his Meditations, apart from his very evident sincerity and the adventitious fact of their author's exalted position, is his repeated inculcation of the idea that, so far as possible, one should observe one's own actions and feelings with a no less cool and critical detachment than those of others. In this he comes close to the moral outlook of Spinoza, who also sought to provide, in the device of seeing all things *sub specie aeternitatis,* what he called a "remedy against the emotions." It seems certain that there will always be many to whom this kind of aim is repulsive; but there are few perhaps for whom it is never at some time tempting; and many again for whom it has the force of an inspiration.

The following selections are from the Meditations.*

1. Every morning repeat to thyself: I shall meet with a busybody, an ingrate, and a bully; with treachery, envy, and selfishness. All these vices have fallen to their share because they know not good and evil. But I have contemplated the nature of the good and seen that it is the beautiful; of evil, and seen that it is deformity; of the sinner, and seen that it is kindred to my own—kindred, not because he shares the same flesh and blood and is sprung from the same seed, but because he partakes of the same reason and the same spark of divinity. How then can any of these harm me? For none can involve me in the shameful save myself. Or how can I be angered with my kith and kin, or cherish hatred towards them?

For we are all created to work together, as the members

* *Thoughts,* translated by John Jackson, London and New York: Oxford University Press, 1906. The opening passage is from Book II, pp. 8-14.

of one body—feet, hands, and eyelids, or the upper and nether teeth. Whence, to work against each other is contrary to nature; —but this is the very essence of anger and aversion.

2. This thing that I call "myself" is compact of flesh, breath, and reason. Thou art even now in the throes of death; despise therefore the flesh. It is but a little blood, a few bones, a paltry net woven from nerves and veins and arteries. Consider next thy breath. What a trifle it is! A little air, and this for ever changing: every minute of every hour we are gasping it forth and sucking it in again!

Only reason is left us. Consider thus: Thou art stricken in years; then suffer it not to remain a bond-servant; suffer it not to be puppet-like, hurried hither and thither by impulses that take no thought of thy fellow-man; suffer it not to murmur at destiny in the present or look askance at it in the future.

3. The works of God are full of providence; the works of Fortune are not independent of Nature, but intertwisted and intertwined with those directed by providence. Thence flow all things. Co-factors, too, are necessity and the common welfare of the whole universe whereof thou art part. Now whatever arises from the nature of the whole, and tends to its well-being, is good also for every part of that nature. But the well-being of the universe depends on change, not merely of the elementary, but also of the compound. Let these dogmas suffice thee, if dogmas thou must have; but put off that thirst for books, and see thou die of good cheer, not with murmurs on thy lips, but blessing God truthfully and with all thy heart.

4. Bethink thee how long thou hast delayed to do these things; how many days of grace heaven hath vouchsafed thee and thou neglected. Now is the time to learn at last what is the nature of the universe whereof thou art part; what of the power that governs the universe, whereof thou art an emanation. Forget not there is a boundary set to thy time, and that if thou use it not to uncloud thy soul it will anon be gone, and thou with it, never to return again.

5. Let it be thy hourly care to do stoutly what thy hand findeth to do, as becomes a man and a Roman, with carefulness, unaffected dignity, humanity, freedom, and justice. Free thyself from the obsession of all other thoughts; for free thyself thou wilt, if thou but perform every action as though it were the last of thy life, without light-mindedness, without swerving through force of passion from the dictates of reason, without hypocrisy, without self-love, without chafing at destiny.

Thou seest how few things are needful for man to live a happy and godlike life: for, if he observe these, heaven will demand no more.

6. Abase thee, abase thee, O my soul! The time is past for exalting thyself. Man hath but a single life; and this thou hast well nigh spent, reverencing not thyself, but dreaming thy happiness is situate in the souls of others!

7. Why suffer the incidence of things external to distract thee? Make for thyself leisure to learn something new of good, and cease this endless round.—And here beware lest the wheel only reverse its motion. For fools, too, are they who have worn out their lives in action, yet never set before themselves a goal to which they could direct every impulse—nay, every thought.

8. Thou mayest search, but wilt hardly find a man made wretched through failing to read another's soul; whereas he who fails to ponder the motions of his own must needs be wretched.

9. Let me ever be mindful what is the nature of the universe, and what my own; how the latter is related to the former, and what part it is of what whole.—And forget not that there is none that can forbid thee to be ever, in deed and word, in harmony with the nature whereof thou art part.

10. Theophrastus spoke with the voice of true philosophy, when he said in his comparison of the vices—though that comparison, in itself, is popular rather than scientific—that the sins of desire are less venial than the sins of anger. For a man in anger seems to turn his back on reason through pain and a sort of unconscious spasm of the mind; while he who sins through desire—that is, because he is too weak to withstand pleasure—would appear to be grosser and more effeminate in his vice.

Hence he considered, justly and philosophically enough, that the sins of pleasure are more reprehensible than the sins of pain. For, on the whole, if you take the two sinners, the one will be found to have been driven to anger through injuries previously sustained; while the other has set out deliberately to do wrong, and been swept along by the current of his own appetites.

11. Let thy every action, word, and thought be that of one who is prepared at any moment to quit this life. For, if God exist, to depart from the fellowship of man has no terrors,— for the divine nature is incapable of involving thee in evil. But

if He exist not, or, existing, reck not of mankind, what profits it to linger in a godless, soul-less universe? But God is, and cares for us and ours. For He has put it wholly in man's power to ensure that he fall not into aught that is evil indeed; and if in the rest of things there had been anything of evil, this too would He have foreseen and enabled us all to avoid.

But how can that which makes not man evil make man's life evil? Universal nature could not have thus sinned by omission: it is omniscient, and, being omniscient, omnipotent to foresee and correct all errors; nor would it have gone so far astray, whether through lack of power or lack of skill, as to allow good and evil to befall the evil and good alike without rhyme or reason.

Rather, life and death, fame and infamy, pain and pleasure, wealth and poverty fall to the lot of both just and unjust because they are neither fair nor foul—neither good nor evil.

12. How speedily change and decay invade all things! In the universe our corporeal substance perishes; in time, its very memory. Look at the things of sense in general: in particular, the allurements of pleasure, the terrors of pain, and all the themes of vanity. Tawdry and despicable, sordid and corruptible, dead and festering are they all!—These are subjects for the intellect to ponder.—And let it ask what are they on whose plaudits and whose fancies fame depends. Let it ask what is death, and reflect that if one look solely to its nature and analyse the idea in itself, plucking off the stage-terrors in which our imagination arrays it, it will be seen to be naught but a function of Nature—and this who but a child would fear? Nay, it is not only a function of Nature but an essential to her well-being.—And let the same reason consider also, how and by what part of himself man can lay hold of God, and under what conditions that part will act for the best.

13. There is no more wretched creature than the man who is ever revolving in a circle, searching, as Pindar says, "the things of the nether realms"; ever striving to read the riddle of another's soul, ever too blind to see that it is enough to observe the godhead within him and devote himself loyally to its service. And this service is to preserve it untainted by passion, light-mindedness, or repinings at the works of God or man. For the decisions of heaven virtue bids us reverence; the deeds of men are the deeds of our kin, and as such we must love them, or, at times, perchance, pity, in that they know not the

better and the worse—a blindness blacker than that which renders darkness and light alike to us.

14. Though the years of thy life should be fixed at three thousand, with three thousand myriads more, remember that no man loses another life than the one he is living, or lives another than that he loses. Thus the longest span is equivalent to the shortest. The present belongs to all in equal measure, so that, when it is lost, the loss, too, must be the same to all. That is to say, through death we lose an infinitesimal portion of time; for we can no more lose the past and the future than be robbed of what we have not.

There are two things, then, which it behoves us to keep in mind: first, that all things from time everlasting have been alike and continue to revolve in the same orbit, so that it matters little whether a man behold the same sights for one century, or two, or through endless aeons: second, that he who dies in the fulness of years and he who is cut down in his youth are losers in like degree. It is the present alone that death tears from us, for the present is all that we have—in other words, all that we can lose.

15. Remember that all is opinion. The saying of Monimus the Cynic is evident enough—as evident as its usefulness, if we accept his jocose remark only so far as it is corroborated by truth.

16. The soul of man may debase itself in many ways, but worst of all when it degenerates, as far as in it lies, into a sort of tumour, an alien excretion on the universe. For to repine at aught that is, is a canker alien to that universal nature, in part of which are comprehended all other natures. Again, it debases itself whenever it conceives aversion for any man or opposes him with purpose of harm; of which type are the souls of those who are possessed by anger. Thirdly, whenever it is overcome by pleasure or pain. Fourthly, when it plays the hypocrite, and is false or feigned in word or deed. Fifthly, whenever it directs an energy or an impulse of itself to no certain mark, but works at random and knows not what it does; whereas, in the least of its actions, it is its duty to look towards the end. And the end of all that has life and reason is to conform to the laws of reason that obtain in the oldest of all bodies politic, the universe.

17. The measure of man's life is a point, substance a perpetual ebb and flow, sense-perception vague and shadowy, the

fabric of his whole body corruptible, the soul past searching out, fortune a whirligig, and fame the decision of unreason. In brief, the things of the body are unstable as water; the things of the soul dreams and vapours; life itself a warfare or a sojourning in a strange land. What then shall be our guide and escort? One thing, and one only—Philosophy. And true Philosophy is to observe the celestial part within us, to keep it inviolate and unscathed, above the power of pain and pleasure, doing nothing at hazard, nothing with falsehood, and nothing with hypocrisy; careless whether another do this or that, or no; accepting every vicissitude and every dispensation as coming from that place which was its own home; and at all times awaiting death with cheerfulness, in the sure knowledge that it is but a dissolution of the elements whereof every life is compound. For if to the elements themselves there is no disaster in that they are forever changing each to other, how shall we fear the change and dissolution of all? It is in harmony with nature, and naught that is evil can be in harmony with nature.

1. When the governing part within us is in harmony with nature it stands in such a relation to the course of events as enables it to adapt itself with ease to the possibilities allowed it. For it requires no specific material to work in, but its efforts to attain its purpose are conditional, and when it encounters an obstacle in lieu of what it sought it converts this into material for itself, much as a fire lays hold of the objects that fall into it. These would have sufficed to extinguish a flickering lamp, but the blazing fire in a moment appropriates the fuel heaped on it and uses it as a means whereby to mount higher and higher.

2. Do not act at random or otherwise than is prescribed by the exact canons of the art of living.

3. Men are continually seeking retreats for themselves, in the country, or by the sea, or among the hills. And thou thyself art wont to yearn after the like.—Yet all this is the sheerest folly, for it is open to thee every hour to retire into thyself. And where can man find a calmer, more restful haven than in his own soul? Most of all he whose inner state is so ordered that he has only to penetrate thither to find himself in the midst of a great peace—a peace that, to my mind, is synonymous with orderliness.

Therefore betake thee freely to this city of refuge, there to be made new. And cherish within thee a few brief and fundamental principles, such as will suffice, so soon as they recur to thee, to wash away all pain and bid thee depart in peace, repining not at the things whereto thou returnest.—For what is it that vexes thee?—The evil of man's heart?—Call to mind the doctrine that all rational beings exist for the sake each of other, that to bear and forbear is part of justice, and that men's sins are not sins of will. Reflect how many before thee have lived in enmity, suspicion, hatred, and strife and then been laid out and reduced to ashes.—Think of this and be at rest.— But, perchance, it is the lot assigned thee from the sum of things that troubles thee.—Then recall the dilemma—"Either Providence or atomic theory," and all the proofs that went to show that the universe is a constitutional state.—Maybe, the ills of the flesh will prick thee somewhat.—Then remember that the mind, when once it has withdrawn itself to itself and realized its own power, has neither part nor lot with the soft and pleasant, or harsh and painful, motions of thy breath; and ponder again the doctrines of pain and pleasure to which thou hast hearkened and assented.—Or, again, thy little meed of glory may cause thee a twinge.—Then look and see how speedily all things fall into oblivion; what a great gulf of infinite time yawns behind thee and before; how empty are the plaudits of men; how fickle and unreasoning are they who feign to praise thee, and within what narrow boundaries that praise is circumscribed. For the whole earth is but a point; and what a fraction of the whole is this corner where we dwell! Nay, how few even here—and they how insignificant!—will be thy panegyrists.

So much is left thee: forget not to retreat into this little plot of thyself. Above all, let nothing distract thee. Do not strain and struggle, but maintain thy freedom and look things in the face as befits a man and a male, a member of the state, and a mortal creature. And, among the principles which are ever most ready to hand for thee to turn to, let these two find a place: first, that things in themselves have no point of contact with the soul, but are stationed motionless without, while all unrest proceeds solely from the opinion within; second, that all the objects thou now beholdest will anon change and be no more. Think, and think often, how many changes thine own eyes have witnessed, and know that the universe is mutation, and life opinion. . . .*

1. What is evil?—It is what thou hast often seen.—Nay more, whatever may chance, let thy first reflection be: "All this have I beheld time and again." In brief, above and below —everywhere thou wilt find the self-same things that have crowded histories, ancient, mediaeval, and modern, and now crowd every city and every house. There is naught new. Everything is as trite as it is ephemeral.

7. Think it no shame to accept help. Thy work in life is to do thy duty like a soldier at the storming of a fortress. How then, if being halt and maimed thou canst not, of thyself, scale the battlements, while with another's aid thou mayest?

26. When any man sins against thee, let thy first reflection be: "With what conception of Good and Evil did he commit this sin?" When this is clear to thee, astonishment and anger will give place to pity. For if thy conception of the Good be still identical with, or similar to, his, it is a matter of duty to pardon him. But if thou hast passed the stage in which these things seem either good or ill, thou wilt be the more ready to show kindness to one who is yet in darkness.

32. Of *death*. It is but dispersal, if the universe be atomic; or, if it be unity, extinction and change.

33. Of *pain*. The pang that cannot be borne soon ends life and itself. That which drags on its course becomes bearable, the mind suspends judgement and preserves its calm, and the rational principle remains unscathed. As for the parts that suffer, let them give evidence if they can.

34. Of *glory*. Look at the minds of them that seek it, and observe their nature, with the character of the objects they pursue and flee. Reflect that as, on the seashore, one layer of sand is buried from sight under another, so in life the exploits of one age are submerged by those of the next.†

1. Injustice is impiety. For if we consider that universal Nature has created all rational beings for mutual service,— that is, to do good to their fellow-creatures in proportion to their deserts, and under no circumstances to do them harm,— it is obvious that a man who transgresses Nature's will is guilty

* *Ibid.*, Book IV, pp. 30-32.
† *Ibid.*, Book VII, pp. 57-62.

of sacrilege against the eldest of the gods. And the same sin against the same divinity is committed by the liar. For the nature of the universe is the nature of the existent, and all things existent are intimately related to each other. Now Truth is only a synonym for Nature as the first cause of all that is true. Hence deliberate falsehood is impiety, inasmuch as deception involves injustice: and involuntary falsehood is impiety, in that it is in discord with the nature of the Whole, and a revolt against order as expressed in the power that orders the world. For a man raises the standard of revolt when he betakes himself, of himself, to the antipode of truth; for he has so neglected the powers with which Nature had endowed him that now he cannot distinguish the false from the true.

Again, another form of impiety is to pursue pleasure as good and flee pain as evil. For it is inevitable that a man so acting will often murmur at the universal Nature as unfair in her dispensations to the just and the unjust, on the ground that nothing is more common than for the unjust to be surrounded with pleasures and richly endowed with means to secure them, while the just have pain and its causes for their only inheritance. Moreover, the man who fears pain must at times fear something that will come into being in the universe; and this is, *ex hypothesi*, a form of impiety. As for the man who pursues pleasure, he will not stop short of injustice in his pursuit; and injustice is flagrant impiety.

The truth is that to whatever the Nature of the universe is indifferent,—and she would not have created both pleasure and pain had she any preference for either,—to these things, I say, we who desire to follow in Nature's footsteps must show like indifference and submit our opinions to hers. It is plain, then, that whoever fails to regard pleasure and pain, life and death, fame and infamy, with the impartiality displayed by Nature in her use of them is guilty of impiety. And when I say that Nature makes impartial use of all these, I mean that they form a necessary sequel to the products and by-products of that Nature, in virtue of a certain primeval activity of Providence, when she set out, from a definite starting-point, on this work of setting all things in order, having conceived within herself certain principles of all that was to be, and determined certain powers generative of existence, transmutation, and all such succession.

14. All is the same: in experience, familiar; in time, ephem-

eral; in matter, sordid; and all in our days is as in the days of those we buried.

15. Things, as such, stand without the door, themselves by themselves, knowing nothing and speaking nothing concerning themselves. What then is it that speaks for them? Reason.

27. Let this thought be ever present to thy mind: that all that now takes place took place in time past in exactly the same fashion; and doubt not the future will see the like. Nay more, conjure up to sight whole dramas with their staging to match; —all thou hast learned from experience or the pages of history. Say, the entire courts of Hadrian and Antoninus, of Philip and Alexander or Croesus. The plays are all the same; the cast only is changed!

29. In every single act of thine pause and ask: "Is it the loss of this that lends death his terrors?"*

18. When thy neighbour sins against thee, consider first what is thy relationship to mankind, reflecting that we all exist to serve each other, and that, in especial, thy life-work is to champion thy fellow-creatures as the bull defends his herd and the ram his flock. Again, approach the matter from the first principle that, if the atomic theory is false, Nature must be the power that governs the universe; and, in this case, the worse is created for the good of the better, and the better for the good of one another.

Secondly, call to mind what manner of men these sinners are, at their tables, on their couches, and in the rest of their life. Chief of all, remember the many forms of constraint laid on them by their principles, and the foolish pride with which their very sins inspire them.

Thirdly, reflect that, if these actions of theirs are right, it is no duty of thine to take them amiss; while if they are wrong it is clear they err through ignorance, not of free-will. For as no soul is willingly deprived of truth, so neither is it willingly deprived of the power of treating every one according to his merits. Whence it comes that nothing pricks a man more than to be spoken of as unjust, cruel, avaricious, or, in a word, as a bad neighbour.

Fourthly, bethink thee thou hast vices enough of thine own, and art a sinner with the rest. True, thou holdest aloof from

* *Ibid.*, Book IX, pp. 80-99, *passim.*

certain errors, yet thy character is prone to fall into them, though cowardice, love of reputation, or some equally despicable motive may save thee from such overt commission.

Fifthly, remember thou hast no sure knowledge that they sin at all. For many acts are merely means to some hidden end, and, in general, much is to learn before one man can pronounce with certainty on the action of another.

Sixthly, when utter vexation and impatience overpower thee, take refuge in the thought that man's life is but for a moment, and anon we shall all be under the sod.

Seventhly, consider that it is not men's actions that trouble us,—for they are situate in the agent's ruling faculty,—but purely our own opinions on them. Then take this judgement of thine that pronounces this or that an object of terror, dare to cast it out, and anger vanishes with it.—"How is this to be done?" you ask.—By reflecting that another's sin is not thy dishonour. For, unless dishonour be the sole evil, it is inevitable that thou must commit untold sins and turn robber, or what not, at the same time as thy neighbour.

Eighthly, bear in mind how much harder to endure are the consequences of the anger and grief that ensue on an act than is the act itself which evoked these feelings.

Ninthly, reflect that kindliness is invincible, provided only it be genuine and not the specious grin of hypocrisy. For how can the extremity of insolence touch thee if thou preserve thy good will to the sinner, meekly admonishing him as opportunity offers and quietly pointing out the error of his ways at the very moment he is meditating thy injury? "Not so, my son; this is not the end for which we were created. True, it will harm me not; but, child, it is harming thee." And show him with tactfulness and friendliness that the case is so, and that not even the bees or the cattle in their herds act as he does. But set about thy demonstration without trace of irony or rebuke, relying simply on affection and a soul free from rancour. Neither treat him as a pedagogue treats his pupil nor strive to inspire the bystander with admiration of thy magnanimity; but, whether alone with him or in the presence of others, be gentle and unaffected.

Remember these nine rules and guard them as though they were so many gifts from the Muses. Begin even now, while life is still left thee, to be a man. But shun flattery as diligently as thou shunnest anger. Both are detrimental to the com-

munity and both lead to harm. And in anger let the thought
be ever present that indignation is not a form of courage,
but that meekness and gentleness are not only more human
but also more manly, and it is he who possesses these that has
strength, nerve and bravery, not the angry and discontented.
For, the nearer patience is to dispassionateness, by so much is
it nearer strength; and as pain is a characteristic of weakness,
so is anger. For their victims have both received their wounds
and both succumbed.

And, if thou wilt, receive this tenth gift from the Muses'
presiding god. To ask that the wicked shall not sin is an act
of madness, inasmuch as it aims at the impossible. But to
give them leave to sin against others and demand they shall
not sin against thee is not madness, but cruelty and tyranny.

36. Friend, thou hast been a citizen in this great city; and
what matters it whether for five years or three? The law is the
same for us all. Where is the hardship, then, if it be no tyrant's
stroke, no unjust judge, that sends thee into exile, but the
same Nature that brought thee hither, even as the master of
the show dismisses the mummer that he put on the stage?—
"But my rôle is unfinished. There are five acts and only the
three are gone!"—Thy words are true; but in life three acts
are all the play. For He decrees it shall end, who was once
the author of thy existence, and now of thy dissolution. But
thou art guiltless of both. Then depart at peace with all men;
for He who bids thee go is at peace with thee.*

* *Ibid.*, Book XI, pp. 108-10, 121.

CHAPTER IX

Two Minor Schools: Cynicism and Scepticism

1. Cynicism

Plato was not the only philosopher to regard himself as the heir and successor of Socrates. This claim was also put forward for himself by Antisthenes. Slightly older than Plato, he was already living in Athens as a sophist before he met Socrates, but thereafter he became Socrates' ardent disciple. That aspect of Socrates which he most fervently admired, and which left its mark later on Antisthenes' own school of Cynics, was the strength and independence of his moral character. By comparison with this quality the Cynics deliberately disparaged all learning, all refinement, all civilization even; they set themselves to ignore, or even (in the case of Diogenes) openly to flout, the customary conventions and proprieties; they determined to reject as superfluous and dispensable worldly goods, worldly positions, even freedom in the ordinary sense—for slavery, they held, can be borne with perfect tranquillity, and leaves it open to the slave to maintain his integrity and virtue. They seem at first to have been inspired, as perhaps no other group of philosophers was, with an active missionary spirit. Instead of pursuing their debates in academic seclusion, they became wandering mendicants, preaching against the shams and corruption of the world, and in favor of a simple, supposedly "natural" life in which all should be equal, the whole of mankind one family. It is plain that we have here a foretaste of Stoicism; and in fact, as Stoicism developed, the Cynics languished. Much later, their doctrines were revived, but in a weakened form. The Hellenistic Cynics, instead of preaching opposition to the forms and conventions of life, favored rather an easy adaptability to them. While still insisting on their triviality as compared with the ways of "nature," still preaching the brotherhood of man, and still disparaging learning, they were ready to approve of an uncommitted acceptance of whatever the world might offer. Wealth, strictly, was worthless; but, if one happened to be rich, one might as well act out the proper part of a rich man. Since the doctrine had never had any great theoretical backing, the later writings of Cynicism tended to become less philosophical, less argumentative, more and more a blend of exhortation and satire. The diatribes of Teles, and the essays and fables of Menippus, contributed little if anything to philosophy; but they provided, apart from the lively satire of their contents, new literary forms that were later adopted by, among many others, Seneca and Lucian.

But later Stoics retained a high respect for the Cynic philosopher. We find in Epictetus* the following words:—

And how is it possible for a man who has nothing, who is naked, without home or hearth, in squalor, without a slave, without a city, to live serenely? Behold, God has sent you the man who will show in practice that it is possible. "Look at me," he says, "I am without a home, without a city, without property, without a slave; I sleep on the ground; I have neither wife nor children, no miserable governor's mansion, but only earth, and sky, and one rough cloak. Yet what do I lack? Am I not free from pain and fear, am I not free? When has anyone among you seen me failing to get what I desire, or falling into what I would avoid? When have I ever found fault with either God or man? When have I ever blamed anyone? Has anyone among you seen me with a gloomy face? And how do I face those persons before whom you stand in fear and awe? Do I not face them as slaves? Who, when he lays eyes upon me, does not feel that he is seeing his king and his master?"

Lo, these are words that befit a Cynic, this is his character, and his plan of life.

* *Op. cit.*, II, Book III, Chap. XXII, pp. 147-48.

2. Scepticism

It seems certain, and would in any case be reasonably expected, that from the earliest days of Greek philosophy the inclination towards bold assertion was accompanied by a contrary tendency towards questioning, doubt, and sometimes despair. Among the pre-Socratics Xenophanes and Empedocles expressed occasionally the gloomy feeling that, in the welter of conflicting doctrines, it was really impossible to find any assertion deserving of full belief; and doubtless many silent members of the philosophers' audiences listened with many reservations to what they were told. But eventually scepticism itself became a doctrine. Pyrrho of Elis, who died at nearly ninety years of age in about 275 B.C., had accompanied Alexander the Great on his expedition to India. Another philosopher present on that occasion was Anaxarchus, a disciple of Metrodorus of Chios, who was in turn an exponent of the theories of Democritus. By Democritus' followers, his view of the insufficiency of mere sense perception had been given a definitely sceptical emphasis, and it may thus be that Pyrrho derived from Anaxarchus the first impulse towards that general questioning and doubt for the propagation of which, almost paradoxically, he later established a school in his native city.

Scepticism as a philosophy shared with all other post-Aristotelian doctrines the characteristic of being directly practical in intention, recommended, like the rest, as a means of achieving non-attachment, thence peace of mind, and therefore such happiness as could be expected in a dangerous world. According to Pyrrho's pupil Timon of Phlius, the nature of things is completely unknowable. If so, the only proper attitude is that of reservation of judgment. Instead, for example, of worrying himself over questions of good and evil, a man should accept with a good grace law and tradition, and find tranquillity in cool conventionality of belief and conduct. It was commonly supposed that knowledge could be acquired by deductive argument. But a deductive argument must start from premises. If these premises are supposed to be known, they must themselves be conclusions in a course of argument which, in the end, can only be circular. And if they are not supposed to be known, then nothing deduced from them can be known either. We may sometimes permit ourselves a judgment of probabilities, but the pursuit of knowledge must simply be abandoned as vain.

It appears that in later life Timon lived at Athens; and while he was there the principles of Pyrrho became evidently the official doctrine of Plato's Academy. The Academy at this time, as Tarn points out, was preoccupied with resistance to Stoicism. Its leader, Arcesilaus of Pitane, who consistently with his principles published no writings, was mainly concerned to attack the admittedly dogmatic Stoic theory of knowledge. Whereas Zeno had vehemently insisted that some "impressions" are so forceful that they compel assent and leave no room for mistake, Arcesilaus asserted that *any* "impression" might be deceptive. Unquestioning conviction was always ill-founded. He appears to have believed that in taking this sceptical line he was being faithful at least to the early Platonic position, in which Socrates is represented as disclaiming knowledge for himself and calling in question all assertions put forward by others. But according to Cicero, he held that even Socrates was mistaken, in that he purported to *know* that nothing could be known with certainty. True scepticism, as the physician Sextus Empiricus expressed it much later, was like a purgative medicine, which carries away itself along with other substances.

Distinguished among later leaders of the Academy, and also a Sceptic, was Carneades, apparently a powerful and vociferous orator, whose readiness to argue with fervor on both sides of any question aroused much excitement and some censure when, in 156 B.C., he lectured in the stern, moralistic atmosphere of Rome. But by far the most extensive and systematic exposition of Sceptical arguments was made much later, at a time when the Academy had made peace with Stoicism, and the Sceptical tradition had been supposedly purified by a return to the pure doctrine of Timon and Pyrrho—indeed revived (by Aenesidemus) after a period of near-extinction.

Sextus Empiricus, who wrote in the second half of the second century A.D., offered in three treatises a complete compendium of sceptical arguments against, in effect, all those who claimed definite knowledge in any field. He included in his attack not only, as one would expect, the philosophers of competing schools, but also mathematicians, such harmless persons as grammarians, and such relatively easy game as astrologers. His work is of some importance in the history of logic, and much of his argumentation is undeniably clever. The effect of his questioning is, however, fatally weakened by its undiscriminating and mechanical character. The reader soon comes to feel that he is resolved to question not only the genuinely questionable, but anything whatever, and that he is prepared to do this, if solid argument will not serve, by any logic-chopping device that will have the effect of producing at least temporary perplexity. There is something disagreeably prolix and pedantic in his incessant criticism, which has in the end the lack of interest of all purely destructive negation. In view of this it is hardly surprising that, although the "dogmatic" philosophers never answered the arguments marshaled by the Sceptics against them, yet these arguments seem to have made almost no effect. By most people the professional Sceptic seems never to have been taken seriously, and this is probably because it was felt that he was not fully in earnest. As Sextus himself insisted, "the Sceptic does not frame his life as a man according to the doctrine which he professes as a philosopher." And although the Sceptic would urge that this is equally true of, for instance, the Stoic, the Stoic paid to his doctrine the tribute at least of *trying* to live as that doctrine prescribed. The tranquillity of mind which it was the aim of Scepticism to provide seemed too empty an affair to tempt many adherents.

One distinguished late disciple of the Sceptical doctrine

was Lucian of Samosata, whose dialogue *Hermotimus* shows an affable Sceptic triumphing over an earnest and laborious student of Stoicism (though most of the arguments are applicable to any fixed doctrine whatever). This is, by contrast with the aridities of Sextus, an unpedantic and even entertaining piece, in which the excesses of solemn philosophy are mildly ridiculed from the standpoint of a critical, detached, easy-minded man of the world. Almost in the spirit of Gibbon, or Hume, or the Earl of Chesterfield, he advocates as suitable for a reasonable man an acceptance of the ordinary ways of the world, since the rivalries of philosophers serve only to make their devotees ill-tempered, unreasonably dogmatic, and ridiculous. There follow extracts, first from Sextus, and then from Lucian.

1. DO GOOD AND EVIL REALLY EXIST?*

Now that the Dogmatists have not described the conception of Good and Evil convincingly we have already argued; but in order to become more easily familiar with the arguments about its existence it is quite sufficient to say that, after all (as Aenesidemus used to assert), whereas all men consider that the good is what attracts them, whatever that may be, the particular views they hold about it are conflicting. And just as, although men agree (shall we say?) that comeliness of body exists yet they are at variance about the comely and beautiful woman,—the Ethiopian preferring the blackest and most snub-nosed, and the Persian approving the whitest and most hook-nosed, and someone else declaring that she who is intermediate both in feature and in colouring is the most beautiful of all,—so in the same way both laymen and philosophers share the same pre-conception and believe that good and evil exist,—good being that which attracts them and is useful, and evil that which is of the opposite nature,—but as to particular instances they are at war with one another:—

* Sextus Empiricus, *Against the Ethicists*, in *Sextus Empiricus,* translated by R. G. Bury. London: William Heinemann Ltd.; Cambridge, Mass.: Harvard University Press, 1936, III, Chap. III, pp. 405-11, 415-29. (The Loeb Classical Library.)

One thing is pleasing to one man, another thing to another. and, in the words of Archilochus,—

> Men differ as to what things cheer their hearts,

seeing that this man welcomes glory, that man wealth, another well-being, and another pleasure. And the same account applies to the philosophers. For the Academics and the Peripatetics assert that there are three classes of goods, and that some belong to the soul, some to the body, and others are external to both soul and body,—the virtues belonging to the soul, and to the body health and well-being and keenness of sense and beauty and everything which is of a similar character, and external to soul and body being wealth, country, parents, children, friends, and the like. But the Stoics, though they too declared that there are three classes of good things, yet classed them differently, saying that some of them belong to the soul, that some are external, and that some are neither psychical nor external, and eliminating the class of bodily goods as not being goods. Thus those belonging to the soul are, they say, the virtues and right actions; and external are the friend and the good man and good children and parents and the like; and neither psychical nor external is the good man in his relation to himself, for it is impossible for him to be either external to himself or psychical; for he is composed of soul and body. And there are some who are so far from eliminating the class of bodily goods that they even assign to them the most principal good; and of this sort are they who approve of carnal pleasure. But lest we may seem now to be unduly prolonging our argument in showing that the judgement of men regarding Good and Evil is discordant and conflicting, we shall base our exposition on one example only—namely health, since the discussion of this is specially familiar to us.

Health, then, is by some considered to be a good, by others not a good; and, of those who suppose it to be a good some have declared it to be the greatest good, others not the greatest; and of those who have said that it is not a good, some have counted it "a preferred indifferent," others an indifferent but not "preferred." Now that health is a good, and the prime good, has been asserted by not a few of the poets and writers and generally by all ordinary folk. Thus Simonides the lyric poet declares that "Even fair Wisdom lacks grace unless a man possesses august Health." And Licymnius, after first uttering this prelude—

Mother sublime, with eyes bright-shining,
Lov'd queen of the holy throne of Apollo,
Gently-smiling Lady of Health—

adds this lofty strain—

Where is the joy of wealth or of kindred,
Or of kingly dominion that maketh man god-like?
Nay, parted from thee can no one be blessed.

And Herophilus in his *Dietetics* affirms that wisdom cannot display itself and art is non-evident and strength unexerted and wealth useless and speech powerless in the absence of health.—Such then are the views of these men. But the Academics and Peripatetics said that health is indeed a good, but not the prime good. For they held that one ought to assign to each of the goods its own proper rank and value. . . .

Thus Crantor put health in the second place, adopting the order of the philosophers previously mentioned; but the Stoics affirmed that it is not a "good" but an "indifferent." They suppose that the term "indifferent" has three senses: in one sense it is applied to that for which there exists neither inclination nor disinclination,—such as the fact that the stars or the hairs of the head are odd in number or even; in another sense it applies to that for which there exists inclination and disinclination but not more for this thing than for that— as in the case of two drachmae indistinguishable both in markings and in brightness, when one is required to choose one of them, for there exists an inclination for one of them but no more for this one than for that. And in the third and last sense the indifferent, they say, is that which contributes neither to happiness nor to unhappiness; and indifferent in this signification, they say, are health and disease and all things of the body and most external things because they tend neither towards happiness nor towards unhappiness. For that which it is possible to use either well or ill will be indifferent; and whereas one always uses virtue well and vice ill, one can use health and the things of the body at one time well and at another ill, and consequently they will be indifferent.—And they say too that of things indifferent some are "preferred," others "rejected," others neither preferred nor rejected, and that the preferred are those which have considerable "worth," and the rejected those which have considerable "unworthiness," and that extending the finger, for example, or contracting it, and everything like that, is neither preferred nor rejected. And amongst the things preferred are ranked health and strength and beauty, wealth and glory and the like; but amongst the things rejected, sickness and poverty and pain and suchlike.—So say the Stoics; but Ariston of Chios affirmed that health, and everything of a similar kind, is not a "preferred indifferent"; for to call it a "preferred indifferent" is equivalent to claiming it to be a "good," and practically differs only in name. For, without exception, amongst the indifferent things which lie between virtue and vice there is no distinction; nor are some of them preferred, others rejected naturally, but owing to the different circumstances of the various occasions; [so that] neither are those said to be preferred inevitably preferred, nor those said to be rejected necessarily rejected. Were it, for instance, obligatory that men in sound health should serve under the tyrant and on this account be destroyed, but that the sick should be set free from that service and freed likewise from destruction, on such an occasion the wise man would choose sickness rather than health. And thus neither is health inevitably preferred nor sickness rejected. As, then, in the writing of names we place different letters first at different times, adapting them to the varying circumstances,— Delta when we are writing the name of Dion, Iota when it is Ion, Omega when it is Orion,—no one letter being preferable to the others by nature, but the occasions compelling us to act thus,—so also in the things which lie between virtue and vice there exists no natural precedence of some before others, but rather a precedence due to circumstance.

But now that we have thus shown, mainly by means of examples, that there is no agreement about the preconception regarding things good and evil, and the indifferent as well, it will be our next task to deal with the arguments of the Sceptics about the problem before us. If, then, there exists anything good by nature or anything evil by nature, this thing ought to be common to all men and be good or evil for all. For just as fire which is warmth-giving by nature warms all men, and does not warm some but chill others,—and like as snow which chills [by nature] does not chill some and warm others, but chills all alike,—so what is good by nature ought to be good for all, and not good for some but not good for others. Wherefore also Plato, in establishing that God is good by nature, argued on similar lines. For, he says, as it is the special property of heat to make hot and the property of cold to chill, so also it is the special property of good to do good; but the Good is God; therefore it is the property of God to do good. So that if there exists anything good by nature, this is good in relation to all men, and if there exists anything evil by nature, that is evil in relation to all. But there is nothing good or evil which is common to all, as we shall establish; therefore there does not exist anything good or evil by nature. For we must declare either that everything which is supposed by anyone to be good is in very truth good, or not everything. But we must not declare that everything is so; for if we should call good everything which is supposed by anyone to be good, then, since the same thing is supposed by one man to be evil, and by another good, and by yet another [is held to be] indifferent, we shall be granting that the same thing is at once both evil and good and indifferent. Epicurus, for example, asserts that pleasure is a good, but he who said "I would rather be mad than enjoy pleasure"* counted it an evil, while the Stoics say it is indifferent and not preferred; but Cleanthes says that neither is it natural nor does it possess value for life, but, like a cosmetic, has no natural existence, whereas Archedemus says that it has a natural existence, like the hairs in the armpit, but possesses no value, and Panaetius that it exists partly by nature and partly contrary to nature.—If, then, everything that seems good to anyone is altogether good, then, since pleasure seems good to Epicurus, and evil to one of the Cynics, and indifferent to the Stoic, pleasure will be at once good and evil and indifferent; but it is impossible for the same thing to be by nature opposite things,—at once good and evil and indifferent; therefore we must not declare that everything which seems good or evil to anyone is good or evil.—But if what seems good to anyone is not in all cases altogether good, we ought to be gifted with discernment and able to distinguish the difference between the supposed goods so as to declare that this thing which is supposed by this man to be good is in very truth good, whereas that thing which is supposed by that man to be good is no longer good by nature. This difference, then, comes to be perceived either through sensible evidence or through a process of reasoning.—But it cannot be through sensible evidence. For everything which causes an impression through sensible

* The Cynic Antisthenes.

experience is of such a nature as to be perceived with one accord by all in common who have their perceptions undistorted, as one may see in the case of nearly all appearances. But the same thing is not accounted good by all with one accord, but by some virtue and what partakes of virtue, by others pleasure, by others painlessness, by others something else. Therefore the really good does not impress all men through sense-evidence.—And if it is perceived by reasoning, then, since each of those persons who are held in honour in the different sects has his own peculiar reason—Zeno one by which he opined that virtue is the good, Epicurus another by which he chose pleasure, Aristotle a different one by which he chose health,—each of them likewise will introduce his own peculiar good, which is not a good by nature nor common to all. So then nothing is good by nature. For if the private good of each is not the good of all nor by nature, and besides the private good of each there exists no good upon which all are agreed, no good exists.

Moreover, if good exists, it ought to be desirable on its own account, since every man desires to obtain it even as he desires to escape evil. But, as we shall show, nothing is desirable on its own account; therefore there does not exist any good. For if there is anything desirable on its own account, either the desire itself is desirable or something other than this,—for example, either the desire for wealth is desirable or wealth itself is desirable. But the desire itself will not be desirable. For if the desire is desirable on its own account, we ought not to be eager to obtain that which we desire lest we should cease from desiring any longer. For just as [we ought to avoid] drinking or eating lest by having eaten or drunk we should cease to wish any longer to drink or eat, so, if the desire for wealth or health is desirable, we ought not to pursue after wealth or health, lest by acquiring them we cease to desire them any longer. But we do desire the acquisition of them; therefore the desire is not desirable but rather to be avoided. And just as the lover is eager to obtain his beloved that he may escape from the distress which love entails, and as the thirsty man hurries to drink that he may escape the torment of thirst, so also he who is distressed through his desire for wealth hurries to obtain wealth that he may be relieved from further desire.—But if the desirable is something other than the desire itself, it is either a thing separate from ourselves or a thing belonging to ourselves. And if it is separate from us and external, either some effect is produced in us by means of it, or no effect; as, for instance, by the friend or the good man or the child, or any other of the so-called external goods, either there is produced in us a pleasing motion and a welcome state and a delightful affection, or no such result occurs and we do not experience any different motion when we regard the friend or the child as desirable. And if absolutely no such effect is produced in us, no external thing at all will be desirable in our eyes. For how can we possibly have a desire for a thing in regard to which we feel no emotion? And besides, if the enjoyable is so conceived because we get joy from it, and the painful because we get pain, and the good because we get delight, it will follow that no desire is implanted by that which produces in us no joy nor delightful feeling nor agreeable emotion. But if there is produced in us by an external object, such as the friend or the child, a welcome state and an agreeable affection, the friend or the child will not be desirable for his own sake but for the sake of this welcome state and agreeable affection. But such a state is not an external thing but is personal to ourselves. Therefore none of the external things is desirable for its own sake or good.—Nor yet is the desirable and good one of the things personal to ourselves. For it is either solely corporeal or psychical. But it will not be solely corporeal; for if it really were solely corporeal, and no longer a psychical affection, it would elude our perception (for all perception is a property of the soul) and it would be on a par with the things which exist externally and have no fellow-feeling with us. But if the pleasure it contains extends to the soul, it will be desirable and good on account of this but not on account of its being a merely corporeal motion. For every desirable thing is judged to be so by means of a sensation or perception and not by means of an irrational body. But the sense or intelligence which apprehends the desirable is of the soul; therefore none of the things which happen to the body is desirable for its own sake and good, but, if any, those which happen to the soul; and this involves us once again in the original difficulty. For since the intelligence of each man disagrees with that of his neighbour in respect of its judgements, each must necessarily regard as good that which appears so to himself. But what appears good to each man is not good by nature. So in this way, too, nothing is good.

And the same argument applies also to evil.

2. "THE RIVAL PHILOSOPHIES."*

HERMOTIMUS: Well, it seems to me perfectly possible, Lycinus, after studying the Stoic doctrines alone, to get at the truth from them, without going through a course of all the others too. Look at it this way: if any one tells you simply, Twice two is four, need you go round all the mathematicians to find out whether there is one who makes it five, or seven; or would you know at once that the man was right?

LYCINUS: Certainly I should.

HERMOTIMUS: Then why should you think it impossible for a man who finds, without going further, that the Stoics make true statements, to believe them and dispense with further witness? He knows that four can never be five, though ten thousand Platos or Pythagorases said it was.

LYCINUS: Not to the point. You compare accepted with disputed facts, whereas they are completely different. Tell me, did you ever meet a man who said twice two was seven or eleven?

HERMOTIMUS: Not I; any one who did not make four of it must be mad.

LYCINUS: But on the other hand—try to tell the truth, I adjure you—, did you ever meet a Stoic and an Epicurean who did *not* differ about principles or ends?

HERMOTIMUS: No.

LYCINUS: You are an honest man; now ask yourself whether you are trapping a friend with false logic. We are trying to find out with whom philosophic truth lies; and you beg the question and make a present of that same truth to the Stoics; for you say (what is quite unproved) that they are the people who make twice two four; the Epicureans or Platonists would say that *they* bring out that result, whereas you get five or seven. Does it not amount to that, when your school reckon goodness the only end, and the Epicureans pleasure? or again when you say everything is material, and Plato recognizes an immaterial element also in all that exists? As I said, you lay hold of the thing in dispute, as though it were the admitted property of the Stoics, and put it into their hands, though the others claim it and maintain that it is theirs; why, it is the

* Lucian, *Hermotimus*, 35-39, 47-57, 83-86, in *The Works of Lucian of Samosata*, translated by H. W. and F. G. Fowler. Oxford: The Clarendon Press, 1905, Vol. II.

very point at issue. If it is once established that Stoics have the monopoly of making four out of twice two, it is time for the rest to hold their tongues; but as long as they refuse to yield that point, we must hear all alike, or be prepared for people's calling us partial judges.

HERMOTIMUS: It seems to me, Lycinus, you do not understand what I mean.

LYCINUS: Very well, put it plainer, if it is something different from that.

HERMOTIMUS: You will see in a minute. Let us suppose two people have gone into the temple of Asclepius or Dionysus, and subsequently one of the sacred cups is missing. Both of them will have to be searched, to see which has it about him.

LYCINUS: Clearly.

HERMOTIMUS: Of course one of them has it.

LYCINUS: Necessarily, if it is missing.

HERMOTIMUS: Then, if you find it on the first, you will not strip the other; it is clear he has not got it.

LYCINUS: Quite.

HERMOTIMUS: And if we fail to find it on the first, the other certainly has it; it is unnecessary to search him that way either.

LYCINUS: Yes, he has it.

HERMOTIMUS: So with us; if we find the cup in the possession of the Stoics, we shall not care to go on and search the others; we have what we were looking for; why trouble further?

LYCINUS: There is no why, if you really find it, and can be certain it is the missing article, the sacred object being unmistakable. But there are some differences in this case, friend; the temple-visitors are not two, so that if one has not got the booty the other has, but many; and the identity of the missing object is also uncertain; it may be cup, or bowl, or garland; every priest gives a different description of it; they do not agree even about the material; bronze, say these, silver, say those—anything from gold to tin. So there is nothing for it but to strip the visitors, if you want to find it; even if you discover a gold cup on the first man, you must go on to the others.

HERMOTIMUS: What for?

LYCINUS: Because it is not certain that the thing was a cup. And even if that is generally admitted, they do not all agree that it was gold; and if it is well known that a gold cup is missing, and you find a gold cup on your first man, even so you are not quit of searching the others; it is not clear that this is *the* sacred cup; do you suppose there is only one gold cup in the world?

HERMOTIMUS: No, indeed.

LYCINUS: So you will have to go the round, and then collect all your finds together and decide which of them is most likely to be divine property.

For the source of all the difficulty is this: every one who is stripped has something or other on him, one a bowl, one a cup, one a garland, which again may be bronze, gold, or silver; but whether the one he has is the sacred one, is not yet clear. It is absolutely impossible to know which man to accuse of sacrilege; even if all the objects were similar, it would be uncertain who had robbed the God; for such things may be private property too. Our perplexity, of course, is simply due to the fact that the missing cup—assume it to be a cup—has no inscription; if either the God's or the donor's name had been on it, we should not have had all this trouble; when we found the inscribed one, we should have stopped stripping and inconveniencing other visitors. . . .

Never despair; I fancy I have found something to hold on to and escape.

HERMOTIMUS: And what is that?

LYCINUS: It is not original; I borrow it from one of the wise men: "Be sober and doubt all things," says he. If we do not believe everything we are told, but behave like jurymen who suspend judgement till they have heard the other side, we may have no difficulty in getting out of the labyrinths.

HERMOTIMUS: A good plan; let us try it.

LYCINUS: Very well, which shall we start with? However, that will make no difference; we may begin with whomsoever we fancy, Pythagoras, say; how long shall we allow for learning the whole of Pythagoreanism? and do not omit the five years of silence; including those, I suppose thirty altogether will do; or, if you do not like that, still we cannot put it lower than twenty.

HERMOTIMUS: Put it at that.

LYCINUS: Plato will come next with as many more, and then Aristotle cannot do with less.

HERMOTIMUS: No.

LYCINUS: As to Chrysippus, I need not ask you; you have told me already that forty is barely enough.

HERMOTIMUS: That is so.

LYCINUS: And we have still Epicurus and the others. I am not taking high figures, either, as you will see if you reflect upon the number of octogenarian Stoics, Epicureans, and Platonists who confess that they have not yet completely mastered their own systems. Or, if they did not confess it, at any rate Chrysippus, Aristotle, and Plato would for them; still more Socrates, who is as good as they; he used to proclaim to all comers that, so far from knowing all, he knew nothing whatever, except the one fact of his own ignorance. Well, let us add up. Twenty years we gave Pythagoras, the same to Plato, and so to the others. What will the total come to, if we assume only ten schools?

HERMOTIMUS: Over two hundred years.

LYCINUS: Shall we deduct a quarter of that, and say a hundred and fifty will do? or can we halve it?

HERMOTIMUS: You must decide about that; but I see that, at the best, it will be but few who will get through the course, though they begin philosophy and life together.

LYCINUS: In that case, what are we to do? Must we withdraw our previous admission, that no one can choose the best out of many without trying all? We thought selection without experiment a method of inquiry savouring more of divination than of judgement, did we not?

HERMOTIMUS: Yes.

LYCINUS: Without such longevity, then, it is absolutely impossible for us to complete the series—experiment, selection, philosophy, Happiness. Yet anything short of that is a mere game of blindman's-buff; whatever we knock against and get hold of we shall be taking for the thing we want, because the truth is hidden from us. Even if a mere piece of luck brings us straight to it, we shall have no grounded conviction of our success; there are so many similar objects, all claiming to be the real thing.

HERMOTIMUS: Ah, Lycinus, your arguments seem to me more or less logical, but—but—to be frank with you—I hate to hear you going through them and wasting your acuteness. I suspect it was in an evil hour that I came out to-day and met you; my hopes were almost in my grasp; and now here are you plunging me into a slough of despond with your demonstrations; truth is undiscoverable, if the search needs so many years.

LYCINUS: My dear friend, it would be much fairer to blame your parents, Menecrates and whatever your mother's name may have been—or indeed to go still further back to human nature. Why did not they make you a Tithonus for years and durability? instead of which, they limited you like other men to a century at the outside. As for me, I have only been helping you to deduce results.

HERMOTIMUS: No, no; it is just your way; you want to crow over me; you detest philosophy—I cannot tell why—and poke fun at philosophers.

LYCINUS: Hermotimus, I cannot show what truth is, so well as wise people like you and your professor; but one thing I do know about it, and that is that it is not pleasant to the ear; falsehood is far more esteemed; it is prettier, and therefore pleasanter; while Truth, conscious of its purity, blurts out downright remarks, and offends people. Here is a case of it: even you are offended with me for having discovered (with your assistance) how this matter really stands, and shown that our common object is hard of attainment. Suppose you had been in love with a statue and hoped to win it, under the impression that it was human, and I had realized that it was only bronze or marble, and given you a friendly warning that your passion was hopeless—you might just as well have thought I was your enemy then, because I would not leave you a prey to extravagant and impracticable delusions.

HERMOTIMUS: Well, well; are we to give up philosophy, then, and idle our lives away like the common herd?

LYCINUS: What have I said to justify that? My point is not that we are to give up philosophy, but this: whereas we are to pursue philosophy, and whereas there are many roads, each professing to lead to philosophy and Virtue, and whereas it is uncertain which of these is the true road, therefore the selection shall be made with care. Now we resolved that it was impossible out of many offers to choose the best, unless a man should try all in turn; and then the process of trial was found to be long. What do *you* propose?—It is the old question again. To follow and join philosophic forces with whomsoever you first fall in with, and let him thank Fortune for his proselyte?

HERMOTIMUS: What is the good of answering your questions? You say no one can judge for himself, unless he can devote the life of a phoenix to going round experimenting; and on the other hand you refuse to trust either previous experience or the multitude of favourable testimony.

LYCINUS: Where is your multitude, with knowledge and ex-

Romans had not, a large and splendid literature; they had living philosophical schools and traditions; in every department of science and art they were exclusive possessors of the knowledge and *expertise* of the age. The Romans had sense enough to wish to preserve and make use of this imposing culture. They accepted, for all purposes of higher education, the use of the Greek language, and frequently, almost pathetically, adopted without question that grand division of the human race into "Greeks and barbarians" which, centuries earlier, had seemed proper to the Greeks at the height of their power. There has probably never occurred before or since, if we except the case of Christianity, so striking an instance of the cultural conquest of military conquerors. Anxious Roman patriots did, from time to time, attempt by decree to keep encroaching Hellenism at any rate out of Rome itself, but such efforts had no chance of long-run success. That Marcus Aurelius, the Emperor of Rome, should have spent much of his time expounding, in Greek, a Greek system of philosophy, would no doubt have horrified some of the early Roman statesmen; but the continuing pre-eminence of Greek culture made it in fact an entirely natural thing for him to do.

The history of philosophical schools in Roman times is a somewhat curious one. The rival traditions of Zeno and Epicurus stand out together for centuries as dominant over all others; but Stoicism, which certainly came to be the characteristic philosophy of the Roman empire, appears to have lagged far behind Epicureanism in the republican period. Cicero, writing in the last days of the republic, gives the impression that this latter system alone was widely popular and generally known, and indeed that it had at that time no effective competitor. The Stoics, it appears, were less skillful at popularization; but it may be true too that, at that particular time, the conditions that prevailed were just those in which Epicureanism might flourish. The last century of the Roman republic was a period, on the whole, of incessant violence and confusion. The domestic politics of Rome were peculiarly embittered, and her ill-governed empire also was in constant peril.

Private fortunes, though sometimes very large, were hardly ever secure, and life itself was precarious even in the streets of Rome. In such conditions the essential moderation of Epicurus, his attempt to make the best of an unambitious, purely private existence, may well have exerted upon many a powerful appeal; it was indeed in very similar circumstances that the doctrine had originally come into being. By contrast the more positive, more active principles of the Stoics may have seemed unattractive to those whose faith in well-meant action had been shaken by too frequent disappointments. This is not to deny, of course, that many successful men of action were also, at that time, Epicureans.

If this were so, we could perhaps also account for the apparently swift change in the position at a later date. After the defeat of Antony at Actium in 31 B.C., the government of the first emperor, Augustus, brought to the world a condition of comparative order and stability such as had been unknown for many decades before. Almost at once the tone of Roman life became stronger, but also more constrained. There was indeed a new enthusiasm for public affairs, a general readiness to labor for the new and beneficent *régime;* but with this there went a constant pressure of official propaganda, moralistic, traditionally religious, rather stiffly self-righteous. In this atmosphere the taste of the Romans for intellectual inquiry, never marked at any time, fell practically to zero, while their devotion to duty, particularly the duties of public life, received every encouragement. Thus Stoicism, in which purely theoretical and scientific doctrine had never been so important as in the system of Epicurus, and in which conversely the stern preaching of virtue had always bulked large, became inevitably the favored philosophy of the day. At the same time the main motive towards Epicureanism— distrust of the perils and treacheries of the great world— was substantially diminished. It would be hard to deny that the resulting tendency towards a somewhat incurious, unimaginative moralizing represents a general decline in philosophy, though Stoic philosophers of a kind were still popular enough. So popular were they, indeed, that for many years controversy almost died out; the doctrines of philosophy were not felt to be matters of dispute, and the emphasis shifted instead onto the personality of the philosopher. It is worth observing too that this prevalent tendency was hostile, on the whole, to literature and to culture in general; the true Stoic regarded all that was not simple virtue as frivolity. We may remember that Marcus Aurelius, when he decided to devote himself seriously to philosophy, felt that this involved the deliberate rejection of those literary arts and interests in which he had been educated.

When Marcus Aurelius, the philosophical emperor, died, the dominance of Stoicism also began rapidly to decline. This decline may well have been connected with a general change for the worse in the conditions of life. The empire henceforward was in almost continuous peril from the pressure of barbarian hordes upon its frontiers. Total failure to solve the problem of orderly succession makes the history of later emperors one of violence, assassination, and civil conflict. It is from this period that Gibbon dates the "decline and fall" of Roman power; and indeed, in considering it, one cannot help feeling that, in spite of the temporary successes of exceptional administrators or military commanders, the downfall of Rome had by this time become inevitable. Furthermore, this seems to have been keenly felt at the time. Roman civilization not only was, but also knew itself to be, in decline; and the literature of the third century A.D. is full, in the pages of both pagan and Christian writers, of prophecies of doom. A striking feature of this unhappy period was a very strange but most vigorous revival of religious feeling. The old Roman pantheon, already almost identified with the Greek, was now subjected—not for the first time—to the encroachment of a number of deities and sets of deities from the East; and, in Rome particularly, a vast number of cults were practiced side by side in mutual toleration, often with the idea that all were perhaps mere variants on some single, vaguely conceived true worship. (Christianity alone not only rejected the divinity of other gods, but actually regarded the gods of other religions as evil demons. It was partly owing to this fervent exclusiveness that the Christians were apt to be singled out for persecution.) Inevitably, this widespread religiosity involved much that we should now consider to be gross superstition. Uncritical belief in so large a number of unseen powers ensured profits for those who purported to communicate with them, and astrology indeed held the place of "the queen of the sciences."

All this being so, it is perhaps not surprising that the next—and last—development in Greek philosophy should have been markedly otherworldly and mystical in character, as complete a break as could be with the morally directed materialism of the Stoics, and the scientifically based moral sobriety of Epicurus. This development took the form, ostensibly, of a return to Plato.

It was regarded as a return to Plato, not to the doctrines of the Academy. It was mentioned earlier that, after Plato's death, the Academy was for a time a center of Scepticism. Later still, in the first century B.C., it became eclectic, its leader Antiochus explicitly contending that between Academic, Stoic, and Peripatetic doctrines there was no real disagreement. This sort of view was all too tempting at a time when genuine intellectual interest was at a low level. It suits very well, for example, with the rather lazy, literary refinement of Cicero, who liked to think of himself as a Neo-Academic. It is probable that the weakness of the Academy at this period was partly due to the fact that Plato himself, being a real philosopher, had never laid down any Platonic dogma. His dialogues certainly would afford small comfort to those more eager for a doctrine than for intellectual stimulation. Apuleius of Madaura, near the end of the first century A.D., wrote a Latin work *De Platone et Ejus Dogmate,* but he was more a rhetorician than a philosopher. A later attempt was made, in the second century, by Atticus to rescue the school from its excessive eclecticism; but Plotinus, the great figure of so-called Neo-Platonism, never regarded himself as an adherent of the Academy. His immediate teacher was an Alexandrian, Ammonius Saccas, apparently a self-taught philosopher; and in his own work he owed more, as will become clear, to the Neo-Pythagoreans, whose singular numerological metaphysics was a development of that aspect of Pythagoreanism which had chiefly influenced Plato himself. They appear to have regarded Pythagoras as a divine being—a status which he shared, in their view, with certain numbers also, particularly one, three, and ten.

CHAPTER XI

Plotinus

Plotinus was born in 204 or 205 A.D., in Egypt, perhaps at Lycopolis, though this is uncertain. He was educated at Alexandria, and seems to have attended there the discourses of various philosophers until, at the age of twenty-eight, he fell in with Ammonius Saccas. Ammonius wrote nothing, and the content of his teaching is quite uncertain; but Plotinus became his eager disciple, and remained under his instruction for about ten years. He next embarked upon an enterprising attempt to investigate the philosophy of the East, by accompanying an expedition of the Emperor Gordian into Persia; but in 244 the young emperor was assassinated, whereupon Plotinus made his way, with some difficulty, to Rome. He lived and taught there for the rest of his life, soon achieving celebrity, and being favored particularly by the Emperor Gallienus, who, according to Gibbon, allowed philosophy and other diversions to interfere with the proper discharge of his imperial duties. Plotinus died in 269 or 270 A.D. It is remarkable that, although he thus lived through one of the most confused, unhappy periods of the Roman empire, his philosophy appears to be quite unrelated to any of the great social, political, or even moral issues of his time—unless, indeed, its marked unworldly character is a kind of negative response to the gloomy condition of his world. But in this respect Plotinus was not exceptional; aversion from the world was a very general feature of the culture of his century.

The philosophy of Plotinus is not, I believe, capable of precise expression; at some crucial points it tends to dissolve into mysticism, and so into a more or less admitted attempt to say the unsayable. However, it may be possible to convey some notion of his leading ideas, even if their articulation must be left obscure.

Plotinus, like the Pythagoreans, had a high respect for the number three; and he makes great use of threefold distinctions. In particular he distinguishes in man Body, Soul and Spirit; and he distinguishes also, corresponding to these, the world as perceived by the senses, the world as a spatial and temporal order, and the spiritual world. (The word "spiritual" is not ideal here; Plotinus' own word implies a reference rather to intelligence, or reason; I accept, however, what has become the conventional translation.) His position is, of course, in very sharp contrast with that of the Stoics or Epicureans, fervently anti-materialist; and in this respect it contains elements which are somewhat hard to reconcile. On the one hand Plotinus certainly wishes to say that Matter—in human beings, the body—is evil and a cause of evil; but also he appears at times to imply that Matter is a pure illusion. But must not what is positively evil be at least real? The fact is that, like most metaphysicians, Plotinus makes a very curious use of the notion of "reality"; he is prepared, that is, to say that matter is "unreal," without thereby intending to deny that (in the ordinary sense) it really exists. In this, of course, he follows Plato, who had certainly held that the Forms alone are really real, while not actually denying the existence of ordinary objects. "Unreality" becomes in this way a term of condemnation, not one that implies nonexistence.

Part of Plotinus' objection to Matter appears to be that, abstractly considered, it is formless or indeterminate; it is something that *can* be this or that in particular, but in itself has no determinate character. (It can, none the less, be positively bad, for any particular thing of which Matter is an element is held to be, to that extent, the worse.) The world of spatially and temporally ordered objects and events is regarded as superior to Matter, in that it is in many ways fully determinate; but the world thus considered is also condemned by Plotinus as no more than an appearance, at best an extremely imperfect counterpart of the real spiritual (intelligible) world. Following Plato again, he regards this imperfection of the world as carrying with it imperfection in our knowledge; about this world he says, as Plato had said, we can achieve no more than "opinion."

This world, according to Plotinus, is the product of "Nature" acting upon indeterminate Matter. "Nature" he conceives as a real spiritual power, though it is the "lowest" in the scale of real existences, and vitiated in a sense by its necessary association with Matter. He speaks of it thus:*

If, before embarking on the serious discussion of Nature, we were to say, speaking lightly, that all living beings, not only rational but irrational, and all vegetables and the earth which produces them, aspire to contemplation and look to this end, and attain to it as far as in them lies; and that some of them arrive truly at contemplation, while others achieve only a reflexion and image of it, would anyone accept so paradoxical a statement? But now that we are discussing the matter among ourselves, there is no objection to our maintaining this paradox in play. Are not we ourselves contemplating while thus playing? And not ourselves only, but all who play, are not they doing the same and aspiring to contemplation? One might say that the child at play, as well as the man in earnest, has the same end, to arrive at contemplation; and that all action earnestly aims at contemplation. Necessary action turns contemplation chiefly towards external things; that which is called free does this less, but itself too exists through desire of contemplation. But we will deal with this subject later. Let us begin by explaining what kind of contemplation may be attributed to the earth, to trees and plants, and how we can ascribe the products and progeny of the earth to the activity of contemplation; how, in a word, Nature, which is regarded as void of reason and imagination, has a power of contemplation in itself and produces all its works in virtue of a power of contemplation which, strictly speaking, it does not possess.

Nature evidently has neither feet nor hands, nor any artificial or natural instrument. It only needs Matter, on which it

* Third Ennead, eighth book, quoted in W. R. Inge, *The Philosophy of Plotinus*, 3rd edition, London and New York: Longmans, Green and Company, 1929, I, pp. 156-60.

works, and to which it gives a Form. The works of Nature are not produced by any mechanical operation. It is not by impulsion, nor by levers and machines that it produces the various colours and forms of objects. Even workers in wax, whose mode of working is often compared with that of Nature, can only give to the objects which they make colours which they bring from elsewhere. We must also remark that these craftsmen have in them a power which remains unmoved, in virtue of which alone they manufacture their works. In the same way there is in Nature a power which remains unmoved, but needs no assistance of hands. This power remains entirely unmoved; it does not need some parts which move and others which do not move. Matter alone is moved; the formative power does not move at all. If the formative power were moved, it would not be the first mover; the first mover would then not be Nature, but that which would be immovable in the whole. No doubt, it may be said, the seminal Reason is immovable; but Nature is distinct from Reason, and does move. But if we speak of Nature in its entirety, we include Reason. If any part of it is immovable, that part will be Reason. Nature must be a form, not a composite of matter and form. . . . In animals and plants, it is the Reasons which produce; Nature is a Reason which produces another Reason, which is its offspring and that on which it works, while remaining itself. The Reason which consists in the visible form holds the last rank; it is dead and cannot produce yet another Reason. The living Reason, being brother of the Reason which produced the visible form, and possessing the same form as that Reason, produces alone in the created being.

How then can Nature produce, and, so producing, to what contemplation can it attain? Since it produces while remaining immovable in itself, and is a Reason, it must itself be a contemplation. Every action is produced according to a Reason, and in consequence differs from it. Reason assists and presides over action, and in consequence is not itself action. Since then it is not action, it must be contemplation. In every chain of reasoning, the last link proceeds from contemplation, and is contemplation in the sense that it has been contemplated. As for the previous link, this may be not Nature but Soul, or again it may be in Nature and be Nature.

Does Reason considered as Nature proceed from contemplation? Certainly; but has it not also contemplated itself? For it is the product of contemplation and of a contemplator. How does it contemplate itself? It has not that kind of contemplation which comes from discursive consideration of what one has. How comes it that being a living Reason, a productive power, it does not consider what it has in itself? It is that one only so considers what one has not got yet. Now, as Nature does possess, it produces because it possesses. To be what it is and to produce what it produces are for Nature the same thing. It is contemplation and the object contemplated because it is Reason. Being contemplation, the object contemplated, and Reason, it produces in virtue of being these things. Production then has been proved to be contemplation; for it is the result of the contemplation, which remains unmovable, which does nothing but contemplate, and which produces in virtue of being contemplation.

If anyone were to demand of Nature why it produces, it would answer, if it were willing to listen and speak: "You should not ask questions, but understand, keeping silence as I keep silence; for I am not in the habit of talking. What ought you to understand? In the first place, that which is produced is the work of my silent contemplation, a contemplation produced by my nature; for being born myself of contemplation, I am naturally contemplative; and that which contemplates in me produces an object of contemplation, as geometers describe figures while contemplating. I, however, do not describe figures, but while I contemplate I let fall, as it were, the lines which mark the forms of bodies. I preserve the disposition of my mother and of the principles which produced me. These too were born of contemplation; and I was born in the same way. They produced me without acting, by virtue of being more potent reasons and contemplating themselves." What do these words mean? That Nature is a Soul engendered by a superior Soul which possesses a more powerful life, and that its silent contemplation is contained in itself, without inclining either to what is above or to what is beneath itself. Remaining in its essence, in its own stability and self-consciousness, it beheld, by this understanding and self-consciousness, that which is below itself, so far as this is possible, and without seeking further produced a brilliant and pleasing object of contemplation. And if anyone wishes to attribute to Nature a kind of understanding or sensation, these will only resemble the knowledge and sensation which we attribute to other things as those of a man asleep resemble those of a man awake. For Nature contemplates its object peaceably, an object born of itself from the fact of its abiding in and with itself, and of its being itself an object of contemplation—a contemplation silent, but feeble. For there is another power which contemplates more clearly; Nature is only the image of a higher contemplation. For this reason that which it produces is altogether weak, because a weak contemplation engenders a weak object.

Consistently of course with his idea that the natural world is an "appearance" only, Plotinus denies the reality of Space and Time. He held however (like Leibniz and Spinoza) that there are real features of reality which appear to us in this guise; he says too that they do so necessarily, "by nature." The "cosmos known to sense" is only the "similitude of the Divine," but its spatial and temporal character is still necessary to it. "To bring this cosmos into existence, Soul laid aside its timelessness and clothed itself with Time. . . . Nature, wishing to become its own mistress and to enter into possession of itself, and to enlarge the sphere of its activities, put itself, and Time together with itself, into motion." Nevertheless, Plotinus holds that it would be demonstrably impossible to deny the existence, beyond or, as he often says, "before" the world of Space and Time, of what is neither spatially extended nor subject to the temporal process.

Are there then, in Plotinus' view, two worlds, one perceived by sense, the other intelligible only? Here it is hard to avoid saying "Yes and No." Certainly, he often speaks of "Here" and "There," as if referring to two distinct places; and very many of his metaphors imply also a similar dualism. On the other hand, he certainly did not believe in two *real* worlds; for only the "spiritual" world is asserted to be real. Nevertheless, he held that the "unreal" world of perception is in some sense *necessary* to the spiritual world; it is a confused manifestation of it, without which the spiritual world would have remained "hidden." The world of perception flows from the spiritual world, like light from an unvarying, undiminishing source. It is not *all* evil, for in some degree it retains the character of the world that is its "pattern." "In order to look downward, the Soul must have forgotten the spiritual world; but if it has forgotten it, how can it create the world? Where could it find its pattern, exc t from what it saw There? But if it remembers the spiritual world in creating, it does not look downwards at all."

What is this notion of "the Soul" in our last quotation? It is for Plotinus the intermediary between his "two worlds." "Besides its spiritual character, Soul has another character, in which its proper nature consists. By looking up to that which is above itself, it sees the spiritual world; by recalling its gaze to itself, it maintains its own life; by looking down at that which is below itself, it adorns, administers, and governs it." Though the soul of each individual man is itself a true individual, not *merely* part of the Soul of the World, yet it is in the Universal Soul that the true character of human souls is made clear:—

The Soul ought first to examine its own nature to know whether it has the faculty of contemplating spiritual things, and whether it has indeed an eye wherewith to see them, and if it ought to embark on the quest. If the spiritual world is foreign to it, what is the use of trying? But if there is a kinship between us and it, we both can and ought to find it. First then let every Soul consider that it is the universal Soul which created all things, breathing into them the breath of life—into all living things which are on earth, in the air, and in the sea, and the Divine stars in heaven, the sun, and the great firmament itself. The Soul sets them in their order and directs their motions, keeping itself apart from the things which it orders and moves and causes to live. The Soul must be more honourable than they, since they are born and perish as the Soul grants them life and leaves them; but the Soul lives for ever and never ceases to be itself. But how is life imparted, in the whole and in individuals? The Great Soul must be contemplated by another Soul, itself no small thing, but one that makes itself worthy to contemplate the Great Soul by ridding itself, through quiet recollection, of deceit and of all that bewitches vulgar souls. For it let all be quiet; not only the body which encompasses it, and the tumult of the senses; but let all its environment be at peace. Let the earth be quiet and the sea and air, and the heaven itself waiting. Let it observe Soul flows in from all sides into the resting world, pours into it, penetrates it and illumines it. Even as the bright beams of the sun enlighten a dark cloud and give it a golden border, so the Soul when it enters into the body of the heaven gives it life and immortality and awakens it from sleep. So the world, guided in an eternal movement by the Soul which directs it with intelligence, becomes a living and blessed being; and the heaven, after the Soul has made it her habitation, becomes a thing of worth, after being, before the advent of the Soul, a dead body, mere earth and water, or rather darkness of Matter and no thing, "hated by the gods," as the poet says. The power and nature of the Soul are revealed still more clearly, if we consider how it encompasses and guides the heaven by its own will. It gives itself to every point in this vast body, and vouchsafes its being to every part, great and small, though these parts are divided in space and manner of disposition, and though some are opposed to each other, others dependent on each other. But the Soul is not divided, nor does it split up in order to give life to each individual. All things live by the Soul in its entirety; it is all present everywhere, like the Father which begat it, both in its unity and in its universality. The heaven, vast and various as it is, is one by the power of the Soul, and by it is this universe of ours Divine. The sun too is Divine, being the abode of Soul, and so are the stars; and we ourselves, if we are worth anything, are so on account of the Soul; for "a dead corpse is viler than dung." But if it is to the Soul that the gods owe their divinity, the Soul itself must be a God higher than the gods. Now our Soul is of one form with the universal Soul; and if you remove from it all that is adventitious, and consider it in its state of purity, you will see how precious the essence of the Soul is, far more precious than anything bodily. . . .*

Inevitably, the "spiritual world" of Plotinus baffles precise description; for the descriptive vocabulary that we employ embodies categories and distinctions drawn from the world of sense perception, which are essentially *not* to be applied to the spiritual world. Accordingly we have to make do with apparent contradictions: "The perceiving spirit must be one and two, simple and not simple"; we

* Inge, *op. cit.*, pp. 205-07.

must, yet we also cannot, distinguish between Spirit, and that real world which Spirit perceives—"each is Spirit and Being, and the whole is all Spirit and all Being." In a sense there are "no separations in the world of Spirit. . . . There, all things are together and yet remain distinct, as the Soul may know many different things without any confusion." Individual spirits—souls in their highest aspects—may come to inhabit this spiritual world, where "they have Truth for mother, nurse, real being, nourishment; they see all things, not those that are born and die, but those that have real being; and they see themselves in others. For them all things are transparent, and there is nothing dark and impenetrable . . . ; for light is manifest to light." The spiritual world, and all that exists therein, is timeless; the notions of past, present, future have no application to it; it is, in that sense, eternal.

Finally, Plotinus seeks to transcend even the spiritual world. For *in a sense* that world contains still an unresolved complexity, *some* distinction between Spirit itself and what Spirit perceives. But "if they are two, we must find that which is before this duality." What is this? Here Plotinus answers, remotely echoing Plato, that this last thing, the thing "beyond existence," is "the One." Of the One, Plotinus holds consistently enough that, strictly, nothing can be said—unless, as in the manner of some theologians, we confine ourselves to saying what the One is *not*. Nevertheless, he certainly holds that there is some sense in which the One is the cause of all that is, and also that towards which all things should strive; and in general he does say, though certainly somewhat darkly, a good deal about the One, much of which is echoed, and indeed in some cases reproduced, in early Christian theological writing about God. Moreover, Plotinus believed that, on rare occasions, direct intuition of the One might be attained, and indeed that he had at times attained it himself. Of this experience he gives* an eloquent description, couched in the curiously unvarying language of mysticism in any period:—

* Inge, *op. cit.* II, pp. 134-36.

For that which we seek to behold is the light which gives us light, even as we can only see the sun by the light of the sun. How then can this come to us? Strip thyself of everything.

We must not be surprised that that which excites the keenest of longings is without any form, even spiritual form, since the Soul itself, when inflamed with love for it, puts off all the form which it had, even that which belongs to the spiritual world. For it is not possible to see it, or to be in harmony with it, while one is occupied with anything else. The Soul must remove from itself good and evil and everything else, that it may receive the One alone, as the One is alone. When the Soul is so blessed, and is come to it, or rather when it manifests its presence, when the Soul turns away from visible things and makes itself as beautiful as possible and becomes like the One; (the manner of preparation and adornment is known to those who practise it;) and seeing the One suddenly appearing in itself, for there is nothing between, nor are they any longer two, but one; for you cannot distinguish between them, while the vision lasts; it is that union of which the union of earthly lovers, who wish to blend their being with each other, is a copy. The Soul is no longer conscious of the body, and cannot tell whether it is a man or a living being or anything real at all; for the contemplation of such things would seem unworthy, and it has no leisure for them; but when, after having sought the One, it finds itself in its presence, it goes to meet it and contemplates it instead of itself. What itself is when it gazes, it has no leisure to see. When in this state the Soul would exchange its present condition for nothing, no, not for the very heaven of heavens; for there is nothing better, nothing more blessed than this. For it can mount no higher; all other things are below it, however exalted they be. It is then that it judges rightly and knows that it has what it desired, and that there is nothing higher. For there is no deception there; where could one find anything truer than the True? What it says, that it is, and it speaks afterwards, and speaks in silence, and is happy, and is not deceived in its happiness. Its happiness is no titillation of the bodily senses; it is that the Soul has become again what it was formerly, when it was blessed. All the things which once pleased it, power, wealth, beauty, science, it declares that it despises; it could not say this if it had not met with something better than these. It fears no evil, while it is with the One, or even while it sees him; though all else perish around it, it is content, if it can only be with him; so happy is it.

The Soul is so exalted that it thinks lightly even of that spiritual intuition which it formerly treasured. For spiritual perception involves movement, and the Soul now does not wish to move. It does not call the object of its vision Spirit, although it has itself been transformed into Spirit before the vision and lifted up into the abode of Spirits. When the Soul arrives at the intuition of the One, it leaves the mode of spiritual perception. Even so a traveller, entering into a palace, admires at first the various beauties which adorn it; but when the Master appears, he alone is the object of attention. By continually contemplating the object before him, the spectator sees it no more. The vision is confounded with the object seen, and that which was before object becomes to him the state of seeing, and he forgets all else. The Spirit has two powers. By one of them it has a spiritual perception of what is within itself, the other is the receptive intuition by which it perceives what is above itself. The former is the vision of the thinking Spirit, the latter is the Spirit in love. For when the Spirit is inebriated with the nectar, it falls in love, in simple contentment and satisfaction; and it is better for it to be so intoxicated than to be too proud for such intoxication.

The philosophy of Plotinus was the last great effort of the Greek genius; it was succeeded by, and powerfully influenced, the more strictly theological writings of Christians. In so far as it makes an appeal beyond the intellect, and still more beyond the emotions in any ordinary sense, it has proved and will prove unattractive to many, in proportion as it is attractive to those who are able to share its mood of mystical fervor. Yet it is by no means intellectually weak; nor is it in the least degree morally objectionable, unless it is rated as a moral defect to lack interest in the most practical daily transactions, and in the advance of the physical sciences. There is of course no doubt that the teaching of Plotinus encouraged an attempt to escape from the preoccupations of the world, particularly oppressive in his own time; but such an attempt can scarcely be condemned as plainly undesirable, without simply assuming the superior importance of precisely what Plotinus tries to show to be without value. In his view, "if we see things as they are, we shall live as we ought." It is not necessary to share, or even to wish to share, his peculiar vision, in order to respect its integrity, richness and imaginative force.

The death of Plotinus is separated by almost nine hundred years from the birth of Thales. It is to this period that we have to look for the origins of almost all that is most valuable in Western civilization—and particularly to the history of the Greeks, the actual inventors of so much that the Romans and others copied or adapted. Very much is owed to the Greeks in detail: metaphysical theories; speculation—and some true science—in astronomy and cosmology; discoveries in mathematics; the analysis of ethical concepts; political philosophy; the first clear statement of several of the great philosophies of conduct—to say nothing, of course, of achievements in literature and the arts. But perhaps most valuable of all was something more general than this, namely, the general conviction that problems are to be solved, questions to be answered, and progress made, by means of the exercise of *human reason*—the conviction that clarity in thought and rigor in argument, though not infallible, are still the best weapons that we can employ in satisfying our needs and our desire for knowledge. It is probably a mistake to think of this conviction as somehow natural to the human species; authority, tradition, habit, superstition, and "wishful thinking" probably have played, and perhaps are still always liable to play, a greater part in determining the beliefs and the behavior of human beings. The Greeks of the early centuries were a tiny island in a sea of what they called, with much justice, barbarism. They believed themselves to be almost of a different species from the rest of the human race; and it is indeed not difficult to feel that in some way they were right. And the essential, immense difference consisted in large part precisely in their faith in articulate argument, in *thinking*. Of course their early thinkers were groping, however boldly; and perhaps also it was not long before the pressure of life repressed in some degree their intellectual vitality, throwing them back first towards predominantly moral preaching, and later still towards old superstitions and new clouds of mysticism. But it remains the case that there did exist for a time, in this not specially favored corner of the world, a center of truly original intellectual power that has been alive and at work in our history ever since. That extraordinary fact seems to baffle complete explanation; but more important, in any case, than to explain it, is for us to remember, appreciate, and learn. If nothing else, it is surely the part of a civilized man to become acquainted with the architects of his own civilization.

Index

233

THE MENTOR PHILOSOPHERS

The entire range of Western speculative thinking from the Middle Ages to modern times is presented in this series of six volumes. Each book contains the basic writings of the leading philosophers of each age, with introductions and interpretive commentary by noted authorities.

"A very important and interesting series."—*Gilbert Highet*

50 cents each

The Age of Belief: The Medieval Philosophers *edited by Anne Fremantle.* (#MD126)

"Highly commendable . . . provides an excellent beginning volume." —*The Classical Bulletin*

The Age of Adventure: The Renaissance Philosophers *edited by Giorgio de Santillana.* (#MD184)

"The most exciting and varied in the series."
—*New York Times*

The Age of Reason: The 17th Century Philosophers *edited by Stuart Hampshire.* (#MD158)

"His (Hampshire's) book is a most satisfactory addition to an excellent series." —*Saturday Review*

The Age of Enlightenment: The 18th Century Philosophers *edited by Sir Isaiah Berlin.* (#MD172)

"(Sir Isaiah) has one of the liveliest and most stimulating minds among contemporary philosophers."
—*N. Y. Herald Tribune*

The Age of Ideology: The 19th Century Philosophers *edited by Henry D. Aiken.* (#MD185)

" . . . perhaps the most distinct intellectual contribution made in the series." —*New York Times*

The Age of Analysis: 20th Century Philosophers *edited by Morton White* (#MD142)

"No other book remotely rivals this as the best available introduction to 20th century philosophy."
—*N. Y. Herald Tribune*

MENTOR Books of Special Interest

Greek Historical Thought *by Arnold J. Toynbee*
Translations of historical works from Homer to Heraclius.
(#MD164—50¢)

The Iliad of Homer *translated by W. H. D. Rouse.* A brilliant prose translation of the epic of the Trojan War.
(#MD110—50¢)

The Odyssey of Homer *translated by W. H. D. Rouse.* The travels of Ulysses told in modern prose. (#MD92—50¢)

Gods, Heroes, and Men of Ancient Greece *by W. H. D. Rouse.* The Greek legends retold in a lively narrative.
(#KD357—50¢)

Life Stories of Men Who Shaped History from Plutarch's Lives (abridged) *edited by Eduard C. Lindeman.*
(#MD166—50¢)

The Anvil of Civilization *by Leonard Cottrell.* A fascinating history of the ancient Mediterranean civilizations.
(#MD197—50¢)

The World of Copernicus (Sun, Stand Thou Still) *by Angus Armitage.* The life story of the radical astronomer.
(#MD65—50¢)

The Inferno by Dante *translated by John Ciardi.* A classic in a new translation by a celebrated poet. (#MD113—50¢)

The Roman Way to Western Civilization *by Edith Hamilton.* The story of the Romans, their lives and thoughts, and works. (#MD213—50¢)

To Our Readers